THE THREE U.S.-MEXICO
BORDER WARS

THE THREE U.S.-MEXICO BORDER WARS

Drugs, Immigration, and Homeland Security

Tony Payan

Foreword by Ed Williams

PRAEGER SECURITY INTERNATIONAL
Westport, Connecticut • London

Library of Congress Cataloging-in-Publication Data

Payan, Tony, 1967–
    The three U.S.-Mexico border wars : drugs, immigration, and Homeland Security /
    Tony Payan; foreword by Ed Williams.
        p.   cm.
    Includes bibliographical references and index.
    ISBN 0–275–98818–X (alk. paper)
    1. Smuggling—Mexican-American Border Region.   2. Drug traffic—Government
    policy—United States.   3. Illegal aliens—Government policy—United States.
    4. United States—Relations—Mexico.   5. Mexico—Relations—United States.
    6. Mexican-American Border Region—Economic conditions.   7. Mexican-
    American Border Region—Politics and government.   8. Mexican-American Border
    Region—Social conditions.   9. Mexican-American Border Region—Ethnic relations.
    I. Title.   II. Title: Three United States-Mexico border wars.
    HV5831.M46T49   2006
    363.0972'1—dc22   2006009796

British Library Cataloguing in Publication Data is available

Library of Congress Catalog Card Number: 2006009796
ISBN: 0–275–98818–X

First published in 2006

Praeger Security International, 88 Post Road West, Westport, CT 06881
An imprint of Greenwood Publishing Group, Inc.
www.praeger.com

Printed in the United States of America

The paper used in this book complies with the
Permanent Paper Standard issued by the National
Information Standards Organization (Z39.48–1984).

10 9 8 7 6 5 4 3 2 1

CONTENTS

FOREWORD

The U.S.-Mexico border is front-page news. The border catalyzes attention from Washington's policymakers, Wall Street's investors, and main street Americans. Sadly enough, the border's new fame defines a mixed blessing. The area is finally gaining the attention it needs to resolve deep-seated problems. But, the saviors' remedies are mostly off the mark, frequently exacerbating rather than resolving the border's woes. Most of the decision makers are appallingly ignorant of the border region.

Decision makers and citizens alike should read, and heed, this splendid study by Professor Tony Payan. Tony Payan knows the border. The book brims with fascinating facts and richly evocative insights into the border region. Beyond capturing the drama of life and death on the border, Professor Payan offers penetrating analysis and sound policy recommendations. The book not only tells it as it is, but also as it ought to be. We hope that Payan gets through to the policymakers before they hatch even more of their harebrained schemes destined to visit even more misery upon we borderlanders, both Americans and *Mexicanos*.

Professor Payan is a first-rate scholar; his research is impeccable. He has read the books, studied the reports, scrutinized the transcripts, and poured over the testimony that frames the context of this study. He has also interviewed the decision makers and cornered the public servants and bureaucrats who implement the decisions. But, he goes beyond the pale in ferreting out reluctant border agents, drug runners, executioners, undocumented workers, and students whose experiences and stories define the stuff of the border. Tony has smelled the streets, mucked around in the washes, kicked up the border's dust, and touched a lot of people in the bargain. Payan has walked the walk. Every paragraph of this study reflects his personal knowledge of the intimate reality of the U.S.-Mexico border.

Professor Payan describes and analyzes three wars declared by policy-makers. They define the nexus of the Washington—border relationship: the war on drugs, the war on terrorists, and, yes, even a war on undocumented workers. As Tony correctly tells us, all are ill-conceived; they are based on false premises and fantastic causes. The war on drugs has chosen the wrong culprit. It is we American consumers, not Mexican suppliers, who define the enemy. The war on terrorism conjures up the image of terrorists crossing from Mexico to wreck destruction on Americans. As the evidence shows, the threat is so egregiously exaggerated as to approach hallucination. Of the three, the present war on undocumented workers may be the most destructive, frightening, and despicable. It evolves from the siege mentality wrought by the security con fomented by ignorant or manipulating policymakers and right-wing zealots. As Americans run scared, they scapegoat poor people crossing the line in search of work.

As Professor Payan unfolds the analysis, the book brims with fascinating facts and rich anecdotes. Some are amusing, others are horrifying, but all are interesting. And, to the point, every one is germane to our understanding the border. He relates the tales of the *sicarios* (executioners) who work with the drug cartels. He describes the numerous tunnels constructed beneath the boundary line. (Mexican engineers are quite skillful!) He chronicles the long, difficult days encountered by hard working, honest, men, women, and students who suffer the indignities of both Mexican and American border officials as they cross from Cuidad Juarez to El Paso to work for Americans or study in El Paso's schools. He reports a poignant and troubling encounter with a Border Patrol Officer who is annoyed by Tony's questions about Mexicans crossing into the United States. The officer responds, "I don't know. That is Mexico on the other side. I don't know anything about it."

Professor Payan's cogent and constructive analysis defines the most significant component of this splendid study. The penetrating insights and analyses number too many to touch in this brief forward, but a few samples may crystallize the sound scholarship and productive policy prescriptions that dignify this book. One of my favorites is Tony's critique of Washington's (and Americans') mindless belief that technology is the Virgin in modern guise. The policymakers embrace indiscriminately and spend riotously on unproved gadgets and wizardry with a childlike belief that they can be rich and safe in one swell foop. In the face of massive data and all logic to the contrary, they ingenuously believe nightscopes, drones, and X-ray machines really can stop poverty-stricken migrants, rich and resourceful drug cartels, and potential terrorists from crossing the line. Not so!

Tony also tells the truth on the North American Free Trade Agreement (NAFTA) and the border as the future of the United States. The NAFTA has succeeded in the areas that it focused upon. It has contributed to significantly increased trade and movement of capital among the three-member nations. It did not substantially better the lives of the overwhelming majority of borderlanders; nor did it improve the region's environment. But, that was not NAFTA's purpose, no matter the fabrications of the spin doctors.

In his treatment of the border as America's future, Professor Payan's truth is a wake-up call. Take heed! The border is largely Hispanic, as the United States will be. Border people are poverty-stricken, unschooled, and physically unwell. If Americans want to avoid the border as a future, we need "a well-devised, *binational* plan to tackle the issues of the border" before they define the plight of the country.

Two other analytical and policy prescriptions form the most significant foci of Professor Payan's study: the imperative of binational efforts and the folly of conflating the three "wars." The imperative of binational cooperation should be obvious to Washington, but evidently not in the age of arrogant unilateralism. We are dealing with a binational border, joining (or separating?) two sovereign countries. It's our binational border; we Americans and Mexicans need to cooperate to repair it. It will not be easy; as Tony notes, the United States and Mexico "are not friends"—less so now than before September 11. But, we had better get on with it.

Finally, and most importantly, Professor Payan offers a penetrating description and analysis of the destructive implications of conflating the three wars. Drug trafficking defines a serious problem for both the United States and Mexico. Undocumented workers crossing the line is not quite a "problem" for the United States or Mexico, but it is fraught with bewildering perplexity and should be addressed. The potential for terrorists infiltrating from Mexico is grossly exaggerated, but sound policy should attend to it.

But, they are separate and distinct issues; conflating them confuses and confounds the issues. It does not crystallize the problems and contribute to intelligent policy. Undocumented migrants crossing the line in search of work almost never transport drugs. Drug runners have nothing in common with potential terrorists. Undocumented workers do not buddy around with terrorists. They practice different religions, they celebrate different fiestas, they speak different languages, their customs and traditions vary, and their dress and manners are dissimilar; their carriage and gait are not the same. Terrorists have not, and almost definitely will not, cross from Mexico. If they come at all, they may cross from Canada, or they may fly into the United States.

As Professor Tony Payan so manifestly documents, militarizing the border will do little but visit even more misery on American borderlanders and our Mexican brethren, while diverting the nation's attention and resources from more productive initiatives.

Tony Payan is right on! You must read on.

Ed Williams
Professor Emeritus of Political Science
and Latin American Studies at the University of Arizona;
Program Scholar with the Arizona Humanities Council

PREFACE

I arrived in El Paso, Texas, on August 22, 2001, from Washington DC, hauling my belongings in a truck, fresh out of Georgetown University. I was moving to the border because I had long felt a call to be there. I had sought to go to the border because it fascinated me and I had diligently worked to get there. Driving into El Paso on I-10, I felt like an Israelite entering the Promised Land. On that hot afternoon of August, I was finally there. My dreamy elation about being on the border was abruptly interrupted about 3 weeks later. On September 11, with my book boxes still unopened, two planes crashed into the World Trade Center in New York, a third into the Pentagon, and a fourth went down in the woods in Pennsylvania. The entire nation was aghast and pained by the events. For a day, anyway, the world stood still, certainly in New York and Washington, and elsewhere too. And thousands of miles away, on the U.S.-Mexico border, we too, were stunned. I remember crossing the Cordoba International Bridge from Ciudad Juárez to El Paso just after 7 a.m. (9 a.m. in New York and Washington). I asked the border officer if he knew what had just happened. He said nothing. He just nodded and waved me through. His bewildered expression, nevertheless, was to me an ominous sign of what was to come.

Border Patrol, U.S. Customs, and Immigration and Naturalization Service agents working the morning shift did not at first realize what happened or how to respond. Their immediate reaction was similar to the bafflement and incomprehension I had seen on that border officer's face that morning of September 11. But within 1 hour of the attack, they had grasped it. They soon found out the extent and the maliciousness of the damage and their rage turned to border crossers. Every one of them became a suspect. All border crossers—shoppers, students, workers, tourists, everyone—could potentially strike terror in America. They were hurt and they responded as best they could: looking at "foreigners" with suspicion. And shortly after, all activity across the border came to a halt. The terrorist plot, its intellectual authors, its executors, and the events themselves had nothing to do with the U.S.-Mexico border. Yet, one of the first sustained responses to the assault on the nation occurred at the border. Within a short time, the international ports of entry along the nearly 2,100-mile southern border had shut down.

Indeed, probably no other region of the country paid as high a price as the U.S.-Mexico border did for the tragic events of that day. In the meeting rooms of every federal agency, in Washington and along the border, much of the discussion focused on what had gone wrong. And the talk often turned to the border. Unfortunately, the debate regarding border security that began with September 11 became highly emotionalized and even irrational. Understandably but unreasonably, it was hard to disentangle the border from September 11. And it would have all been good if the debate had focused on securing the border from those who would want to harm the United States, but allowing the rest to continue with their normal lives. But it was not so. Soon all sorts of issues became conflated on the border. The discourse on the border has metamorphosed several times and taken many shapes: drugs, immigration, terrorists, smugglers, economic integration, trade, investment, etc. Every one of the issues on the border is not a national security concern. Yet, the national security debate absorbed every aspect of the border: trade, immigration, drugs, terrorism, tourism, economic integration, cross-border workers and residents, students, etc. And the result has been a massive mobilization of government resources to "protect" the border, to plug its "holes," to end its "porousness," etc. The high intensity conflict that began in Afghanistan and went on to Iraq had also intensified the ongoing low intensity conflict on the U.S.-Mexico border.

This is what motivated me to take a 1-month-long trip along the U.S.-Mexico border in the summer of 2005. I felt the urge to see with my own eyes what was happening along the border, what the effects of that fated attack were on us, border residents. I knew nothing was the same after September 11, but I needed to see it with my own eyes. What I saw shocked me but did not surprise me. Whoever I talked to perplexed me. What I heard baffled me. The border is today a "soft war" zone. There is, I concluded, a low intensity war along the border. And I sadly concluded that there is probably no real solution in hand to this low intensity conflict. A real solution to the border would require a political will and resources that no one, from Washington DC to Mexico City, is willing to invest on this god-forsaken part of the globe that clamors for attention. One can only hope that both Congress and President George W. Bush see the light of the border needs.

Still, the thought of a low intensity war occupied many of my hours in the summer of 2005. I thought then that in fact to say that there is a war on the border is simplistic. There are in fact three major wars going on at the border—each taking the front stage at different times. But, increasingly, these "wars" are becoming indistinguishable, and they are still three different endeavors at the border. What connects these wars is their geographical location; they are happening on the U.S.-Mexico border. They extend from the Tijuana–San Diego border at the Pacific Ocean to the Rio Grande delta at the Gulf of Mexico. These wars have all the accoutrements of regular war. There is the rhetoric of an enemy and an invasion. There is the hardware: from guns to vehicles, to helicopters and planes, to high-tech devices. There are the fences and the trenches. There are the exorbitant budgets to finance them and tens of thousands of personnel to fight them. And there are the civil society mobilizations for and against the war, with full-fledged Web pages as a necessary accompaniment of modern conflict and public debate. These three wars, the war on drugs, the war on immigration, and the war for Homeland Security, are now a daily fixture of the lives of the border people.

The war on drugs is not so new. In reality, it may be America's longest war. It began in the 1970s, when President Richard Nixon declared a "war on drugs." The border has for a long time experienced what it is like to be caught in the middle of a sustained effort to stop the manufacturing, trafficking, and consumption of illegal drugs. The big difference now is that this war has been elevated to a war of national security. It is no longer simply a law enforcement operation. The efforts and the resources are increasingly those of a low intensity conflict and the rhetoric is more and more that of a fight to death.

The second border war is one that has come to be labeled a war more recently, although it has been a growing problem since 1964, when the United States ended its *bracero* guest worker agreement with Mexico: the war on immigration. Here, too, the rhetoric has turned to terms like "enemy," "invasion," "frontlines," etc. The resources, the personnel, and the technological gadgets against these "would-be invaders" have also grown exponentially. This escalation of efforts to stem the flow of illegal immigrations into the United States seems to be a myopic low intensity conflict strategy that promises to be costly and resolve very little.

The last border war began on September 11, and juxtaposed on the other two. It is the war on terror and it too came to the border, and 5 years later it is still here and likely to stay for generations to come. The Homeland Security strategy on the border is now a full-blown war on largely imaginary terrorists crossing the U.S.-Mexico border. With the terrorist attacks of 2001, trade, trucks, vehicles, student and tourist visa holders, cross-border workers, etc.—all border crossers—became suspect. As such, the view of them changed. Officers came to regard them as guilty of wanting to harm America until they proved themselves innocent, rather than innocent until they prove themselves an enemy of America. Every vehicle came to be seen as carrying a potential threat to the United States. Every person was first assumed to have bad intentions until they demonstrated that they meant no harm. Everyone was affected by this new way of looking at border crossers. To this new Weltanschauung on border crossers, there had to be a consequent investment in resources and manpower to fight this new war, the war of suspicion.

Although the Homeland Security Department reorganization of 2002 conflated these three issues into one, these three issues are in fact quite separate from each other. They have different origins, they have different processes, and they require different strategies, etc. Yet since September 11, the United States government has bundled them into a single "mother of all battles" that has turned the border into a front line of national security. To conduct this comprehensive war, the U.S. government lumped all issues together, employed harsh rhetoric, and increased the expenditures, which are now reaching exorbitant amounts, in order to fight a comprehensive war that is simply unwinnable, at least in the ram-it-down-your-throat way the government insists in solving its border problems.

As I said, all the elements of a war are there: the strategy, the tactics, the personnel, the resources, the rhetoric, and the hardware, etc. The war has been declared and it has trickled from Washington down to tiny ports of entry like Antelope Wells, New Mexico, to huge urban centers like El Paso–Ciudad Juárez and Tijuana–San Diego. The strategy obeys the lines of a low intensity conflict; the tactics are often those of a war; the hardware is increasingly militarized; the training of officers has turned to war talk. The resources have been increased accordingly. And the American society has been duly polarized around the issues that concern the border. Thus, over the last few years since September 11, 2001, the U.S. bureaucracy has been reorganized and geared to fight this war. It is ironic that it was not the intelligence community that underwent the deepest reorganization—it took until 2005 to finally even barely touch its structure, although there was a consensus that intelligence had failed miserably. Instead, all the agencies that had something to do with the border were reorganized. The resources have also been increased considerably to the tune of billions of dollars a year. The technology has been jacked up to include some of the latest technology available for war.

Winston Churchill once said that Americans could always be counted on to do the right thing ... after they have exhausted all other possibilities. It is likely that the U.S. government will continue to deal with the border in the most myopic way possible, throwing resources at it that will not help solve any problems, denying the motivations behind border activity, and refusing to go to the negotiating table to find long-term useful solutions. In the end, however, the border has no solution but to do just that: solve its "problems" as a matter of a comprehensive plan to integrate North America into a sphere of greater security and cooperation for the benefit of all.

This book offers an examination of these three border wars. It peppers this examination with a historical perspective, necessary to understand the border today. Finally, the book turns to a long-term solution to the border problems. The solution, North American integration, is not easy, but it is likely inevitable if we are to survive as a free society and a prosperous nation.

I want to thank many people who helped me discern the problems of the border by listening to my long monologues. I thank Kenn Kern, Nivien Saleh, Irasema Coronado, and many other friends and colleagues who read my writing and gave me enormously useful feedback. I dedicate this book to Ralph L. Scott, my mentor, counselor, and life-guide who passed away on January 5, 2006, just as I was putting the finishing touches to this preface.

CHAPTER 1

The Three Border Wars

A TALE WITH TWO SIDES

Héctor Rodríguez gets up in the morning before the crack of dawn. He showers, shaves, and gets dressed quickly. By the time he gets out of his bedroom, his wife, a Mexican citizen, has already packed a brown-bag lunch for him and their two children. Héctor is a U.S. citizen who works for a construction company in El Paso, Texas, but lives in Ciudad Juárez, across from El Paso. His wife works at a local radio station in Ciudad Juárez. The children attend elementary school in the United States. Hector and the children cross the international bridge to El Paso every morning as early as they can to avoid the long waiting lines at the port of entry every morning. Once on the U.S. side, he drops the children at school before heading to his workplace. He picks up the children in the late afternoon and makes his way back home. His wife comes in later in the day. They have supper together and prepare to go to sleep.

Martín Sánchez has always been considered the "black sheep" of the family. Unable to pay for school beyond grade six, he started doing drugs early on. He hung around with some local gang members suspected of robbing several local banks in Nuevo Laredo. From there he was recruited by the powerful drug smuggling organization known as the Juárez Cartel. He now works for them. Martín has a criminal mind in every way. He has even participated in several kidnappings and killings.

The stories of Héctor and Martín are a powerful image of the border. The two men and their lives are representative illustrations of life at the southern edge of the American empire. These men embody the good and the bad; the beautiful and the ugly; the ordinary and the anomalous of life where Mexico, a developing nation, and the United States, the world's only superpower, meet.

Indeed, the United States is recognized as the most powerful nation in the world. Its economy is the largest; its technological advances are phenomenal; the accumulated wealth of the country is enormous; its military is unparalleled in the history of the humankind; its achievements are admirable. You would think, like almost any impoverished Central American or Mexican peasant working hard on his small patch of land, that the United States is a paradise on earth. But, according to many, all is not well in Paradise. Well, at least, all is not well on the borders of Paradise. These days, it is enough to turn to the news to see that the U.S. media has long been offering a harrowing view of the "turmoil, chaos and lawlessness" of the U.S.-Mexico border. There are stories of drug traffickers running life on the border[1]; there are stories of illegal alien invasions coming from the south[2]; and lately there are stories of Middle East terrorists trying to enter the United States from Mexico by sneaking across through Arizona or New Mexico. U.S. Representative Sue Myrick stated for example that al-Qaeda operatives have been detained along the U.S.-Mexico border. She suggested that "terror was spilling across the border." Representative Myrick is not the only one sounding this trumpet. The U.S. Congress has periodically entered the fray calling the border a "frightening place" and a place where "business centers are closing down, tourism is declining, and the general population is demoralized by the level of lawlessness."[3] This is the world where Martín Sánchez lives. By the stories of the media and the speeches of Congress members, if you live in the United States away from the border, you would think that the U.S.-Mexico borderlands are a wild, wild West where living conditions are unbearable and life is "solitary, poor, nasty, brutish and short."[4] And there is some truth to this view of the border. Anyone familiar with Martín Sánchez's life as a gang member or a drug trafficker or who has read the stories of the hundreds of women assassinated on the border can have a look at the kind of border that Representative Myrick described. But the world of Héctor Rodríguez is seldom paid attention to or covered by the media, even if it really is much more common on the border than the life of Martín Sánchez.

Today more than ever, the U.S.-Mexico border is experiencing one of its most difficult and defining periods of its 150-plus year history, particularly since September 11. As the next chapters will make clear, the problems of the border are serious. The Martín Sánchezes of the border are also many, and they make life on the border a frightening place. But there is also plenty of evidence to tell another story that can debunk some of the dizzying rhetoric regarding the border. There are also the millions of Héctor Rodríguezes. In other words, there are two sides to the border tale.

For those of us, 14 million people,[5] like Héctor Rodríguez, who live on and move across the border on a regular basis, the portrayal of our strip of land, running nearly 2,100 miles along the southwest and about 100 miles wide on both sides of the international boundary, as a violent, chaotic, lawless war front is largely inaccurate.[6] Most border residents are law-abiding, hardworking citizens of either Mexico or the United States. Most people who live on the border get up every day, with the same preoccupations of any other family in the United States: work, school, family life, and in general carving a good life for their community. The overwhelming majority of border crossers do so to shop, work, study, visit family, and seek good entertainment. They are men and women who view themselves as bridging two worlds. Just as there are terrible stories of crime and violence, there are also stories of heroism and courage on the border. And the story of Héctor Rodríguez is not unique. Frank is a maquiladora manager from Michigan who goes to Ciudad Juárez to work everyday. Robin is a housewife in Chula Vista who likes to go shopping in Tijuana. Maria takes her two children to school from Nuevo Laredo to Laredo every morning and picks them up at three in the afternoon. Raúl is a dedicated husband who takes his family shopping from Monterrey to McAllen every year. Mariana and Mabel are two students at the University of Texas at El Paso who commute every day from Ciudad Juárez to El Paso. Like Héctor, Frank, Robin, Maria, Raúl, Mariana, and Mabel, there are millions of stories of border residents who live cherished lives on the U.S.-Mexican border. Unfortunately, it is not the millions of good lives on the border that give it its reputation. It is the thousands of bad lives that determine what the border is for the rest of the world. The bad seems to outweigh the good.

But before I delve into the border today, it is important to take a closer look at the history of the border over time with a view to how this strategy of escalation has worked through nearly a century of U.S. efforts to control the border. This exercise can help enlighten our view of what is happening at the border at present, and perhaps even give us an opportunity to glance at where the border is going in the future.

THE MEANING OF THE BORDER

When one thinks about the U.S.-Mexico border, images of chaos, disorder, poverty, pollution, crime, and insecurity are often evoked. An American tourist who arrives at the border and crosses to Tijuana from San Diego or Ciudad Juárez from El Paso often testifies to this. In 1999, Scott Rogerson, a *Weekly Alibi* journalist traveling on I-10 at 70 mph, wrote his impressions regarding the border:

> Driving south to El Paso you come over a rise and the first thing you see is a vast sprawling city choking the Rio Grande valley. If you were on vacation and had never been there before, you would think El Paso is a much larger city than what your map indicates. But as you descend further and draw nearer you notice the rat maze of shacks covering

the hillside along the valley and realize it looks like no other American city you have ever seen before. Then you grasp the reality. The hillside is Mexico. The rat maze of shacks is a cardboard colonia.[7]

His rather unflattering portrayal of "the border" constitutes a common impression by visitors to almost any town along the nearly 2,100-mile stretch that separates the United States and Mexico. But those who dismiss the area as a dusty, poor, and wretched land miss the long and magnificent history of the U.S.-Mexico border and the varied tapestry of wealth and poverty, hope and despair, backwardness and progress that is manifest, for example, in the lives of its residents, who number nearly 14 million and live in fourteen pairs of cities that dot the border. Regardless of the impressions the occasional visitor may have, few can capture the flavor of the border that do not live and move and have their being there.

Rogerson's description of the border reflects a temptation to lump three distinct concepts together: the boundary, the border, and the borderlands. The boundary is the physical line between the two countries. It was set in 1853 in the Gadsden Purchase Treaty, which reads:

Article I: The Mexican Republic agrees to designate the following as her true limits with the United States for the future: retaining the same dividing line between the two Californias as already defined and established . . . the limits between the two republics shall be as follows: Beginning in the Gulf of Mexico, three leagues from land, opposite the mouth of the Rio Grande . . . thence . . . up the middle of that river to the point where the parallel of 31°47′ north latitude crosses the same; thence due west one hundred miles; then south to the parallel of 31°20′ north latitude; thence along the said parallel of 31°20′ to the 111th meridian of longitude west of Greenwich; then in a straight line to a point on the Colorado River twenty English miles below the junction of the Gila and Colorado rivers; thence up the middle of the said river Colorado until it intersects the present line between the United States and Mexico.[8]

If the boundary refers to the physical line drawn between the two countries, defining the border is much more difficult because it is the geographical area where the national and cultural characteristics of the two nations meet and mix and where their respective governments implement policies concerning the international boundary. This geographical area varies depending on where one is along the nearly 2,100-mile boundary line. Moreover, the 1983 La Paz agreement between the United States and Mexico defines the borderlands as the band of land that stretches about 62.5 miles north and south of the boundary line. This region includes communities not on the border itself, but in relative proximity to it. The U.S.-Mexico borderlands therefore contain nearly 14 million residents in both countries. Their number is projected to reach between 20 and 25 million people by 2030.[9]

These residents of the U.S.-Mexico border straddle two languages, two cultures, two legal systems, two economic systems, two currencies, and two political systems, and most of them do so with great ease. This fact may surprise many a Midwestern who finds himself/herself in a place that does not resemble either Mexico or the United States.

What the border looks like today and what its 14 million residents experience day to day is the product of its historical legacies and its political, social, and economic context. To understand—to truly understand—the border one has to look to the past as much as to the present. In effect, the border has not always been the way it is today. There is a natural tendency to freeze the border in time as a bedlam, as if it had always been a place of great turmoil and disarray. In reality it is an extremely dynamic place whose meaning and physical appearance, whose practices and activities have shifted continuously for a period of 150 years, even as the physical line has remained unmoved. A look at the U.S.-Mexico border across time will quickly reveal that it has suffered a substantial transformation over the last century and a half, and current perceptions of the border as an immoral, dirty space are relatively new. To understand the evolution of the area and to appreciate what is happening there today, we need to take a look at its major transformations since 1853.

The history of the U.S.-Mexico border begins in the mid-nineteenth century. Although the physical boundary between the two countries took its final shape in 1848 with the Treaty of Guadalupe-Hidalgo and in 1853 with the Gadsden Purchase, the way in which we view the border has changed over time. Its meaning to people living on it has undergone dramatic changes, which can be categorized as different stages of meaning, according to the emphasis given to the border, principally by the United States government. In effect, the U.S. government is the primary agent determining the face of the border, by dictating how open or closed it should be and what the rules governing transboundary activity should be. Residents on both sides of the physical boundary are generally left to adjust, adapt, and react to Washington's decisions. They do so by accommodating their lives and routines as best they can to the newest policy whims that come from Capitol Hill.

Shaped largely by the United States federal government, the meaning of the border to its residents went through four stages, which I will label as follows: the frontier border, the customs border, the law enforcement border, and the security border. Each of these stages can be measured by specific changes on the ground along the border, changes that have taken us to the current situation on the ground: the three border wars analyzed in this volume.

THE FRONTIER ERA

Between 1848 and roughly 1910, the prevalent meaning of the border was that of a "frontier." The Southwest of the United States was a place of open spaces and expressions of freedom. The boundary line that separated the United States from Mexico defined citizenship and civic duty, but it did not constrain mobility or access. People and cattle were free to roam back and forth without impediments. The spirit of the U.S.-Mexico border at this time is best captured in the romantic narratives of the cowboy and the cattleman. The region was marked by weak ties to centralized authority and removed from the large-scale economic activity of the Eastern United States.[10] It was a place left to its own devices and border crossers traveled freely, uncontested by governmental institutions. During these decades, there were no border bureaucracies to speak of, with the exception of a handful of U.S. customs agents who worked only a few hours a day at certain checkpoints.

On matters of immigration, there were few laws regulating immigration on the U.S.-Mexico border in the second half of the nineteenth century. Congress was preoccupied with immigration from Europe and overlooked migration movements from the southwest border. The Chinese Exclusion Act of 1882 targeted the Chinese immigrants who came to work on the railroad lines of the southwest. It did not refer to Mexican immigration at all and it barely mentioned land borders. Four intervening congressional immigration acts[11] also said nothing about immigration laws governing the U.S.-Mexico border. All of the acts of Congress of that time related closely to labor laws, indicating that immigration was viewed more as an economic or rather a labor issue rather than a law enforcement issue. The Immigration Act of 1891 instructed the Treasury Secretary "to prescribe rules for inspection along the borders of Canada, British Columbia, and Mexico so as not to obstruct or unnecessarily delay, impede, or annoy passengers in ordinary travel between these countries and the United States."[12] The Immigration Service it created focused on immigration arriving "by water" but not by land, and it is likely that there were no Immigration Service officers along the border, perhaps with the exception of Leonidas B. Giles, who was stationed at El Paso, Texas, in 1893. In that year, 119 of the 180 Immigration Service officers were stationed in Ellis Island alone compared to one along the U.S.-Mexico border. In 1899 there were only about four Immigration Service inspectors along the entire border.[13] It is worth noting that the Immigration Service at that time was under the Treasury Department and on February 14, 1903, it moved to the Department of Commerce and Labor, a fact that reflected a preoccupation with the relationship between immigrants and economic issues, particularly labor, rather a preoccupation with immigrants and law enforcement or immigrants and national security. The government considered immigrants as workers, not as potential criminals who posed problems of law enforcement or national security. Even if the immigration acts well into the 1900s were increasingly restrictive, there was almost no preoccupation with land immigration either from Canada or Mexico. Both the economic and labor orientation of most immigration controls and the absence of concern with the U.S.-Mexico border lead us to conclude that the mood of the U.S.-Mexico border at the time was that of the frontier. Persons, goods, services, and vehicles moved freely across the border subject to hardly any inspection. Into the first decade of the 1900s, Mexicans were still allowed to move in and out of the United States unencumbered by any bureaucracies. Typically, Mexicans arrived in the United States, were questioned, their entry was recorded, and they were free to enter the United States and even settle there. In the first decade of the 1900s the mood began to shift along the border, but the focus was not on immigrants of Mexican origin. Marcus Braun, an Immigration Service inspector, investigated the U.S.-Mexico border in 1907 and found that Syrians, Japanese, Greeks, Chinese, and other third-country unskilled labor were using the U.S.-Mexico border as a passageway to the United States. This led the Immigration Service to classify immigrants through the Mexican border into "legitimate immigration" and "illegitimate immigration." Chinese, Japanese, Middle Easterners, and others coming in through Mexico were considered "illegitimate immigrants." Mexicans continued to be considered "legitimate immigrants." It was at this time, 1908, when the government began to keep complete records of arrivals across the U.S.-Mexico border.[14]

The national mood that demanded immigration controls at the turn of the century originated in the industrial areas of the east coast and slowly expanded to the south and northwest. The southwest, however, was largely indifferent to the national mood to control immigration. It did not embrace the notion that border crossers had to be controlled. Other than the occasional political rhetoric concerning the Chinese or the Japanese in California, the Mexican border was largely exempt from the anti-immigrant movement that marked other parts of the United States. Mexican border crossers were made liable for a head tax upon crossing. Those who could not afford to pay the head tax did not enter through an official port of entry. Instead, they crossed at some other unguarded point between ports of entry. Importantly, there are no records of anyone arrested, detained, or deported on account of such "illegal" entries. In the words of Theodore Roosevelt, the U.S.-Mexican border was to be "closed to all but citizens and bona fide residents of Mexico." Such was the frontier border.

Soon after the final settlement of the boundary line in 1848 and 1853, border towns sprang up, many of them such as Laredo and El Paso, Texas, heavily identified with Mexico. Mexicans also crossed into the United States and founded entirely new towns such as Brownsville, Texas. In fact, the lower valley of Texas saw the greatest creation of towns, although the Western border in New Mexico, Arizona, and California remained largely empty. For decades only U.S. cattle barons and agricultural interests profited from the abundant empty lands by monopolizing the trade routes across the border. An examination of photographs of the time shows that on most of the nearly 2,100-mile long boundary there were no fences or significant obstacles to the movement of persons. The pairs of towns along the border were divided by a short wire fence just a few feet high, when there was a fence at all!

Like immigration, trade across the U.S.-Mexico border went unregulated for a long time. It was the railroad that connected the border with zones of major economic significance in the United States and thereby cities like Nuevo Laredo, Piedras Negras, Paso del Norte, and Nogales on the Mexican side and Laredo, El Paso, Nogales, and others began to prosper on the United States side. Products, like people, could easily cross from one side to the other. Contrabandists were an important part of the border economy. They smuggled anything into Mexico, from coffee to textiles. Smuggling has been part of the border since its inception because "one side of the river always had something that was lacking on the other side." By 1850, the Mexican government saw contrabandists as criminals. With their activities, contrabandists deprived Mexican producers of their Mexican market share and the Mexican government of its revenue. Meanwhile, border residents considered trading across boundaries an acceptable and even respectable activity.

Smuggling, as a border reality, has thus always been present. What has changed over time is the nature of the goods smuggled. During the second half of the nineteenth century the government of Mexico, in order to remedy revenue losses, imposed tariffs on the importation of numerous agrarian and manufactured goods. To enforce these laws it created a special customs police (*contraresguardos*), which was far too small to prevent smuggling. Mexicans and Americans, therefore, continued their nearly free trade practices across the border without much difficulty. Smuggling was facilitated by the general lack of governmental bureaucracies on the border. At that time, drugs were not a concern to central authorities on either side. For one thing, drugs had not yet been made illegal. In addition, drug use among border residents—or in the country as a whole—was minimal, if it existed at all.

The U.S.-Mexico border was an open border where individuals could cross at will. Even though, strictly speaking, it was illegal to cross between official ports of entry, the United States government had neither the wherewithal nor the desire to guard the border, and bureaucrats on the border were limited to a few at official ports of entry, and no one patrolled the line between them. In the 1880s, Jeff Milton was the first border patrolman to ride along the Texas border on horseback with a revolver on his belt. Still much of the efforts of the early pioneers of border patrolling were directed against "illegitimate" immigration, that is Chinese and other "undesirables," but not against Mexicans. When Congress began to require Mexicans and Canadians to pass literacy tests and pay a head tax of $8, many avoided the official ports of entry and crossed between these. The real struggle with illegal immigration begins here, with these requirements now imposed on Mexicans and with the increasing abuse of the openness of the border by Asian and European immigrants, who preferred to skip the cumbersome process at New York and other ports and decided to enter the United States from Mexico.

Although many have complained that cowboy and frontier narratives often romanticize the nineteenth century border, this century was, in a way, an era of bliss characterized by a lack of attention to the border, unimpeded mobility, free trade, and practically no inspection of border-crossers. This era of absolute and relative bliss for border crossers came to an end with the turn of the century. The pressures of twentieth century modernization were gathering on the border like dark clouds in the sky.

THE CUSTOMS ERA

Three major events changed the face of the border forever. These events had little to do with the border itself, but they changed it profoundly. They ended the frontier era and rang in the Customs Era.

The first great nail on the coffin of the frontier border was the advent of the Mexican Revolution, which began on November 20, 1910. To prevent the turmoil from spilling into U.S. territory, the government established a series of forts along the border. During this time, the number of illegal crossers decreased considerably only to rise again after 1920, when the Mexican Revolution ended. The 1917 $8 head tax and the literacy tests were making it very hard for many Mexicans to migrate or even just to travel to the United States as easily as they had done for decades before. Many, however, had become eligible to move to the United States because of persecution during the Mexican revolution. The Mexican upper class, for example, immigrated en masse to the United States, with all their capital, much of which began to feed business financing in the southwest. Others were simply refugees of the violence of the revolution. The Hispanic character of many border cities was reinforced at that time by mass migration into cities like Nogales, El Paso, Laredo, and Brownsville.

The second major circumstance that was to transform the character of the border was the growing anti-immigration wave in the United States that reached the southwest via the Chinese Exclusion Act of 1882, intended to exclude all Chinese from migrating into the United States. Amendments to this Act extended the provision for another ten years in 1892. By 1902, the Chinese Exclusion Act was further extended, this time indefinitely. Although Mexicans had been able to move back and forth freely for decades, suddenly they were no longer part of the daily life of the American side of the border. Instead, they were considered "foreigners" who did not possess the right to mobility across the boundary. This was a fundamental shift in attitude brought about by the growth of the state and the consolidation of nationhood in the empty lands of the southwest. This attitude of the American public, translated into harder legislation, began a century of gradual closing of the border. The U.S. government began to bureaucratize the border and systematize inspections. In 1924, the U.S. Congress created the Border Patrol as part of the Immigration Service. Their duty was to guard the border to prevent illegal crossings of both persons and merchandise, and to apprehend those who would aid a migrant who had not gone through the normal immigration clearing process. The Border Patrol began with just a few hundred agents but they continued to increase over time, reaching about 11,000 agents today. In fact, it was not until World War II that the Border Patrol reached 1,500 agents responsible for guarding the entire United States' borders, not only the Southwest. By the 1930s, the Border Patrol was reorganizing, introducing new technology and professionalizing its training. The stricter immigration laws had translated on the border ground to a much larger, professional border patrol force integrating the latest in surveillance technology. The Border Patrol numbers would only grow and their use of technology would only get more sophisticated. There was no turning back.

A second factor that changed the meaning of the border was the prohibition era. On January 16, 1920, Americans woke up under the Eighteenth Amendment of the Constitution forbidding the manufacture, sale, or importation of alcoholic beverages. As a result, customs inspections became more prominent to enforce prohibitionist laws. The new amendment created a new black market that demanded most of the attention of Customs inspectors and even the Border Patrol. The U.S.-Mexican border began to see the smuggling of alcohol hidden in other cargo or crossed by mule between ports of entry. An increasing number of customs agents had to focus on enforcing Customs laws derived from the prohibition era. Because the new quotas on immigration imposed by Congress in 1921 and 1924 only fueled the market for illegal labor, bureaucrats along the border came under growing pressure to enforce not only immigration laws, but also customs laws, and the latter occupied more and more of their time. Even after the prohibition laws were repealed, customs inspections continued to focus on numerous other goods crossing the border. Customs exemplifies what some call "the natural law of bureaucracy:" it is easier to create and grow a bureaucracy than it is to dismantle and control it. Customs, like the Border Patrol, would only expand in size over the next few decades. By 1929, a new Act of Congress began to require Mexicans a visa to enter the United States and stiffened the penalties for entering the country between official ports of entry. This was indeed the end of a privilege enjoyed by Mexicans for decades and further divided local communities.

The third element that changed the border was the First World War. Although its effect was not felt directly on the border, the Second World War made clear that the United States was becoming a mature power, a prosperous economy, even as Mexico turned on the wheels of a revolution that would barely place it on the path to modernity. This drove a wedge between the two countries, driving home the economic disparities that have marked the border to this day. Mexicans would begin to view the United States as a place of both political and economic refuge. Eventually, this disparity grew and determined the current geopolitical relationship of the two nations in its modern outlook. If immigration works somewhat like osmosis, the wealthier side will inevitably attract people from the poorer sides. Asymmetry works to create incentives and disincentives to move, often illegally to the more prosperous side of the border. Much of what occurred in the twentieth century and is likely to occur in the first part of this century will be largely determined by this unequal relationship, including another potential bracero (guest worker) program that has already been proposed in various immigration reform bills in 2005.

These three chains of events conspired to close the border in two important directions: to restrict the movement of persons and to regulate the traffic of all commercial goods between the two countries. During this "Customs Era," the border was characterized by a fixed, harder line that revoked the frontier milieu permanently. The United States increased its surveillance and stiffened its customs protections. Bureaucrats began to keep records of all cross-border transactions, which increased their paperwork, and which in turn increased the number of agents working on the border. The momentum was toward greater vigilance at the border, creating a deep sense of separation between the two nations. Still, much of the inspection activity was focused on goods being transported across the border. Surveillance between ports of entry remained very light and sporadic and cross-border interaction, even undocumented interaction was relatively easy. People still went back and forth between ports of entry. In fact, up to the 1970s, it was quite easy to cross the border, even illegally.

THE LAW ENFORCEMENT ERA

There is no single dramatic event that inaugurated the "law enforcement border." Instead, the transition to this era on the border occurred slowly over time. Beginning with the Nixon administration, ideologically conservative forces in the United States rose to prominence. Their prominence began an emphasis on law and order that dominated the American political landscape by the 1980s. This new conservative revolution left no stone unturned. Ronald Reagan's Administration was sent to Washington in 1980 to do just that: bring "law and order" to its fullest expression. In this scheme of things, the border could not be the exception, and so it underwent a quiet revolution, further restricting mobility between the two countries.

The focus of the law enforcement era was on two major issues. One was the massive undocumented migration that had been rising with Mexico's rapid urbanization in the 1960s and 1970s and culminated with several million Mexican citizens living without authorization inside the United States. In the view of many, the flood of undocumented border crossers who took advantage of the relative openness of the border between official ports of entry to settle in the United States was now unacceptably high. Indeed, the number of illegal entries in the South Texas border even in the 1950s had risen so rapidly that the Border Patrol began to transfer Border Patrol agents from the Canadian border to the Mexican border. With the number of undocumented workers, the Border Patrol saw a considerable increase in its own budgets and personnel. There was a sustained sense of urgency regarding the problem of undocumented migration and the U.S. government began to step up its efforts to "guard" the border against this "alien invasion."

Moreover, in 1982 the U.S. government began to put pressure on the Colombian drug cartels that smuggled cocaine via the Caribbean. Because of the squeeze on the Caribbean, the Colombian drug lords sought an alliance with the Mexican drug smuggling organization of Miguel Angel Félix Gallardo, which operated on the U.S.-Mexico border. This new alliance brought the cocaine trade to the border, in addition to the existing heroin and marijuana trade that had already flourished on the largely unguarded border in the 1970s. By the mid-1980s, the Colombian-Mexican drug cartel alliances were smuggling tons of drugs across the border. This raised some serious concerns and the U.S. government began to beef up its efforts to combat drugs on the U.S.-Mexico border. This, added to the problem of immigration, which had already been redefined as a law enforcement problem and concentrated in the Justice Department, made the border a place where law and order had to be imposed from above. Evidence suggests that the overall funding to combat drug trafficking focused on the U.S.-Mexico border, mostly devoted to law enforcement measures. Policing became the new way of dealing with any issues along the border.

The law enforcement era was reinforced in the 1990s. By 1993 and 1994, three law enforcement operations to guard the border were set up. One was Operation Hold the Line in El Paso, Texas; a second was Operation Safeguard in Arizona; and the third was Operation Gatekeeper in California. These three operations were military-style operations with new hi-tech gadgets and added patrolmen and vehicles. They were supposed to be posted every quarter of a mile (within sight of each other) in order to stop the flow of undocumented workers and illegal drugs. Although this was unsustainable as a general strategy, it reinforced the view that the border was a lawless place where more law and order was required.

It was at this time that some local communities on both sides of the border began to lose the historical connections that had bound them together and cross-border social and family relations began to weaken. Fences began to go up and there were already some proposals to build a steel wall along the border, principally in urban areas. Some walls were in fact built.

THE NATIONAL SECURITY BORDER

Unlike the "law enforcement era," which descended on the border with the transformation of the United States into a more conservative society, the national security era of the border was inaugurated with a single event: the attack of September 11 on New York and Washington. With the post-September 11 lash out, perhaps no other area of the country was as affected as the U.S.-Mexico border. But the response of the U.S. government *on the border* was to some extent a curious response. Those who diagnosed the failure to deter the terrorist attacks of that day focused on immigration procedures; on cross-border commercial practices; on the openness of the border, etc. Thus, the diagnosis of the failure of the government fell heavily on the U.S.-Mexico border, even though the border had very little to do with the terrorists of September 11. Few focused originally on the real failure: a lack of intelligence coordination to detect and apprehend potential terrorists in the United States entering anywhere, whether at sea ports, airports or land ports of entry.

With this border-centered diagnosis of the terrorists attacks came the many short- and long-term reactions of the U.S. government and their costs, many of which also focused on the border. In the short term, the border was temporarily shut down. Families were separated; students could not get to school; cross-border commuters could not get to their jobs; and the retail business experienced a slowdown. In El Paso alone, there were 50,000 fewer business transactions in the month following September 11. The waiting time to cross the border increased up to 4 to 5 hours due to the careful inspection of every vehicle crossing the border. The import/export sector, too, experienced additional costs because of the delays in trucking their merchandise across the ports of inspection. The added fuel, hours spent on waiting, and man-hours lost represented a considerable expense in the days following September 11.

The long-term effect was also important. The first and most important effect was the redefinition of the issues along the border. Whereas border issues were previously a matter of law enforcement, everything was redefined as a matter of national security. There was a "securitization" of all border issues that was made permanent by the creation of the Department of Homeland

Security, where many of the agencies that deal with border issues are now located. Besides the redefinition of border politics as national security issues, the focus of the Department of Homeland Security reorganization was to a large extent the border and its activities, not so much the interior of the country, except perhaps for the international airports. After September 11, the budgets for border security and surveillance increased even more than they had in the 1980s and 1990s, reaching $7 billion dollars in 2006. Some budget proposals called for much more. In 2005, for instance, Congressman Bennie Thompson demanded an increase in the number of Border Patrol agents, from 11,000 to 21,000. President Bush, however, vetoed that increase.

With the "securitization" of all matters pertaining to the border and the increases in budget and personnel came also a change in the general attitude toward border-crossers. Before September 11, officers on the border tended to treat border crossers poorly. Now every vehicle and every person entering the United States is considered a suspect, a potential harm to America.

It is interesting to observe that five years after September 11, not much has changed on the border. Two important factors make this evident. First, illegal drugs and undocumented workers continue to stream in at the same levels as before, despite increased budgets, personnel, and a new Homeland Security Department notwithstanding. All that these changes and the reforms seem to have accomplished is a redefinition of the concept of security to include all border issues, a new and more hostile attitude toward border crossers, and a new layer of bureaucratic paperwork for all. But none of these reforms seem to have fixed the more fundamental problems of the border. To do so, what is required is a long-term plan, with a much wider vision and political leadership than the current political leaders of either country are willing to provide. For now, the security era is here to stay.

One can only hope that the fifth era of the border will be one where the border will be dismantled, rather than reinforced, by conceptions of law enforcement and national security. "Debordering" will likely become a historical necessity for both countries. The question is when it will happen and whether things will get worse before we get there.

THE CLOSING OF THE BORDER

An examination of the history of the border over its 150 years or so reveals that the border is closing. With every era, the border has become even more guarded and more tightly controlled. The result of every escalation along the border has been massive bureaucratic reorganizations and the addition of more resources and personnel to control the border. However, the approach throughout the twentieth century has been quite the same: more law enforcement with greater punishment for border lawbreakers. And yet, the approach is the equivalent of an escalation that has not paid off.

OUR LIVES IN THE HANDS OF OTHERS

Unfortunately, border residents have little control over the image and reputation of their homeland. They do not even control their cross-border life. They certainly do not make or even influence the policies and rules that structure their cross-border interaction. Those policies are made in the capitals, like Mexico City and, more specifically, in Washington DC, thousands of miles away from the border itself. Through border policy, the lives of millions of people who reside in the borderlands are strongly contoured by policies from far away. This is why the perceptions of politicians and policy makers regarding the border matter. It is their perceptions that give rise to policies presumably designed to determine how the border and its "intractable" problems are to be dealt with. Border residents simply live with the consequences of the decisions made in the halls of Congress or the corridors of bureaucracy. For this reason, an alert border resident shudders when politicians grandstand to talk about illegal drugs, undocumented immigration, and homeland security on the border.

Yet these are the three issues that are most talked about today when it comes to the border. There are thousands of media stories, congressional hearings, statements by various groups of civil society, press releases, and declarations by governments and leaders on the wretched condition of the U.S.-Mexico border.[15] Illegal drugs, undocumented immigration, and the potential for a terror attack filtering through the border are the most often cited reasons for a governmental impetus for a new border security policy coming down from Washington DC.[16] This is particularly true since September 11, although the terrorist attacks of that day have only accelerated a trend already in progress. How the lives of the vast majority of those living along the border are affected or what their needs may be is largely irrelevant. Washington DC has decided that the border is a chaotic, lawless, unwieldy place that must be brought "under control."[17] To that effect, the United States government speaks of the drug war, the efforts to combat undocumented migration, and the war on terror. Drug traffickers, undocumented workers, and terrorists must be stopped at the border. The rhetoric is couched in militarized language. These three "border wars" consume most of the time of any politician or policy-maker even willing to take a hard look at this troubled part of Paradise.

The perception of the border as a bedlam has clearly not been good for the border or the people who live on it. But it has not been good for decades now. For nearly forty years, the United States government has waged its two longest wars on the border: the war on drugs and the war on undocumented migration. To these two wars, the last five years have seen the development of yet a third border war: the war on terror, as it manifests itself on the border. To the three fundamentally distinct problems of the border: illegal drugs, undocumented migration, and homeland security (guarding against terrorists), the U.S. government has come up with three similar solutions: a border war. And these wars are largely fought on the U.S.-Mexico border.

A DEMOCRATIC DEFICIT

The talk of "border wars" is particularly disturbing to border residents when it comes from Washington DC. If politicians and policy makers perceive the U.S.-Mexico border as a dangerous place that poses a threat to the national security of the United States, they will be inclined to create and implement policies to "close the border" or to "bring it under control."[18] Many of them are fond of declaring a war on this or that problem, with an even stronger centralizing effect in dealing with border issues. Thus, when it comes to the border, decisions on how to deal with its issues come from above, not from below. Over the history of the twentieth century and into the twenty-first century, most laws and policies relating to border control were created in Washington. Yet, their deepest effects have been felt by the people who live, work, do business, and study on the borderlands—those who live on the frontlines, so to speak. Moreover, whenever politicians change the laws and establish new rules that govern cross-border interaction and create new bureaucracies, residents of the borderlands are never consulted. They are denied the fundamental right to a level of self-government in their cross-border interactions because boundaries are a "federal jurisdiction."[19] The fact that borderland residents do not have an input into how the government deals with the area's issues indicates a democratic deficit. Border residents do not govern themselves; they are governed from above.

CONFLATING THE ISSUES

In Ciudad Juárez, I interviewed a former drug trafficker, who wanted to remain anonymous. My interviewee told me a joke when I asked him about the interrelation between drug trafficking, human smuggling, and the war on terror. He said that he saw some connections between the first two—and he showed me some of these connections, but he did not see a connection with the third. He joked and said that no decent drug trafficker would want to be seen with a terror suspect because then the U.S. government would really come after him. This joke made me think about how these three wars are different on the border, and how they are interrelated. In the eyes of the U.S. government today, they are today one and the same thing.

President George W. Bush declared a global war on terror in September 2001.[20] It soon became obvious that this global war would necessarily have consequences for border management. That was a logical follow up. What was not logical was the fact that this new global war on terror would conflate the issues into a single image of a dangerous border that posed a national security threat to the very survival of the United States and then proceed to declare an all-out war to "control the border." Robert Bonner, former director of Customs and Border Protection (CBP), best illustrated this conflation of the issues. He said that "the existence of CBP makes us vastly better able to protect our nation from all external threats, whether illegal migrants and illegal drugs, terrorists, terrorist weapons, including weapons of mass destruction."[21] Bonner's words clearly show that the U.S. government was not interested in disaggregating the border into various regions or component problems, even for the purposes of analysis. His words also show that the government was not interested in dealing with each one of these issues at a time. Instead, the government was going to view a lack of control of the border as a single national security threat and it was going to deal with it with a single strategy: by declaring war on the presumed threats coming through the southern border.

To the observant border resident and the trained academic eye, illegal drug trafficking, undocumented migration, and homeland security at the border are very different problems. Yet the United States has lumped them together by creating a single Homeland Security Department and dumping most border issues into it.[22] Moreover, every one of these issues was given a similar treatment. It would be very hard to make the case that the Border Patrol, with the same training, personnel, equipment, and manuals could fight drug traffickers, undocumented workers, and prevent terrorists from crossing the border. Yet, they are commissioned to do all three. But it is absurd to think that these border phenomena are the same. And it is even more absurd to imagine that the solution to all three is the same, waging a generalized war that has made the border more insufferable than it already is. It is incongruous to think that drugs are smuggled the same way as human beings or that either of these is a national security threat as opposed to being a serious crime or that drug traffickers would necessarily associate with Middle Eastern terrorists when they do not share the same motive for their activities, etc. In sum, neither the problem nor the United States' blanket solution to these distinct problems is a long-term, wise strategy for the border. Conflating the issues can only prevent the U.S. government from dealing more effectively with each of them. Creating what looks like a single strategy with a unilateral, short-term focus seems counterproductive as well, given that the problems of the border are better solved in partnership with one's neighbor, with a long-term focus to tackle the very origins of each concern.

PLANNING TO SECURE THE BORDER: SAME OLD, SAME OLD

The National Intelligence Reform Act of 2005 included a request for 10,000 more Border Patrol agents, to take the total to about 21,000 agents. Eighty percent of the new agents would patrol the U.S.-Mexico force. That would bring the total number of agents guarding the southern border to nearly 18,000, a veritable army. President Bush cut that number and his FY2006 Budget authorized only 210 more agents. A January 24, 2005, letter signed by many Republicans asked President Bush to reinstate the request "in order to secure our borders against terrorists."[23] The request for an increase of 10,000 more Border Patrol agents is the type of request that has been repeated in Washington for decades when it comes to the border. Timothy Dunn has argued that the U.S. government has one single approach to deal with the border: to move steadily to a militarized strategy with increased personnel and resources and a low-intensity conflict strategy.[24]

Nowhere is this logic of escalation more evident than on the ground along the nearly 2,100-mile southern boundary. Throughout the twentieth century, when a problem surfaces or spirals out of control along the border, the U.S. government has defined it and then responded with an escalation strategy.[25] The rhetoric too escalates. Instead of law and order, over time the discourse has turned to a word of invasions, wars, national security threats, lack of control, and now, terror. September 11 only sped up this logic of escalation. Even as late as 2005, the White House proposed a Secure Border Initiative (SBI) that would represent more of the same: a unilateral, law enforcement approach. The SBI focuses on:

- More agents to patrol our borders, secure our ports of entry, and enforce immigration laws;
- Expanded detention and removal capabilities to eliminate "catch and release" once and for all;
- A comprehensive and systemic upgrading of the technology used in controlling the border, including increased manned aerial assets, expanded use of UAVs, and next-generation detection technology;
- Increased investment in infrastructure improvements at the border—providing additional physical security to sharply reduce illegal border crossings; and
- Greatly increased interior enforcement of our immigration laws—including more robust worksite enforcement.[26]

Thus, over the heads of the nearly 14 million residents along the border, the U.S. government bureaucracies operating on the U.S.-Mexico boundary engage drug traffickers, undocumented workers, and presumed border-jumping terrorists with little regard to local solutions or the creation of a larger frame within which to solve these issue—ideally together with Mexico—in order to secure the border once and for all. Instead, the focus is a unilateral, short-term approach centered largely on law enforcement. No attention is paid to either the larger social and economic forces that motivate people to smuggle drugs, or to cross the border to work without documents and now, say many in the U.S. government, or to jump the border as terrorists with the intention to "harm America."[27] There is indeed little thought to the construction of a long-term, bilateral solution to the troubles that plague the border. The European way of dealing with its internal border issues is nowhere to be found in North America.[28]

In sum, border control programs have come and gone and what they have in common is that they have largely relied on more agents, more facilities for detention, more technology, and generally more enforcement. Every proposal and bill includes more of the same. Thus, the border today constitutes the frontline of three ongoing wars that need to be analyzed as such, as the continuation of the same old strategies and tactics. This book will argue, however, that so far the three border wars have been utter failures, given the poor results the U.S. government has had overtime. Drugs are just as abundant; undocumented workers continue to cross over; and no credible reports of terrorists crossing the border to blow themselves up in the United States have been recorded publicly.

ARE THE THREE BORDER WARS JUSTIFIED?

The issue of a logical law enforcement escalation along the border is important. The problem of unilateral action by the United States is also crucial. The economic sustainability of the approach is fundamental.[29] But there is an even more critical question that must be asked about the three border wars that we are about to examine in this book. Even if it were fully justified to view these three great issues on the border as the same problem and to wage a massive law enforcement, quasi-military war against them, using the same strategies, the same tactics, the same bureaucracies, the same training, the same equipment, etc., at an increasing cost, we would have to look at whether the wars of the border are both limited and successful.[30] In other words, the question of whether there is in the future a successful end to the problems of the border is key. Unfortunately, there is no end in sight to the battles of the border. They seem to be unlimited and, worse yet, unsuccessful. Nearly all historical evidence over decades shows that the border has never been under control and is not likely to be under control in the near future. More of the same guarantees only a less democratic borderland with a more repressive police state operating along the border.

A close look at the history of the border can help us put the U.S. approach in perspective. The war on drugs has been going on for nearly forty years.[31] The war on undocumented migration has been going on for over forty years.[32] These two wars are in fact America's longest wars. And now we have the war on terror coming to the border. The war on terror, away or at the border, has no end in sight and has not produced a single successful "terror bust" on the border. The government's inability to declare victory in these wars is particularly serious if we consider that the current approach is not only monetarily unsustainable in the long run—it is an expensive approach—but that it has also not solved and is not likely to solve the problems of the border.

Moreover, the approach also often alienates Mexico diplomatically and there is little reason for that country to cooperate with U.S. border issues. The United States insists in going it alone, with an expensive border apparatus, and a law enforcement approach that has not paid off. This is the path of empire, attempting to secure its outer perimeters at an increasingly higher cost. History has shown that this path is doomed. Consequently, in the process of analyzing what it is like to live and work and study and move about on the frontlines of these border wars, I also want to expose the absurdity of dealing with the border unilaterally. That is, the United States treats the boundary as if beyond the borderline there were simply an abyss, and the "national security threats" on it came from that dark chasm that Mexico is assumed to be.

THE SCOPE OF THE BOOK

It is against this background: a mixed picture of the border, a democratic deficit, three distinct border problems and a single government response to them, that this book is written. These pages argue that illegal drugs, undocumented migration, and homeland security at the border are three problems interrelated mostly by the fact that they happen on the border. They need to be analyzed independently, taking into account their unique characteristics. Each problem has its own dynamics, its own actors, its own motives, and its own scenarios—even when there are points of interception among them. Bluntly put, they are not the same issue and they should not be treated as such. To examine each of them and to demonstrate why a single U.S. strategy against three distinct problems is not a workable solution in the long term, I rely on real-life border stories to draw attention to these issues, their origin, their nature, and their day-to-day development. I try to bring the reader to the daily activities of a drug trafficker, or the ordeals of an undocumented worker, or the way the border is changing by the new homeland security regime. Although all these stories happen along the same geographical location, it is important to separate them because it becomes easier to see the absurdity of dealing with three entirely different issues in the same way, waging an all-out war on the border that is at once transforming and hurting life on the border and driving a wedge between two neighbors.

At the end of the book, I outline a longer term solution to the problems of the border. But that long-term solution is one that requires hard work, much patience, and strategic investments by both the United States and the Mexican governments. I also argue that the political will and the leadership vision, however, are not there. No one yet, in either country, has dealt with the border within the larger framework of an integrating North America. The solution, by default, has been a border strategy that has not paid off and is not likely to pay off in the near future, but whose costs keep mounting. Law enforcement is expensive, alienates neighbors, and has proven an inefficient solver of long-term, deep-seated issues such as illegal drug trafficking, undocumented migration, and now terror (if any) at the border. A war of attrition on the border does not seem to be successful today or in the future.

Let us now disaggregate the three fundamental border issues to show the logic behind each of these border problems. This separation of the issues will help analyze them separately and understand what is behind each of them. This same examination should expose the futility of the twentieth-century approach ratcheted up further by the Bush administration in the early years of the twenty-first century.

CHAPTER 2

The Drug War on the Border

A BIRD'S EYE VIEW

In November 2005, a marijuana-laden dump truck got stuck in the Rio Grande in Hudspeth County, Texas, while fleeing back to Mexico from U.S. law enforcement officials.[1] In September 2005, Aldo Manuel Erives, a former Border Patrol agent in El Paso, was sentenced to ten and a half years in federal prison for allowing drug couriers through a checkpoint without inspection.[2] In December 2004, Robert Dean Harper and Timothy Gavin Hynd were arrested by the Highway Patrol in Tucson, Arizona, for attempting to smuggle 610 pounds of marijuana inside coffins.[3] In July 2003, Ismael "El Mayo" Zambada, Mexico's number one drug trafficker, evaded the Drug Enforcement Agency's 19-month-old "Operation Trifecta," even while U.S. authorities reported capturing 240 suspected drug smugglers in the United States and Mexico, and seizing 6 tons of cocaine.[4]

All these stories have something in common—they are part of a war on drugs, which the U.S. government is waging on the U.S.-Mexican border. Mexican and American newspapers and magazines are full of stories like these. A quick Internet search will yield thousands of drug war stories over the last years of what is now America's longest war.

When President Richard Nixon declared a war on drugs in 1969, the U.S.-Mexico border became, for all practical purposes, the frontline of a never-ending war between the U.S. government and the drug-smuggling cartels. The border is where the government and the drug smuggling organizations wage their fiercest battles, and where both sides suffer most of their defeats and score most of their victories. Thus, it is worth asking: what exactly is the relationship between the border and the drug war? The answer is, simultaneously, simple and complex.

ECONOMICS AND GEOGRAPHY

Two fundamental truisms combine to explain America's longest war. The first of these was pronounced by Charles Caleb Colton (1780–1832) who wrote that "[c]ommerce flourishes by circumstances, precarious, transitory, contingent, almost as the winds and waves that bring it to our shores." The other maxim is even simpler: geography is destiny. That is, a standard map can reveal more about the fortunes and strategies of the players in a given issue than all other explanations combined. Analyzing the war on drugs on the border requires that we consider these rather deceptively mundane observations because they are nevertheless the key to uncovering the dynamics and fate of the struggle to eliminate the production, trade, and consumption of mind-altering substances in the United States. The supply route flourishes along the border because of these two forces: economics and geography.

It's Economics

To begin to understand the illegal drug business, we need to recognize that humans have innate desires, especially for pleasure. Almost all human desires produce economic activity. When one is hungry, there is resort to a supplier of food. When one desires stimulation, one seeks a place for entertainment. In the United States, there are some 20 million people who regularly desire and gratify the pleasure that mind-altering drugs produce. Just as grocers provide food and entertainers provide entertainment, so do illegal drug dealers provide mind-altering drugs. The market for psychotropic drugs is like any other commodity. There is a product, there is a supplier, there is a middleman, and there is a consumer. Economics, then, can help explain the entire activity of the drug trade.

Even when a government makes the gratification for an innate desire illegal, the innate desire still remains; and very likely there are still willing suppliers of the desired good. The result is the creation of a black market. In the illegal drug black market, all the elements of a normal economy are distorted. In such an economy the rewards and risks are both magnified. For example, a unit of marijuana of 0.5 grams costs about $1.70 to produce. On the street, it sells for $8.60. A profit margin of $6.90 per unit of 0.5 grams in a free and open market would not last long. In an open market, competition would eliminate this excessive profit. The $6.90 profit per unit is the risk premium that draws the "criminal" to willingly engage in a highly dangerous activity: producing and trading marijuana. A black market creates a class of criminals because government prohibition of the product will drive the market players underground creating a clandestine network of producers, traders, and consumers. Participants in such a market are thereby made criminals.

Throughout the history of humankind, borders and black markets have been closely related, usually because individuals are willing to engage in smuggling the forbidden goods across the borderline. With this understanding, it is easy to see why smuggling is pervasive. The connection between economic incentives and criminal behavior was intuited by Adam Smith in *The Wealth of Nations* when he said that "[n]obody will be so mad as to expose himself upon the highway, when he can make better bread in an honest and industrious way." And yet, on the Mexican border, there are people mad enough to engage in organized crime on the sheer basis of the profits to be made from the drug trade. These can be exorbitant. Drug trafficking is the most profitable organized crime in the world and America is the most important market for illegal drugs. The estimated annual income from drug trafficking and dealing is virtually impossible to calculate. The United Nations Office of Drug Control and Crime Prevention estimated it could be as much as $400 billion worldwide and *The Economist* argues that it could be as high as $150 billion.[5] On the U.S.-Mexico border, the profits are estimated to be $80 billion. The reality is that no one knows accurately how much money there is to be made, but it is easily in the tens of billions of dollars. The sheer profit incentive for anyone to partake in this activity is enormous.

To the estimated annual profits from the drug trafficking business add the current conditions of high unemployment and low income in Mexico. This will yield a tremendously fertile ground of thousands of men who are willing to risk their lives for a share of the drug trade profit. According to the International Labor Organization, in 1995 there were 1.1 million unemployed men in Mexico. Although unemployment went down, as of 2003 there were still 560,000 unemployed Mexican men.[6] Considering that in Mexico even part-time and self-employed persons (e.g., vendors in the streets) are considered employed, we are left with an exorbitant number of men able and willing to pick up a trade that promises quick riches. Moreover, the Mexican labor force adds 1 million workers per year but has steadily produced only about 500,000 jobs per annum. That means that every year 500,000 people are very much on their own. Many choose to enter organized crime networks and even more move on to the United States as undocumented workers. These individuals—and they are overwhelmingly men—are rationally making their calculations on the basis of utility maximization. They measure both benefits and risks to the best of their knowledge and many conclude that it is worth risking life and liberty for the kind of profits that can be made in the drug trade.[7] What else can explain the fact that most drug traffickers die young and the rest get old in jail, and there remains a never-ending supply of men willing to take the place of the dead or the jailed?

Furthermore, the income levels in Mexico are still well below those of the United States. The minimum wage in Mexico is between $4 and $5 a day. In the United States, the minimum wage exceeds $5 an hour. As one climbs up the wage ladder, the disparities between the two countries generally grow even starker. Whatever scale one uses, however, the wage disparity across the U.S.-Mexico border is enormous, even in the context of the greater prosperity of the Mexican border states and the lesser prosperity of the U.S. border counties, particularly in the lower Rio Grande valley in Texas. These border asymmetries have a strong effect on the incentives for individuals to participate in the drug trade. It is quite common in El Paso, Texas, to see young Mexican and Mexican-American men and women being led in handcuffs to jail where they are processed for attempting to smuggle drugs hidden in their vehicles. These young men and women—as young as 18 years—are often convinced by drug traffickers to cross a load of drugs on a one-time basis in exchange for hundreds or even thousands of dollars. The amount of money offered to many of these B1-B2 visa holders (crossing card) is several times what it would take them to make in a single month. If they get away with crossing the load of drugs—and many do— they receive a handsome reward with hardly any strings attached.

In addition, human development in Mexico is still lacking. Many of these men (and some women) are unskilled labor. As such they cannot obtain well-paying jobs. They are willing to try a trade that requires only the ability to behave like a thug, handle a gun, be a bodyguard, or drive a vehicle loaded with illicit drugs. These are skills that are easy to acquire because they do not require long-term training. When in the 1980s Mexico became a chosen transshipment point for drug cartels from Colombia—which had been squeezed by U.S. counter drug efforts in the Caribbean—the initial scouts sent by the Colombian drug lords to liaison their organizations in Mexico found many Mexican men willing to collaborate with them.

The attraction to the drug trade is, albeit not absolutely, fed by wealth disparities along the border. Thus, much of the drug trade along the border cannot be attributed to the morality or immorality of the border, or the good or ill intentions of those who participate in the production and trafficking of illicit drugs, but to the sheer economic incentives that the business itself offers and the structural forces influencing border asymmetries such as differences in income levels, unemployment, and the low-skill levels of many Mexican workers. Such is the "dark force" against which the U.S. government directs its drug war.

The Explanatory Power of a Standard Map

Real estate agents have long known that their business is about location, location, location. For drugs and the border, the same rule holds. The U.S.-Mexico border is the busiest border in the world. According to the

Bureau of Transportation Statistics, 4.23 million trucks with 2.6 million loaded truck containers, 7,774 trains with 266,469 loaded train cars, 88 million personal vehicles with 194 million persons, 319,087 buses with 3,747,337 million bus passengers, and 48,663,773 pedestrians crossed the border on the U.S.-Mexico border in 2003.[8] This is in addition to the million-plus individuals who attempt to cross illegally every year between ports of entry (POEs). That number of crossings is staggering for any agency to keep track of and to inspect thoroughly. Border inspectors must necessarily rely on random checks to detect illegal drugs or contraband coming from Mexico. The windows of opportunity for those who would use the border to smuggle illegal drugs is enormous. According to a former drug trafficker I interviewed in Ciudad Juárez, many of the tons of drugs such as cocaine, heroin, and methamphetamines smuggled into the United States make it across through POEs, rather than between them. And many of them make it across the border hidden in trucks. The Drug Enforcement Administration's (DEA) own Web page proudly exhibits several narratives and pictures of operations conducted along the U.S.-Mexico border. And surely they cannot themselves estimate very accurately how much drug smuggling actually goes on.

With all the opportunities for smuggling drugs, the many men willing to work in the drug trade, the economic incentives to do so, the unabated appetite for drugs in the American public, and the nearly 2,100-mile U.S.-Mexico boundary, the border and illegal drugs cannot be separated. An estimated 70 percent of all the drugs consumed in the United States come across its Southwest border. The general routing through Mexico is certainly determined by the map; cocaine is a perfect example of this. Mexican traffickers obtain the cocaine from South American businessmen and transport it into and through Mexico. This is not difficult to accomplish. The Mexican police are nearly completely unable to stop this. In fact, some segments of the police actually cooperate with the drug dealers. Once the drugs reach the warehouses within Mexico, they are moved overland to the border and then into the United States by various methods discussed later in this chapter. Mexican rural areas are peppered with clandestine air strips where drugs arrive or where planes refuel on their way to their final destinations. Even well established airports serve as the entry for South American drugs into Mexico.

THE BEGINNING OF THE WAR

The border and illegal drugs do not have a long history. The relationship between illegal drugs and the border begins in the 1960s. America's love affair with illegal drugs began in the counterculture of that decade. Since then, the country's appetite for psychotropic substances has escalated from marijuana to heroin, cocaine, and the hardcore chemical drugs consumed in nightclubs around the country.[9] Because mind-altering drugs were already illegal, the growing appetite for them increased not only the risks of dealing in drugs, but also the profits of doing so. These profits, however, increased more than the risks because the incentives for people to deal in drugs grew considerably, not only in Mexico, but also inside the United States.[10] An increasing number of illegal drug producers and smugglers found it profitable to enter the business of selling illegal drugs.

Because the border was wide open, the costs of smuggling drugs into the United States through the 1960s and 1970s and by the 1970s, the illegal drug smuggling business was booming along the border. There were numerous small gang-like groups in Mexico that operated to smuggle drugs into the United States. The market was large and growing, and the willing suppliers were also many. Mexico was a major supplier of marijuana and heroin, particularly Mexican brown heroin. Cocaine came mostly from Colombia via the Caribbean.

During the early 1980s, the United States implemented a series of operations in the Caribbean to stem the flow of cocaine from Colombia.[11] In response, the Colombians began to look for different routes to smuggle their cocaine, thus expanding the drug war strategic game. They discovered Mexico, whose location and open border with the United States could be remarkable assets. Over two thousand miles of largely unguarded border into the largest drug market in the world could not go unnoticed. The Colombians found a willing counterpart in Mexico, Miguel Angel Félix Gallardo, a well-known Mexican drug smuggler who had consolidated many of the small time smugglers in the 1970s into a single organization and by then controlled much of the illegal drug trade along the border. His marijuana and heroin-based organization was already in place and ready to serve as a conveyor belt for Colombian cocaine. The alliance between the Colombian drug lords and Félix Gallardo's organization produced a formidable drug cartel that would operate through most of the 1980s. Félix Gallardo, a quiet man who preferred to negotiate and avoided violence for the most part, became the drug lord of the border. He consolidated the Colombian-Mexican multi-drug corridor into a formidable business.

Again, the drug war is a strategic game. In response to the development of the Colombian-Mexican connection, the United States redirected massive anti-drug efforts to the U.S.-Mexico border.[12] The efforts were largely expended with considerable insensitivity, bringing the U.S.-Mexico relationship to some of its lowest points.[13]

Félix Gallardo was finally arrested in 1989 in Mexico. He continued to run his operations from inside his prison cell, but his collaborators outside were in a constant struggle for control of the organization's operations on the border. With his many lieutenants vying for control of the drug business, Mr. Félix Gallardo sent a message to them from his prison cell. To receive his message they met in a posh hotel in Acapulco. Through his messenger,

Gallardo told them that given that the U.S. government, "the real enemy," was stepping up its efforts to destroy his organization, intra-organizational disputes had to be settled. In response to U.S. action, he ordered a territorial division of his organization. Each "lieutenant" would control one smuggling corridor. He then exhorted them to live in peace among themselves and to stay within their own territories. Thus, it was at this meeting that the modern drug cartels with their respective corridors would emerge: (1) the Tijuana Cartel, (2) the Sinaloa–Sonora Cartel, (3) the Juárez Cartel, and (4) the Gulf Cartel.[14] Starting in 1989 then, the U.S. government would not have one criminal organization to fight but four. These are the same organizations that today move at least 70 percent of all the drugs that enter the United States. American counter drug measures did little to undermine the Félix Gallardo cartel but did do enough to inspire the 1989 division of his organization into a group of drug smuggling oligopolies (cartels) that have been even more difficult to fight.

BETWEEN BUSINESS AND WAR

This brief, historical even if impressionistic view of the birth of the drug cartels, together with a quick look at the market forces that operate behind the drug trade, shows that the illegal drug business and the U.S. drug war on the border is a strategic game, strangely lodged between market forces and warlike strategies to fight it. As the United States squeezed the Colombian drug cartels headed by savvy "businessmen" in the Caribbean, the Colombians sought an alliance with the Félix Gallardo organization in Mexico. This led to a formidable business-like alliance and an increase in drug trafficking on the U.S.-Mexico border even as the United States and the Mexican governments made inroads into fighting the drug trafficking activities of the Félix Gallardo organization in the 1980s. After the reorganization, the four cartels have proven resilient against nearly all drug war strategies and tactics. To every attempted crack-down by the United States government, the cartels have responded by becoming highly flexible organizations that can adapt and adjust quickly to nearly any adverse circumstance. Whenever the U.S. government attempts to escalate the drug war, the cartels change their modus operandi: they invest in more sophisticated methods to smuggle drugs across the border, they recruit new members, they corrupt more officials, and they seek innovative ways to remove obstacles to the business of the organization, etc. The four drug cartels are by now veritable business corporations that have outlived their original founders. In spite of the approximately $12 billion that the U.S. federal government spends on the drug war every year, the four cartels continue to thrive and smuggle in nearly 70 percent of all drugs consumed in the country. And like corporations, they continue well after the entire workforce has changed—always refreshed by new ever more astute illegal drug entrepreneurs who are willing to take the risks in exchange for the profits. In effect, in regard to the drug cartels and U.S. tactics to destroy them, what does not kill them makes them stronger.

The drug war on the border is just such a cat-and-mouse game between law enforcement agencies and drug cartels. This game is a constant process of escalation.[15] Law enforcement agencies increase their resources, hire more personnel, and introduce the latest technology to intercept illegal drugs. The drug cartels respond with ever more creative ways to go around the latest law enforcement efforts. In this escalation game, the U.S. government is the general loser, scoring tactical victories (drug busts and arrests) but losing the overall war against the flow of illegal drugs. A diachronic analysis of illegal drug quality and availability in the U.S. streets shows that in spite of all the United States' tactical victories, illegal drugs are just as abundant as they have ever been and there is evidence that their price is dropping and their quality is increasing, signaling a steady, unabated supply.[16]

BUREAUCRATS VERSUS DRUG CARTELS: UNEQUAL ENEMIES

Just as in any war, where no two armies use the same manuals containing the standard operating procedures or train in the same strategies or tactics, the U.S. government's drug war has forced two very different types of "enemies" to confront each other. These important differences have resulted in a distinct disadvantage for the U.S. drug war bureaucracies vis-à-vis the drug cartels.

First, bureaucracies are very rigid hierarchical structures that do not allow for much flexibility in responding to contingencies. Any substantial changes in the budget or personnel or in the programs and operations take a long time and often legislative action, a notoriously slow process. The decision-making is also a process that requires many meetings and much planning. Although the drug cartels are somewhat pyramidal, they are not rigid structures at all. Changes in the organization are made very quickly, largely because the decision-making is centralized in a few capos and their lieutenants. This enables the cartels to be extremely flexible and adaptable. Often changes are implemented as a matter of routine to stay ahead of law enforcement organizations. In general, cartels respond very quickly to any contingencies or emergencies.

Second, U.S. drug war bureaucracies are saddled with handbooks full of ethical and legal rules and requirements. In addition, the labor force has certain rights and benefits. They often enforce their rights rather vigorously. They are not available 24 hours a day. Any law enforcement bureaucrat is accountable for human rights and for due process. A sloppy law enforcement officer not only makes his agency liable but can also cause the criminal to escape from the U.S. judicial system because of due process violations.

In contrast, in a drug cartel, there is no handbook and there are no ethical and legal requirements. The only handbook is the decisive calculations and will of the capos, which trickle down the workforce mostly through word of mouth. Cartel communications are relatively quick, without the long memoranda and paperwork trail that is required of a bureaucracy. In a criminal organization, there is no paperwork because there is no accountability to a public or its representatives. Moreover, there is no due process to speak of. Cartels are not accountable for due process or human rights, inside the organization or outside. Deception, lying, and murder are legitimate weapons in the arsenal of operating procedures of a drug cartel. Such instruments are obviously not available to a disciplined bureaucracy.

The result is that whereas bureaucracies do not change or adapt easily, drug cartels can change swiftly and adapt upon command. Their workforce is available 24 hours a day and it is generally highly disciplined. Death awaits a cartel member who fails to follow orders. This makes them highly flexible organizations that are able to respond to contingencies immediately.[17] That is the difference between the U.S. drug war bureaucracies and the criminal organizations they are up against. These conditions constitute a nearly insurmountable structural difference between U.S. anti-illegal drug bureaucracies and the four large cartels and it likely contributes to the ability of criminal organizations to defeat most U.S. drug war strategies and tactics and maintain their business booming all along the border and in the U.S. illegal drug market.

MODUS SMUGGLANDI

On a midday afternoon, Pedro, a 26-year-old, sits nervously waiting on line at a Nogales POE. He finally makes it to the inspection point. The U.S. border official leans toward the window of the car on the driver's side. He looks at Pedro who flashes his crossing card to the officer. The officer asks Pedro where he is going. Pedro, fashionably dressed, says that he is going shopping. Pedro is very nervous but contains himself quite well. His heart is racing, but he disguises his nervousness well. The official stands back up and waves him through. Pedro has just made it. His car has several kilograms of cocaine hidden in a secret compartment behind the dashboard. He drives the car to a house in Nogales where an automatic garage door opens. Once inside the locked garage, the drugs will be recovered from the car and stored; they will be readied to be taken to Tucson the next day, and from there on to Phoenix and Denver.

Smuggling drugs in a "fixed" vehicle, known as a "clavo" (nail), like the one Pedro was driving, is one way to smuggle drugs. But there is no single method for transporting drugs across the border. The drug cartels employ a variety of smuggling methods. Still, it is possible to classify their modus operandi.

The Port of Entry versus the Non-Port of Entry Axis

Most drugs enter the United States through the ports of entry (POEs) at the border. According to a former member of a drug cartel I interviewed in Ciudad Juárez, cocaine, heroin, and methamphetamines are too valuable to risk crossing between POEs, in the wilderness. They can be intercepted by a Border Patrol agent and the loss to the organization would be considerable.[18]

Like in any other business, drug smugglers prefer to minimize risk and reduce uncertainty. The method to accomplish this is by working hard to build "networks" of employees and bureaucrats who are willing to offer protection to the organization's operations through payoffs (corruption). This ensures that the cargo crosses safely into the United States. They are willing to pay not only Mexican but also American officials handsome rewards in order to minimize the risk of losing the merchandise. It is mostly small-time drug smugglers that risk crossing drugs between POEs, and usually only marijuana. Marijuana is not as valuable, hence potential losses are not so high and the risk of crossing between POEs is often worth it, as the Hudspeth incident referred to earlier shows.

The People versus the Vehicles Axis

In spite of the occasional media hype regarding the intersection between undocumented migration and drugs, the overwhelming majority of undocumented migrants cross on foot between POEs, while most drugs are hidden in vehicles that cross at POEs. Very few risk crossing the border on foot carrying illegal drugs. These are mostly novices or work for small-time drug dealers. Some may pose as backpackers or attempt to cross drugs hidden on their bodies or clothing at POEs. They are recruited by small-time smugglers and trained to hike certain routes that may or may not coincide with the preferred routes of undocumented workers. The Tohono O'odham Nation of Arizona has reported the arrest of some drug smugglers who cross on foot with their knapsacks full of cocaine or marijuana. Their reservation in south central Arizona has witnessed this problem.[19]

Smuggling drugs on foot between POEs is rare, however. An internet search for stories of individuals "busted" crossing drugs by walking either between POEs or even at POEs renders very few cases of this modus operandi. There are, of course, stories of people caught trying to smuggle illegal drugs hidden on their bodies and clothing or in their bags and luggage through legitimate POEs, but as U.S. officials get better at detecting the nervousness of a border crosser or odd shapes on their bodies or in their bags, crossing drugs on foot is just too risky. Also, the amount of drugs that a pedestrian can cross is small, compared to the amounts that can be crossed hidden in a vehicle. Those who get caught end up in local courts, rather than federal courts because they tend not to exceed the amounts that would force them into federal court with higher penalties. These pedestrian drug-crossers cannot provide much intelligence either, because they tend not to work for the large drug cartels but for smaller entrepreneurs and sometimes are hired on the spot for a few dollars! One individual reported that he was offered $50 to cross drugs on himself. Others reported that they did it because they were coerced or threatened. Yet others reported sheer economic need.[20] What a drug dealer offers is sometimes several times a Mexican resident's monthly salary, which can go a long way to help their families. But overall, pedestrians are not anywhere near the favored modus operandi of drug smugglers. They are inefficient and too risky.

A more favored method for smuggling drugs is vehicles (cars, vans, and pickup trucks). Vehicles are often modified to build in special compartments where drugs can be hidden. A vehicle prepared in such a way is known as a "clavo" ("nail"). The secret compartments tend to be in the gas tank, behind the dashboard, the spare tire, or some other non-suspicious compartment in the body of the vehicle. The drugs are wrapped in tin foil, saran wrap, or other packaging material. The packages are sometimes basted in substances from that range from gasoline to oils and perfumes so as to disguise the smell, permitting the load to be undetected by the sniffing dogs. According to my interviewee in Ciudad Juárez, the drug cartels have sniffing dogs to test the "clavos." If their sniffing dogs detect the smell, the appropriate steps are taken until they cannot detect it. Only then is the vehicle sent to the POE.

A "clavo" can make it across the border in two ways. The first is by taking a chance. The vehicle shows up in the hope of not being detected. Sometimes they are, sometimes they are not. Whether they are detected or not depends on a number of factors, including the presence of sniffing dogs, the nervousness of the driver, and the thoroughness of the inspection. "Clavos" are sometimes sent in groups, with one easily detectable so that agents are distracted by that one "bust" and neglect thorough inspection of the other vehicles crossing at that moment. The busted "clavo" is the price to pay for reducing the risk of the other "clavos" being caught. This works partly thanks to the "spies" posted on both sides of the border by the drug cartels. It is not uncommon to see idle men, often posing as vendors, whose job is to "spot" for the cartel, watching the work patterns of U.S. officials and looking for a "lazy" or "distracted" officer who might not bother to double-check a vehicle. This information is relayed to the cartel operatives who immediately send a pre-prepared "clavo" to that checkpoint at the POE.

A better way to reduce uncertainty and risk for a cartel is to smuggle a "clavo" in an operation that has been prearranged with a U.S. official working at a POE. This modus operandi involves the corruption of U.S. officials. Every year produces several dozen cases of corrupt U.S. officials who are willing to cooperate with a drug cartel. Most U.S. agents that become corrupt are motivated by greed. An agent usually makes an annual salary between $30,000 and $50,000 depending on rank and longevity in the job. A drug cartel is willing to pay anywhere between $10,000 and $20,000 to that same agent for allowing a "clavo" to come across by waving it through the POE inspection point.

A 2-day documentary on corruption by National Public Radio showed that several factors matter in tempting a U.S. official to become corrupt. One is greed, of course, but blood ties also matter. Many officials are tempted by their own relatives across the border. Corruption by U.S. officials has an enormous impact on facilitating the drug trade and is perhaps more perverse than the corruption of Mexican officials. A corrupt Mexican official may offer protection by overlooking the operations of the drug cartels, but the drugs are still in Mexico. A corrupt U.S. official may allow tons of marijuana and produce millions of dollars in profits by waving dozens of "clavos" through over time. That one official undermines all the efforts of his organization and constitutes a considerable loophole through which the drug business can profit enormously.[21]

The NAFTA Connection

The favored method of the drug cartels to smuggle their drugs across the border today is not "clavos"—though they, unlike pedestrians, are still extensively used. The large cartels now ride the formal NAFTA economy. There are nearly 5 million semi-trucks that cross the U.S.-Mexico border every year.[22] They carry 70 percent of all U.S.-Mexico trade, now an estimated total value of around $250 billion. NAFTA is turning out to be a heaven-sent blessing to the drug cartels. Over time, the four large cartels have come to rely on trucking as the primary conveyor belt of illegal drugs across the border. Tons of marijuana, cocaine, heroin, and now methamphetamines ride hidden in the millions of trucks that cross the border. These same millions of trucks also move the drugs on U.S. highways to the major metropolitan areas throughout the country.

What makes this possible is revealed in a simple mathematical reflection. Of the 5 million trucks that cross the border, only a fraction of them is inspected. It would be extremely costly and time-consuming to run a thorough inspection of every truck. Technology is helping to catch more of the hidden drugs: the infrared and X-ray scanners similar to a car wash sprayer that trucks now go through are helping considerably, but still only a fraction are detected. Cartel technicians are also looking for ways to beat the newest technology. Their oligopolies give them the resources to invest in such research.

The C-TPAT

U.S. bureaucracies realize the impossibility of inspecting every truck crossing the border and catching every load of drugs hidden in them. To circumvent this problem—and the potential of a terrorist attack on the border, the Homeland Security Department is building a new system called Customs and Trade Partners against Terrorism (C-TPAT).

C-TPAT is largely a trust-based system that consists of networks of intimate knowledge between U.S. officials, importers and exporters, and truck drivers. The drivers and the trucking companies are registered and precleared with Customs and Border Protection (CBP) as is the merchandise. C-TPAT participants are required to apply for preclearance to avoid delays at inspection points. The trucks are loaded at the warehouse or factory in the Mexican border town and a seal is placed on the cargo container to expose any break-ins or subsequent opening in order to hide illegal drugs in them. CBP agents may or may not break the seal upon inspection at the POE, but when they break it, they do not generally replace it. This sometimes allows a trucker to load illegal drugs kept in stash houses in border towns and move them via the major highways into metropolitan areas throughout the United States. C-TPAT, billed as essentially a supply chain security program for international businesses, is supposed to prevent such cheating and build trust among those participating in cross-border businesses.[23]

The C-TPAT system has proven to be fallible. The rewards the cartels offer to anyone willing to break the rules are just too high. Truckers can be tempted into breaking the trust. A truck operator from Laredo explained that some trucks, after leaving the warehouse in Mexico and before they arrive at the POE, take a "detour." At an appointed place, the seals are broken, the drugs loaded, and the seals replaced. Sometimes, it is not noticeable that the seals have been violated, although CBP inspectors are gaining experience in detecting whether a seal has been tampered with.[24]

Sometimes, the Mexican police, principally at the local level, offer protection to these trucks and escort them on their routes in Mexican border towns. My guide in Ciudad Juárez took me to Avenida Américas where a local policeman was standing directing traffic. The guide and I approached the police officer. The officer, who knew the guide, described the police force's willingness to "escort" a load of drugs in town so that no one would stop the truck on its route to the POE. Such services are regularly offered by the Mexican local police forces. At a May 2004 Conference on *Border Security: the New Realities*' lunch in El Paso, a Mexican businessman bitterly stated that their cargo was sometimes "contaminated" by corrupt drivers. Businesses often lose the merchandise and even the semi-truck, which are seized by CBP, when the truck is found to be carrying illegal drugs. To avoid this, many business owners and managers in Mexican border towns had bought small cars and hired drivers to "escort" the trucks all the way to the POE. This effort turned out to be very expensive and was largely scrapped. Besides, nothing guaranteed that the driver of the escorting vehicle was not in on the take as well.

New technology is being introduced to keep track of the 18-wheelers carrying the majority of trade between the United States and Mexico. GPS devices are being installed in the trucks to ensure that the company knows where a truck is at all times. Even so, there are too many transactions to keep track of. My Laredo interviewee said that often trucks are detected off their appointed route, perhaps even 30 or 40 miles south of the border. At that point, the trucking company must decide what to do. If they decide to report it to law enforcement authorities on the Mexican side, they risk losing the semi-truck and having the driver jailed. Generally, they first call a lawyer who can deal with the issue before reporting it to the authorities. The extremely risky legal protocol often leads to informal inquiries with the driver, without involving any government authorities at all. No real follow-up may happen at all.[25] The following table summarizes the current state of affairs in regard to smuggling methods.

	Pedestrians	"Clavos"	Trucks
POE	Older method. No longer preferred and almost never used	Increasingly favored by small-timer drug smugglers but still used extensively by cartels	Preferred method of the four largest cartels
Between POEs	Not preferred and hardly ever used. If used, it is mostly small loads of marijuana by "backpackers"	Not preferred and seldom, if ever, practiced	Nonexistent

The Narco-Tunnels

On February 27, 2002, U.S. officials discovered a 1,200-foot tunnel running between a private home in a farm east of San Diego and a home in the town of Tecate, Baja California. This sophisticated tunnel was used to smuggle tons of cocaine, marijuana, and other drugs between Mexico and the United States for perhaps as long as 3 years. On April 19, 2004, U.S. officials reported that they had discovered more underground tunnels that were being used by drug traffickers. Since September 11, U.S. drug officials have discovered more than ten passageways that usually run between buildings on the Mexican side to a house on the U.S. side. More than thirty tunnels have been discovered between Mexico and the United States since 1990. These tunnels have been used by drug traffickers to transport tons of cocaine and other drugs into the United States. Thus, in addition to the surface patrolling, U.S. border officials now have to use equipment such as ground-penetrating radars and large earth-excavating drills in order to discover the tunnels running between the two countries.

Driving along the border highway in Mexicali, Baja California, it is easy to see how building a tunnel in certain areas could be easily accomplished. In some areas close to downtown Mexicali, a stone's throw to my left was a regular Mexican neighborhood. Peering through the fence to the American side, I observed a paved street with a typical U.S. neighborhood row of homes. The distance between the two houses on my right and on my left could not have been more than the distance of a four-lane avenue with the median serving as the border between the two countries. Carefully planning and building a tunnel connecting two of these houses is entirely feasible.

The tunnels are yet another indication that the drug war is a strategic game. As the U.S. government makes it more difficult to cross drugs over the border, drug cartels respond by appealing to ever more creative ways of doing business. The narco-tunnels are one more strategic response by the drug capos in the never-ending drug war.

CORRUPTING THE WARRIORS

Nearly everyone who lives along the U.S.-Mexico border knows that Mexican officials are corrupt. The corruption is no secret to officials either. Anthony Placido, the DEA's top intelligence official has testified that "the single largest impediment to seriously impacting the drug-trafficking problem in Mexico" is Mexico's police corruption.[26] I, too, have personally witnessed acts of corruption by Mexican customs officials. Most Americans, however, would like to believe that U.S. border officials are not corrupt. And yet many are. The culture of payoffs flourishes on both sides of the border.

Walking into the Federal Court room in El Paso, any researcher becomes quickly aware that there are always ongoing corruption cases against U.S. officials. Recently, for example, a U.S. official used his personal vehicle to drive into Ciudad Juárez from El Paso and bring back a load of drugs. Because the officer was well known among his peers, they would usually wave him through. Very often, he would then drive the same car past the second checkpoint, in Sierra Blanca, Texas, and then turn in the drugs on the other side, safely on their route to Dallas or Houston or elsewhere. He was discovered only because someone else driving his vehicle was stopped beyond Sierra Blanca. Upon inquiry, it was discovered that he had crossed the same vehicle not long before and had turned it over to someone else at Sierra Blanca. A sting operation caught him in the act and he is now serving time.

The rewards for corrupting a drug warrior on the border are potentially very high. U.S. officials are powerful figures on the U.S.-Mexico border and the interior checkpoints, such as Sierra Blanca, Texas. They can stop you in your tracks or they can let you move freely inside the United States. And they guard the richest illegal drug market in the world. Drug cartels are constantly looking for the lazy or the greedy official and the incentives may pay an officer's income many times over. A U.S. official may make anywhere between $34,000 and $40,000 a year, while a drug lord may offer to pay him $15,000–20,000 for every drug load he waves through at the POE.[27]

Federal investigators are convinced that corruption among U.S. officials is a serious problem and they are constantly investigating discrepancies in officials' incomes and their lifestyles, etc., in order to follow threads that often lead to entire rings of corruption, such as the sting in Chicago where eighteen U.S. officials were caught. While upwards of fifty to sixty cases of corruption per year are open on account of drug smuggling or alien smuggling, only a fraction of them are probably being caught, and drug cartels are constantly recruiting new officers. The cartels have an entire team looking for ways to make connections with U.S. officials and tempt them to join the other side. This group is, according to a member of the Juárez cartel I interviewed, part of the Public Relations division of the Juárez Cartel.

Corruption among U.S. officials is particularly damaging because, with a wave of his hand, a single official can be responsible for tons of drugs that make it to the streets of U.S. cities and provide millions of dollars in profit for a drug cartel. Again, all the officer has to do is wave a vehicle through in exchange for handsome rewards. Although Mexican corruption is widespread and systemic, American corruption can go an even longer way toward producing enormous profits for everyone involved. A single U.S. official can do much harm and essentially undermine the work of all his coworkers by opening a huge hole on the border protection net that they are supposed to constitute.

Corruption is a fundamental component of any illegal industry. Drug trafficking could not be the exception. Corruption greases the wheels of the drug smuggling business and assures its flow. Corruption is not exclusively a Mexican phenomenon. It takes place on both sides of the border. The motivation is the same: greed. Corruption practices have also contributed to strengthening the hand of the large drug cartels because they are increasingly the only ones that can afford the millions of dollars that it takes to keep the wheels of the drug smuggling business rolling. The small-timers simply cannot afford to corrupt officials on either side of the border who increasingly demand more and more of the drug smugglers in a perverse game of reverse extortion.[28]

Mexican illegal drug-driven corruption is pervasive. It is systemic. It reaches thousands of individuals both horizontally and vertically within the country. A drug cartel may have several thousand direct employees—from buyers to spotters to smugglers to weapons procurers to sicarios (or gunmen) to accountants—but indirectly it pays off hundreds, if not thousands, of people, particularly law enforcement officials and politicians. Border law

enforcement agencies in Mexico are heavily penetrated by the drug cartels because they are indispensable in ensuring that the operations of the
drug cartels can be conducted without interference by government operatives not on the payroll of the drug cartels. Cartels are now becoming more
professionalized, hiring highly educated individuals who serve as Public Relations Officers that recruit the help of other professionals, including accountants, businessmen (to launder money), law enforcement officials, doctors,
lawyers, etc.

American officials do not offer this kind of protection to cartels or their operatives. American corruption is considerably less extensive and it is nowhere
near as systemic as Mexican corruption. But American corruption has a
much larger concentrated impact than Mexican corruption. It goes a much
longer way than Mexican corruption. Crossing the international border is
the riskiest operation for a drug smuggler. It is the toughest link in the chain.
A single corrupt American official is enough to let through tons of illegal
drugs producing hundreds of millions of dollars in profits for a cartel, by a
simple act as waving a "clavo" or a truck through a checkpoint. Corrupting
a U.S. official pays much more handsomely than corrupting nearly any official in Mexico. Most of the time, a U.S. official's corruption is uncovered
because their lifestyle appears to surpass their earnings.

Interestingly, the escalation of U.S. anti-drug efforts and the increased
effectiveness of U.S. officials at POEs have made it increasingly expensive
to bribe them. The higher the risk for the corrupt official implies higher
payoffs by the drug cartels. Often, a corrupt official will even demand more
money to wave a "clavo" through the inspection point. Cartels now dis-
burse millions of dollars to buy officials on both sides of the border. Both
the heightened vigilance and its consequent higher payoffs are squeezing the
small-time smugglers out of business. They cannot afford the bribes. This
in turn concentrates the ability to do business in the hands of the four large
cartels.

THE PROTECTIVE SHIELD OF THE BORDER POLICE

Walking along Avenida López Mateos in Nogales, Sonora, I came to a
corner where a young woman was selling newspapers. The headline of the
local paper, *El Imparcial*, was more than clear: *Tres Ex-Policías Ejecutados*
(Three Former Policemen Executed). Digging into the newspaper columns,
it became clear that these former policemen had actually been drug-law
enforcement agents in the states of Sonora and Sinaloa in the past. These
men are examples of the conditions of law enforcement in Mexico today.
It is very difficult in any one Mexican border town today to disentangle
drug trafficking and law enforcement. Almost all Mexican law enforcement
officials along the border with the United States are bought off by the drug
trafficking cartels or neutralized by explicit or implicit threats. The strategy

has long been the same: "plata o plomo" (silver or lead). In other words, you either take the bribe (silver) or a bullet to the head (lead). At a minimum, a police officer that does not want to become corrupt will simply keep silence to protect himself and cover the corruption of his fellow officers. This is a rough equivalent to the "blue wall" in U.S. police departments. Whatever the situation of the police officer, the choice that any new police officer in Mexico faces is to keep silent, to actively participate in protecting the drug trade or to resist and be killed. Such was the case of the new chief of police in Nuevo Laredo in June 2005. For weeks no one would accept the job in that drug cartel-controlled border town in the state of Tamaulipas. Finally, Alejandro Domínguez was convinced to take the job. On that hot day of June 8, 2005, only a few hours after taking the job of city Police Chief, Mr. Domínguez was gunned down. Even though the Mexican federal government practically occupied the city with federal police agents and Army soldiers and placed nearly 700 police officers under house arrest, more deaths continued to occur over the following days. Many argued that the major battle was between the Zetas, a group of Army soldiers who have organized to provide protection to the Gulf Drug Cartel that controls the region and the Men in Black, a group fighting for control of the territory on behalf of the Juárez and Sinaloa Cartels. Regardless of the unprecedented presence of Mexican federal policy and military, the choices for any police officer in a Mexican border town remain unchanged. Most cannot remain neutral and sooner or later take sides.

The choices do not end there, however. Often, police officers desert the force to become more active members of the drug trade. They become bodyguards, operatives, or even sicarios who carry out the executions of those "condemned to death" by a drug lord. Drug lords prefer to recruit former policemen because they are already trained in the use of weapons, and torture techniques, and know everyone else inside the police force, not to mention the weak points of the law enforcement organizations.

Thus, in nearly every case, the job of the police forces in border towns becomes serving as a protective shield for the drug lords and neutralizing any real government action against the drug cartels, and they do a very good job of it. Street level cops provide day-to-day protection to the drug lords. They often give advanced warnings of any government action against a cartel. They moonlight guarding drug shipments and warehouses. And many of them serve as sicarios for the drug lords when there is the need to eliminate a rival. In fact, the actual operative personnel of any given drug cartel is often composed of former policemen or policemen moonlighting for the drug cartel. The drug trade is so profitable that many policemen are tempted to leave their jobs outright and join the drug organizations. Such was the case of the three former policemen executed in Nogales the day before I arrived there—Pablo Gracia Noriega, Jesús Martínez Luna, and Jesús Heriberto García Valenzuela.[29] One of these three had been in charge of directing the major operations by the state police against the drug lords.

VICTIMIZING THE CRIMINALS WITH BRIBES

My interviewee in Ciudad Juárez attempted to disentangle for me the relationship between the cartels and law enforcement officials in Mexico. He argued that sometimes the cartels are the "victims" of law enforcement officials because they often extort criminal organizations attempting to obtain a greater share of the profits than the cartel is naturally accustomed to giving up. Law enforcement officials and even some politicians become extortion entrepreneurs and demand increasing amounts of money in exchange for allowing the cartel to operate freely within their jurisdiction or for offering protection. Many do not passively take what the cartel is willing to give. Instead, they demand their own price. If the cartel does not deliver, its operations can be made quite difficult. Occasionally, there will be a police officer or even a politician executed because their demands on the cartel far exceed what the cartel is willing to pay for help or protection.

VIOLENCE AND THE DRUG TRAFFICKING BUSINESS

For a long time, the border's image has been that of a violent place. Nevertheless, there are certain discernible principles that can help us understand illegal drug-related violence on the border. In fact, illegal drug-related border violence is seldom random, even in these circumstances. Instead, border violence obeys certain patterns and necessities by the actors that perpetrate it and suffer it.

When a government makes a commodity, such as psychotropic substances, illegal, but the human desire for them remains unabated: the result is the creation of a black market. In any market, disputes inevitably arise; so also in a black market. But in a black market, the dispute resolution procedures that exist in a legal, regulated market do not exist. Those who participate in an illegal market, such as drug dealers, retain an acute awareness of the risks involved and know that all kinds of procedures might be used, even illegal practices, up to and including violence, in order to resolve disputes among the participants. Sometimes nonviolent procedures, such as negotiations, are used, even as a first instance of dispute resolution. But then, sometimes, the dispute escalates to the use of illegal practices. They may only threaten the use of violence, but sometimes, they may actually use it. Often, violence is used not only to regulate competition, but also to adjust accounts. Illegal drug-related violence for the most part is not random. It has a purpose and even a meaning. Let us explore further the two specific reasons why a cartel would resort to violence: competition and adjustment of accounts.

Competition: Violence between Cartels

As explained earlier, the border is divided into four great territories or smuggling corridors: the Tijuana Cartel, the Sinaloa–Sonora Cartel, the Juárez Cartel, and the Gulf Cartel. Every so often, there is a breakdown into violence because the lords of one or more cartels decide to compete with another for control of a given drug smuggling corridor. This competition, as in Nuevo Laredo in the summer of 2005, and in Ciudad Juárez in 1996, can lead to extreme and sometimes very public inter-cartel violence. Nuevo Laredo is a highly profitable corridor because nearly 1.5 million trucks coming from Southern Mexico (Mexico City, Guadalajara, etc.) and from Monterrey take the Nuevo Laredo-Laredo POE route. It is not surprising that the Gulf Cartel's operatives and the Sinaloa–Sonora cartel were vying for control of this corridor. Competition between them resulted in a violent summer in 2005.

Competition: Intra-Cartel Violence

At times, a capo is killed or captured and jailed. This can provoke a struggle among his potential successors and sometimes this intra-cartel violence becomes public. This can lead to an outburst of public violence that often involves dozens if not hundreds of dead and disappeared, as in the Nuevo Laredo case in the summer of 2005. Still, it is rare when a person who has nothing to do with the drug cartels gets killed. Most violence in these cases is intra-cartel, although it nevertheless projects a negative image of the border. When Osiel Cárdenas, the head of the Gulf Cartel was imprisoned, competition among his potential successors, including his brother, became ferocious and this also contributed to the Nuevo Laredo violence of 2005. Thus, intra-cartel violence exacerbated the violence already in progress by inter-cartel competition for control of this profitable corridor.

Taking Sides: The Mexican Government

Besides inter- and intra-cartel rivalries, what can exacerbate border, illegal drug-related violence is the level of willingness of the Mexican government to cut an explicit or implicit deal with the drug cartels designed to maintain public order. It is generally acknowledged that the Mexican government— federal or state—will favor one group over its competitors. The deal generally implies that the protected group will keep its executions to a minimum and its operations out of the public's eye.

President Vicente Fox's administration (2000–2006) has largely refused to compromise along these lines. Instead, he has declared an all-out war on the cartels making it very difficult for any group to establish most-favored status anywhere. The cartels have had to defend their corridors with increased violence not only against opportunistic violence from their competitors but also from a government, which has not let up the fight against the cartels. The capture of several capos by the Mexican federal government has created instability inside the cartels and between them. The result is worsened violence. Consequently, Nuevo Laredo's summer 2005 violence was compounded by the decision of the Mexican government not to negotiate.

Often the Mexican government or specific state governments will negotiate with a cartel explicitly allowing their operations to continue and "faking" a drug war by going after the small, illegal drug entrepreneurs and taking credit for a drug war, which punishes the small-time smuggler while allowing the large cartels to operate unhindered.

"Plata o Plomo": Silver or Lead

The fundamental modus operandi of a cartel vis-à-vis the government and its officials in Mexico is "plata o plomo" (silver or lead). When a cartel requires the protection of a law enforcement agency, or at least needs it to stay out of its way, the officials are both incentivized and threatened at the same time. You either take the bribe (silver) or get killed (lead). Simply staking out a neutral position is not always a prerogative allowed to Mexican government officials by the cartels—although there are those who have managed to remain somewhat neutral and not be bothered by the cartels. However, when an official decides to stay away from the criminal organizations and not take their bribe, the result is that he becomes mostly ineffective in combating drug trafficking. More often than not, officials take the money. The sums are too tempting and the alternative, to die, is just too extreme. Neutrality of course means becoming ineffective at doing one's work.

Taking money from a cartel always creates a liability for a government official. Drug cartels will sometimes not kill an official who remains neutral or even who harasses their operations somewhat but who has never taken anything from them. Executing a government official who is not involved with a drug cartel at all is a step capos prefer to avoid.[30] They prefer instead to neutralize the incorruptible official by buying off those around him. But if someone has taken money from a cartel and then turns on it, death is the certain payback. Their bodies are often found tortured in back alleys or empty lots.

Disciplining the Workforce

Most day-to-day illegal drug-related violence, however, originates in the cartels' tactics used to discipline the workforce. Nearly all the bodies found scattered around the border cities, tortured and dead, have to do with "ajuste de cuentas" ("account adjustment"). This is an issue of justice among drug lords and their employees, suppliers, or clients. Account adjustment occurs because in the clandestine business of drugs there are no legal mechanisms for the resolution of disputes, particularly between the capos and their employees, suppliers, and clients. Thus, when one of these cheats the cartel, he is usually dealt with swiftly. He is tortured, killed, or "disappeared." Cheating cannot be allowed in an illegal market and because it cannot be dealt with legally, it is generally punished severely. In a formal economy, these relationships have law enforcement and judicial systems to resolve this kind of cheating and maintain labor relations relatively peaceful. Such mechanisms are not available in a black market and threats and violence are nearly the only way that cheating is resolved.

The violence, with its torturing and deaths, can happen for several reasons. A few instances are illustrative. First, a member of the cartel may "shave off" a portion of the drugs from a bundle in his care. He may then try to sell it on his own to make a profit on the side. Similarly, an employee of the cartel may try to dilute a drug load by adding other substances to it in order to keep a certain amount of the drugs and either consume or sell them. Someone may also make off with a load of drugs or cash—a type of activity known as "bañarse" or "to take a shower." A client can also feel tempted to do this. An employee, supplier, or client may become an informant of the law enforcement authorities as well, usually the Drug Enforcement Administration (DEA). Sometimes a "bocón" ("big mouth")," someone who "talks too much" and blabs unnecessary information, can also get in trouble. Even taking unnecessary risks in crossing a "clavo" that is captured by the inspectors at the POE can be a reason for punishment by torture or death. Punishing cheating or mistakes sends a strong message to the cartel's employees and keeps the workforce, suppliers, and clients disciplined, although at the same time, it projects an image of extreme violence along the border.

Random Violence: The Exception to the Rule

Seldom will drug lords and their lieutenants employ strictly senseless violence. Although sometimes passersby may become victims of illegal drug-related violence, their wounding or death is nearly always accidental. A Cartel's violent act is always related to a target on account of treason, cheating, whistle blowing, competition, etc. The innocent victims are "collateral damage"—usually passersby. Nevertheless, from time to time, a drug lord emerges who is particularly brutal and does not care to be discreet. The Arellano Félix brothers in Tijuana were particularly brutal and often killed for the sake of killing or because they felt annoyed at someone. Ramón Arellano Félix in particular was well-known for using unnecessary violence, for being particularly cruel, and for avenging petty peeves. Blancornelas recounts, for example, how Ramón shot a neighbor dead for complaining that the music was too loud; or how he shot the son of a prominent Tijuana family for arguing outside a bar with a young man who happened to be his friend; or how he shot a waiter for warning him that he could not take the drink outside the bar building. But this seems to have been his personality trait more than the regular modus operandi of the cartel capos. Most prefer to do their business quietly, including their most violent actions.

THE SICARIOS

The executioners for a cartel are known as "sicarios." These are death squads that the drug lords handle as discreetly as possible. Their work is gruesome. The sicarios torture, maim, or kill, and take care of the dead bodies. Sometimes they dispose of the dead by either burying them clandestinely or by leaving them in a public space in order to send a message to the cartel's employees, to the government, or to society in general. Sicarios are men hired elsewhere, often squads put together for a single job. The men are brought to the place where they are to carry out their executions. Their mission is usually narrow and well specified in advance. They live together, usually in houses, and come out only when the job is ready to be done. Their work usually takes place at night, although they may also work during the day. Most of them are drug addicts and operate under the influence of some drug in order to mitigate any emotional reactions of remorse or revulsion while torturing or killing someone. When they are finished with their assigned task, they are sent back to their hometowns elsewhere in Mexico. Occasionally, an American citizen with specific skills, such as sharp shooter, will also be hired for a specific job. In general, only a cartel can afford a death squad. The small-time smugglers cannot. If they are cheated out of their merchandise or cash, they lose it all; they are left to take revenge with their own hands.

Handling the Disloyal

Another common feature of the border is the dead body found randomly here and there, usually tortured. To this too, there is a method. Once an individual has been identified by the drug lords as a target for torture or death, the sicarios are brought in and prepared to do the job. Intelligence is gathered on the whereabouts of the target. A propitious moment is chosen to execute the target or to kidnap him and take him to a chosen place for torturing—sometimes houses rented or bought for that purpose. If the house was bought, after it is used, it is cleaned out and sold. It is almost always preferable to kidnap the target and conduct the ghastly task of torturing him or killing him in a house where there are no witnesses. Many of the bodies are never actually found. Quite a few of them are buried in these same houses, under concrete slabs, in back patios. Other times, the bodies are buried under the floors of the house. According to my guide in Ciudad Juárez, there are hundreds, possibly thousands of bodies buried under the backyards and patios and rooms of houses all along the border. This particular interviewee told me that he could personally point out several houses where bodies are buried, very often unknown to the current occupants of the house.

Those buried in houses constitute "los desaparecidos" or "the disappeared." Sometimes, however, the cartel needs to "send a message." In this case, the body disposal is public. To send a message, the bodies of "cheaters" (employees, clients, or suppliers) are disposed of in a public place. These are usually found by some passerby early in the morning of the next day. There are several well-known methods to dispose of a body. One is known as "encajuelados" or "en-trunked" because they are generally found in the trunks of stolen cars. There is in fact an ongoing business of stealing cars on U.S. border towns to sell them to the drug dealers for needs such as this one. Another disposal method is "encobijados" or bodies found wrapped in a rug or a blanket, just thrown out in the desert, empty lots, drainage ditches, or back alleys. Another method is the "entambados" or men who are stuffed into an empty oil barrel and disposed of anywhere in the city, as well. Almost always these men show signs of torture and sometimes specific signs that reflect their "crime" or "mistake." A man with his finger cut off and stuffed in his mouth was probably an informant. A man with gunshots in the palms of his hands probably stole drugs or money ("took a shower"), and so forth.

MONEY AND DRUGS: NORTH AND SOUTH

On a weekday afternoon, Juan, a thirty-something Ciudad Juárez resident, got out of a taxi at the Santa Fe Bridge and ran across the border. He went straight to a U.S. official and asked for his help. He claimed that he was about to be killed by a sicario from the Juárez Cartel. Juan's job had been to collect the cash coming from the sale of drugs from all over the United States and to then transport it across into Mexico; he was paid $20,000 to $30,000 for every $1 million that he transported into Mexico.

That fated day, Juan thought it harmless to take his mother along on his trip. When he drove to the house where he was to deliver the money, the Juárez Cartel members waiting for him saw him as an undisciplined worker because he had been instructed to always ride alone. They took him outside the house to the backyard. As he was pacing, guarded by the sicarios, he could see through the window that his mother was lying in a pool of blood. She had been killed inside the house. He kept his cool and on the first opportunity made a run from the sicarios. He managed to make it to a major street and to flag down a taxi, which took him to the border.

The American appetite for illegal drugs is enormous; it constitutes a huge, northward pull. The border is caught in the drug war as the passageway for drugs to satisfy this insatiable demand. But, what happens to the money gathered in the millions of daily illegal drug transactions that occur in bars, clubs, restaurants, street corners, houses, and elsewhere, throughout the United States? A ton of cocaine may produce "tons of cash." How is it possible to hide and transport all this money? How does the money make its way down to Mexico and Colombia?

This is a complicated and increasingly dangerous process as well. Cartels send drugs north, accepting the risk of not being paid after delivery. There is a small chance of this as the local dealer can lose his or her client. There are disciplinary measures that are taken in these cases as well. My Ciudad Juárez interviewee informed me of three African–American women who failed to pay the cartel for the drugs sold to them. These three women were kidnapped and brought to Ciudad Juárez in the trunk of a car to force them to pay.

Most drugs move across the border and then north to the rest of the United States, an enormous majority of them in trucks and other vehicles. The money collected in those areas is warehoused in homes in major U.S. cities and then carefully packaged to be smuggled south. The money is concealed in trucks and vehicles traveling south. These same vehicles take it across the border into Mexico. Just as drug lords worry about packaging their drugs so that they are not detected, they also worry about packaging the money so that it is not detected by U.S. or Mexican authorities, who can confiscate it. The money must then be warehoused in places scattered along the border and prepared for money laundering. Cartels today have sophisticated finance and accounting divisions that find creative ways to hide the cash and then to launder it. Professionals are hired for that purpose.

Sometimes, when the cash makes it to the U.S. border town, it is then crossed in smaller amounts into Mexico. Individuals are often hired to cross the cash into Mexico. They make trips south with cash hidden in various compartments in their vehicles. Moving cash south is increasingly as delicate as moving drugs north. Cheating by cash smugglers is just as likely to be punished as cheating by other cartel employees. Treason, shaving cash off the stashes, or stealing is punishable by torture and death as well. A person is paid up to $30,000 for crossing anywhere between $500,000 and $1 million south in his car, truck, or van. Increasingly, Public Relations specialists are hired by the cartels to find people who can cross the cash south without raising anyone's suspicions. Millions of cars cross the border every year and some of them do so with cash stashed inside. This is made somewhat easier by the fact that the Mexican customs system relies on random checks where only about one in ten or twenty vehicles is checked—if it triggers the red inspection light upon crossing. Most vehicles simply cross right through into

Mexico without being bothered. This enables the drug lords to cross tons of cash going south.

Efficient money smuggling contributes to the maintenance of the large cartel operations in Mexico and beyond. The cartels can take losses. They can bribe a considerable number of people. They can invest in R&D to go around the use of technology by U.S. law enforcement officials. In general, the enormous amounts of cash have created veritable oligopolies that can operate massively and turn a profit, even when the United States steps up the pressure on their organizations.

THE MEDIA AND THE DRUG WAR

Most Americans get their news regarding the drug war from the media. The media not only chooses the content of drug war stories, but they frame the issue as well, providing the general public with a certain view of the border. Sometimes the media focus on the number of overdoses that end up in hospitals, the ups and downs of drug use, street-level drug dealing, the ravages of drug consumption in U.S. cities, and law enforcement drug busts. They sometimes focus on the actors of the drug war: the criminals, the organizations, the capos, or the law enforcement officials. But when the media focuses on the drug war on the border, they generally tend to sound a note of doom. Often, the portrayal of the border is a largely lop-sided view of how the drug war and the border relate to each other. The words of U.S. Ambassador to Mexico on June 9, 2005, regarding the Nuevo Laredo violence of that summer could be the words of nearly any story covering the drug war on the border. His declarations received extensive coverage in both the U.S. and the Mexican media. He said,

A few weeks ago, I asked the State Department to re-issue a public announcement about the on-going violence in the border region. This violence, combined with previous murders and numerous kidnappings involving U.S. citizens, remains a priority concern for state and municipal leaders and U.S. citizens along the border. And while I have no interest in criticizing the Mexican Government, given my responsibility to promote the safety and security of U.S. citizens, I will not shy away from speaking out when their safety is at stake... As friends and neighbors, we should be honest with each other about the rapidly degenerating situation along the border and the near-lawlessness in some parts. I absolutely recognize that the security of the border region around Nuevo Laredo is a shared responsibility and we are committed to doing our part. The bottom line is that we simply can't allow drug traffickers to place in jeopardy the lives of our citizens and the safety of our communities.[31]

Then coverage of the bloody 2005 summer of Nuevo Laredo died down by the fall. Thus, the media's sporadic, incomplete, and largely scandal-driven coverage of illegal drugs contributes to this generalized, partial understanding of illegal drugs and the drug war, particularly on the border. It also contributes to the largely negative image that the border has both among Americans and Mexicans. Media coverage, even in that bloody summer, completely ignored the positive aspects of what is going on in Nuevo Laredo, including, for example, that most people continued living their daily lives worrying about the same thing that everyone else does: work, school, and so on.

Worse yet, for the bulk of the population, the border and its relationship with the illegal drugs some 20 million Americans consume regularly and many more consume casually is a problem others focus on.[32] Most Americans do not frequently think of the border and illegal drugs and they seldom connect the appetite for illegal drugs in major U.S. cities with the smuggling operations of criminal organizations on the border. Even border residents have learned to live with the drug war as part of their communities. They hardly pay attention to it anymore. On the border, the drug war is part of the landscape.

THE WEALTH OF DRUGS: ON NARCO MANSIONS AND NARCO-JUNIORS

Rio Grande City, the county seat of Starr County, is one of the oldest settlements in South Texas. Rio Grande City is located on the Rio Grande 100 miles from both Brownsville and Laredo. It is an international POE connected by bridge to the town of Camargo, Tamaulipas. Driving through Rio Grande City, the visitor can easily be surprised by the various mansions that sprawl around the area. Speaking with a native of Rio Grande City, I was "confidentially" told that some of these houses, like many in Laredo, Brownsville, and McAllen, are narco-mansions. A narco-mansion is defined by the locals as a house that belongs to someone who is making his money in the drug business. It can be a mansion that belongs to a drug trafficker, to his family, to a partner working in money laundering operations, or in other capacity. Often, the wives and children of various capos and lieutenants live in those narco-mansions. And more often than not, locals avoid even talking about them. It is simply "known" to whom these houses belong to; no one dares to acknowledge this reality in public.

Interestingly, however, the children of the large drug traffickers do study and travel extensively throughout the United States. They attend colleges and universities and shop at the most expensive malls in large U.S. cities. They drive luxurious cars and spend money lavishly. None of them seem to have trouble obtaining visas to enter the United States. This is partly because of the fact that the visa-issuing process in American consulates in Mexico places an inordinate importance on the number of zeros that the bank account of the visa applicant has. It is nearly always sufficient to show a bulky bank account to obtain a visa to travel and study in the United States. This has allowed a number of relatives of drug traffickers to live in relative safety inside the country that is waging war on their fathers! These privileged offspring of cartel capos and lieutenants are better known in Mexico as narco-juniors, the children of those who would smuggle drugs today and send their children to a posh liberal arts college in California or Texas.

THE BIG CARTELS VERSUS THE SMALL TIME PLAYERS

The large cartels do most of the illegal drug smuggling. But there are also a number of small, illegal drug entrepreneurs. I interviewed one of them in Parral, Chihuahua, Mexico. Every so often, he goes up to the mountains of Chihuahua and buys marijuana by the kilogram. He recruits the occasional worker to help him bring it down from the mountains and drive it to the border. There he generally hires a "clavo" entrepreneur or a truck driver to bring it across the border. He may also go out to the night clubs and recruit someone there to help cross a load, often a few dozen pounds at a time to minimize losses and to protect the smuggler whose sentence may be lighter if caught with a smaller load.

The small-time smuggler may sometimes pay a few hundred dollars to a naïve teenager or barfly to hide the drugs and sneak them across the border in his vehicle. Sometimes, imprudent partygoers are also willing to do so as they return across the border from "clubbing" in Mexico. It is not uncommon to see late-night drug busts and young people being led away in handcuffs for trying to cross a load of illegal drugs in their car in exchange for a few dollars.

For some time, the favorite group to recruit was Hispanic single mothers who were U.S. citizens and sometimes had their children with them to distract the inspection officer. Once the border inspectors caught on to this trend, this modus operandi disappeared almost entirely. To these women, the few hundreds of dollars earned smuggling drugs often made a big difference in their personal or family finances.

In an ironic twist, the Homeland Security strategy of the post-September 11 era is hurting these small time smugglers in higher numbers. As new technology is introduced, as border law enforcement resources and personnel increase, and as inspectors get more savvy at finding the drugs hidden in "clavos," the small, illegal drug entrepreneurs are being detected and caught in higher numbers.

The drug cartels, however, have the wherewithal to invest heavily in corrupting truckers, and U.S. and Mexican officials, and to invest in more sophisticated technology to get around Homeland Security tactics. They also invest in building better "clavos." If caught, they can also take larger losses, given the volume of drugs they handle. Unlike the small-time entrepreneurs, they enjoy an economy of scale that affords them higher risks. Thus Homeland Security effectiveness has contributed to strengthening veritable oligopolies in the drug cartels. This is further evidenced by the kinds of cases that come to the federal court along the border. Most of those arrested and hauled to court for smuggling are, or work for, small-time smugglers. Seldom is someone working for a large drug cartel arrested crossing a "clavo."[33] The testimony of many of those that end up in court shows that they are often inexperienced smugglers hired haplessly through a friend, at a bar, or on the streets. A quick analysis of court cases and testimony corroborates this consolidation of large cartels along the border because of enhanced Homeland Security tactics.

THE BORDER GEOGRAPHY OF THE DRUG WAR

Traveling along Highway 2 in Sonora, going west through the high desert reserve, I wondered at what point I had crossed over the territory that the drug lords agreed to as the line between their great cartels. The U.S. drug market is vast and the borderline long. It is nearly impossible for anyone to build an empire that can control the entire border and the entire market. Thus, just like the U.S. drug warriors are divided into two groups: prohibitionists and permissivists, the Mexican drug lords have had to make their own arrangements, corporate-style, to divide the borderlands and create peace among them. That is what a cartel consists of: a series of providers who agree to coordinate their actions in order to organize and maximize the profit for all. Because no corporation can survive if it has to defend its assets from the violence of others, the Mexican drug lords met to divide the border into what are essentially four great drug suppliers. The Gulf Cartel operates out of northeastern Mexico and supplies drugs going to the east. The Juárez Cartel operates out of northern Mexico and supplies drugs to the Midwest and east of the Rockies. The Sinaloa–Sonora Cartel operates out of western and southern Mexico, except for Baja California, and supplies drugs from west of the Rockies to the California border. The Tijuana Cartel operates out of the Baja California peninsula and supplies drugs to the west coast. The negotiations occurred mostly among the great lords in the 1990s, when the drug trade began to flow through Mexico rather than the Caribbean, which became unprofitable due to effective interception of drugs by the United States drug war troops. One of those great meetings occurred in Ciudad Juárez. There, the capos agreed to respect the boundaries of each Cartel.

CONCLUSION

There is a dire need to understand how the drug war interacts with the border. The study of drug trafficking organizations, their motivations, their operations, and their strategies is still highly underdeveloped. Yet, criminal organizations and their operations are not outside the reach of our study. In spite of their complexity, it is possible to understand and make sense of how these criminal organizations interact with the other dynamics of the border. Several things have to be kept in mind to make sense of this: the economics and geography of the border, the nature of underground business, the entrepreneurship and creativity of criminal organizations, the escalation character of U.S. anti-drug policy, the use of violence and corruption by drug cartels, and the attention of the media to the issue. Without considering these crucial pieces of the puzzle, it is nearly impossible to understand how drug smuggling organizations work and why the border is such a propitious place for them to prosper. And I say to prosper because up to today drug cartels continue to do their business as usual along the border, even as the United States government continues to struggle to eliminate them.

From an academic perspective, combining the study of the border and drug smuggling organizations is an exciting prospective. As this chapter demonstrates, all of these elements, put together, can help describe and explain the "problem of the border" and then propose potential solutions to the issue of illegal drugs on the border. Doing the hard work of studying these criminal organizations' modus operandi and classifying their work is an indispensable element if we are to succeed in "cleaning" the image of the border. Of course, this kind of work has, undoubtedly, enormous implications for policy makers in Washington DC as well. Clearly, the interplay of the drug war and the border is not easy to disentangle. But the major conclusion of this chapter is that over time, the U.S. drug war on the border has forced the cartels to consolidate their operations, to make their practices more efficient, and to make use of the economies of scale. Cartels have become flexible hierarchies, capable of responding to the contingencies of the drug war. And they generally succeed in doing so. The border drug war waged by the United States has consolidated drug smuggling into four large oligopolies that continue to send massive supplies of illegal drugs to the country. There are no strategic successes in the drug war, and the tactical successes of the drug war have only squeezed the small-time smugglers out and made it easier for the four large, consolidated drug smuggling cartels to operate more efficiently. Such conclusions, which should be important to everyone, can only be drawn if we dedicate the time and energy to a careful consideration of all the forces that interact across the border to make drugs the profitable business that it is and to make the U.S. drug war the great failure that it is.

CHAPTER 3

Immigration and the U.S.-Mexico Border

THE SCENE AT THE BORDER

Driving down the border from Columbus, New Mexico, one runs into James Johnson's farm right up next to the U.S.-Mexico border. Every night, about 500 immigrants use Johnson's farm to make their way into the United States. These undocumented migrants are generally dropped a few feet from the border by a yellow school bus that they catch at the main square in Palomas, Chihuahua, across from Columbus. Like Johnson, many farmers and ranchers in New Mexico and Arizona complain that the undocumented migrants tear their fences, spoil their crops, and foul their water wells; in addition, a lost sense of security wakes them up in the wee hours of the morning.

Driving on New Mexico's Highway 9, going west and hugging the border, I came back to the town of Columbus. The town's claim to fame is the armed invasion by Pancho Villa on March 9, 1916. Across from Columbus is the town of Palomas, Chihuahua. The first thing that strikes the visitor to Palomas is the dust. It is very fine and clings to everything. I drove around and found numerous hotels in the rather small town. Tourism could not be the main reason for so many hotels. The annual memorial occasioned by Pancho Villa's "raid" on Columbus never really attracts any large crowds; but the lodging industry seemed disproportionately large and included makeshift hotels, houses really, where signs read: "Se rentan cuartos" (Rooms for rent). I set out to talk to the townsfolk about this mystery.

Several men standing around explained to me that Palomas has become a major crossing point for people to enter illegally into the United States. This was particularly true, said one, since they began to "put the squeeze" on the Arizona border and the "sharpshooters" (referring to the Minutemen) began to guard the line there. While in town, these immigrants rent rooms and stay five or six in one, while they make contact with the coyote (human smuggler) that is going to lead them across the border.

The one thing common to the dozens of men waiting around in the streets and the squares of Palomas was their knapsacks. They carry the minimum, as recommended by the coyotes and those who have made the trek before. Several of these men were waiting for the yellow school bus that would drop them right up against the border, perhaps on the Johnson's farm, that night.

After talking to that group of men, I made my way to the main square, which was nearly as dusty as the rest of the town. There, lying on a patch of grass was another group of men. I approached them and asked some questions. The most outspoken of the group told me that they were from Chiapas, a southernmost state in Mexico. They had just arrived that same morning and were waiting for a "contact" to take them to the coyote, which was to charge them $2,000 each to guarantee their way to Phoenix, where they would work in a farm or in the construction industry.

Visits to the New Mexico border with Mexico offer firsthand views of the political battle that is brewing over undocumented immigration in the United States. It is like visiting the frontlines of the coming war over immigration in America. Politicians, bureaucrats, the media, the public, the local ranchers, and farmers in California, Arizona, New Mexico, and Texas, U.S. businesses, the American consumer—everyone has a stake in undocumented migration. But from the border, the issue looks more pressing, more chaotic, and in need of much more attention than anyone is willing to give it beyond the border at least until the summer of 2006. While driving along the rugged road between Sonora and Arizona, just before Ambos Nacos, I got out of the car and walked along the fence. I saw numerous water bottles, clothing, and other personal items that surely had belonged to men and women trying to make their way across the border without documents. Most striking was a pair of toothbrushes, one blue and one purple. These were scattered right along the fence, next to other items. My mind flashed to the people to whom these items belonged and I wondered who they were and even whether they "made it." On the frontlines of the war on immigration, even these small items can give us the frames to put together the puzzle that is the border.

THE BEGINNING

The problem of undocumented immigration on the U.S.-Mexico border is relatively recent. From 1848 to 1929, Mexicans crossed the border freely. In this period, it was not illegal to cross the border without papers. It sufficed to declare one's citizenship, if there was anyone even guarding the port of entry (POE). The immigration acts prior to 1929 included provisions that allowed Mexicans to cross without papers. These acts were designed to exclude persons of nationalities other than Mexican—some actively targeted Asians, particularly the Chinese. But the 1929 Immigration Act made it illegal to cross the border from Mexico without papers. This was, in some ways, a response to the economic hardship of the 1920s. With this Act, open immigration was drastically curtailed.

By the 1940s, however, the United States entered World War II and, with an enormous number of persons occupied by the war effort, its labor needs skyrocketed. To tap into Mexican labor, the U.S. Congress created a guest worker program known as the Bracero (literally "Arm") Program in 1943. This program would bring about a somewhat privileged status for Mexican laborers. Many Mexicans who came to the United States under that program were poor peasants but also very hard workers and their labor was needed to fill the gap left by the mobilization of Americans to the war effort. The Bracero Program inaugurated an exodus of economic refugees from Mexico to the United States. And although they were supposed to leave when their contracts expired, many of them would eventually settle in border towns, many of which began to see their Hispanic population explode, beginning about that time. The Bracero program continued until 1964. In 1956, The El Paso-Herald Post wrote, "More than 80,000 braceros pass through the El Paso Center annually. They're part of an army of 350,000 or more that marches across the border each year to help plant, cultivate, and harvest cotton and other crops throughout the United States."[1] Some 4 million Mexicans worked in the United States between 1943 and 1964, when the program was cancelled.

With the cancellation of the Bracero Program the current state of affairs on immigration began. Many Mexicans could not find work in Mexico, a rapidly urbanizing society in the 1960s and 1970s, with an exploding population growth. Many came back to the border and attempted to cross, this time without a guest worker visa, to work in the farms and other industries in the United States. Many succeeded in crossing a relatively open border and settling in various parts of the United States. By the early 1980s, the problem of undocumented migration reached new levels. By 1986 there were an estimated 4 to 5 million undocumented migrants in the United States.

Thus, the current undocumented migration "problem" on the border is about 40 years old, because the cancellation of the Bracero Program forced Mexicans to attempt access to the U.S. labor market without documentation. Between 1965 and 1985, the pace of Mexican undocumented migration on the U.S.-Mexico border grew steadily albeit still slowly. The major debate around undocumented migration during this period centered on the idea that undocumented migrants displaced American workers because they worked "hard and scared."

THE BREAKING POINT: 1986

In 1986, the U.S. Congress passed the 1986 Immigration Reform and Control Act, granting amnesty to nearly 3 million undocumented migrants, most of them Mexicans. The Act would regularize the situation of those already in the United States, increase border patrolling to prevent more workers from coming in, and penalize employers who would hire undocumented workers. The combination of these three would, in the eyes of Congress, solve the problem of undocumented migration across the U.S.-Mexico border.

But the 1986 Act did no more than focus on the problem of undocumented migration as a border problem. It did nothing to solve the issue of migration between Mexico and the United States beyond reinforcing patrols along the border. From 1986 to 2006, the Border Patrol grew from 2,000 to about 12,200 agents and its budget expanded from $200 million to $1.213 billion—although the 2006 figure was a decline from the $1.4 billion budget of 2002.[2] Most of these agents (about 9,000) guard the nearly 2,100-mile U.S.-Mexico border. The rest guard the Canadian border and other POEs. The Border Patrol today, with all its staff and resources, represents where American immigration controls have gone wrong. The 2007 budget provides for even more resources and for hiring another 1,500 agents.

By 1986, undocumented immigration from Mexico was being conceived as a border law enforcement problem, rather than a general labor policy problem. The United States had made the Border Patrol the "army" in its new war on undocumented migration and was fully engaged in a logic of escalation, much like in the war on drugs. It was in the 1980s that the U.S. Congress forced the military to aid the Border Patrol in guarding the border. A reluctant military conducted various operations along the border with relatively little success beyond what the Border Patrol could effectively do by itself. Thus the U.S. government's war on undocumented immigration was based on a logic consisting in throwing more people, more resources, and more vehicles at the problem. Most efforts against undocumented immigrants centered on the international borderline rather than in the major metropolitan areas where undocumented immigrants live and work. They focused on the undocumented workers, rather than those who employed them. They focused on the problem of law enforcement on the U.S.-Mexico border rather than on the issues of increasing economic integration in North America.

This law enforcement bent had two important consequences. First, among undocumented workers it is well known that the real danger is on the border. Once they make it to Chicago, Denver, or Atlanta, they are safe. No one will go after them. This situation benefits U.S. employers who benefit from relatively inexpensive and flexible labor. Second, increasingly strict law enforcement on the border has discouraged many undocumented immigrants from returning to Mexico. Instead, they prefer to stay put in the cities, thereby increasing pressure on many local governments around the country and causing a political storm,[3] halted temporarily by the Hurricane Katrina disaster.

A FAILED LOGIC FOR A FAILED WAR

The U.S. government, with all its Border Patrolmen, its helicopters, its trucks and jeeps, its fancy night-vision goggles, its underground sensors, and all its operations on the nearly 2,100-mile U.S.-Mexico border, has made no inroads into the problem. Congress continues to trust that its law enforcement strategies on undocumented immigration from Mexico work. Yet, all evidence points to the contrary. Since 1986, undocumented migration through the U.S.-Mexico border has only grown. There are now anywhere between 6 and 12 million undocumented workers in the United States, based on the high and low estimates, most of them Mexican.[4]

Curiously enough, Congress continues to call for repeats of the strategies already in place—just more of the same. There are calls on Capitol Hill to strengthen the Border Patrol with 10,000 more agents, to increase its budget by hundreds of millions of dollars every year, and to introduce new hi-tech gadgets to "guard" the border. The strategy of the Border Patrol today, according to its own documents, is to stop terrorists attempting to cross between POEs, to stop illegal entries through improved enforcement at the border, and to detect anyone smuggling drugs, humans, and other contraband.[5] In other words, instead of looking at the immigration issue as a comprehensive policy issue occasioned by globalization and North American integration forces, the U.S. Border Patrol insists on looking at it exclusively as a narrow law enforcement issue, focalized on the border, and as an action against undocumented migrants and their smugglers. However, the statistics show that the number of undocumented workers in the United States keeps growing. Not only are there perhaps as many as 12 million of them working inside the country today, but also some 300,000 to 400,000 undocumented workers make it into the country every year. The numbers alone demonstrate that the war on undocumented migration is a 40-year failure, and that its strategy is thoroughly bankrupt, even if there are tactical successes here and there along the border.

THE BALLOON EFFECT

In considering my next point regarding the war on undocumented migration, my mind returns to my visit in Columbus and Palomas. Walking across the dusty town of Palomas, two things struck me immediately. The first was one I mentioned already, the number of hotels and the number of "room for rent" signs everywhere. Palomas is a small town. Who could possibly need so many hotel rooms? Second, there was a very the large number of idle men hanging around the Main Square and surrounding streets. They were obviously not local men. Most carried a knapsack with them. I had approached another group of them, lying on the grass, and struck up a conversation with them. They were very reluctant to talk to me at first. But after a while, I managed to gain their trust and they opened up. Their honesty about what they were seeking surprised me. Bulmaro, the most outspoken of them, told me that all five of them came from the same town in Oaxaca. They were heading to Denver where jobs in the construction industry were waiting for them. They were patiently waiting for the border runner who would take them to Las Chepas, a dusty, mostly abandoned town 20 miles west of Columbus, New Mexico, where they would make the run into the United States walking long hours in the wilderness. A yellow school bus, whose driver refused to talk to me, would take them to Las Chepas. Eventually, someone would pick them up on the other side, well into the United States, and smuggle them to Denver. The undocumented worker smuggling rings are well developed and there are certain routes and routines in place to convey humans across the border and into the United States. These smuggling rings are now veritable criminal organizations, with their own networks of contacts on both sides of the border and with their flexible systems for transporting undocumented workers sometimes from the worker's hometown all the way to a major metropolitan area in the United States. Their operations around the New Mexico-Chihuahua border have increased, particularly since the U.S. government "put the squeeze" on undocumented migration through Arizona. Undocumented migration in Arizona had increased, of course, since the squeeze was put on the California and Texas borders with Mexico.

The narrow law enforcement focus on immigration at the border by the U.S. government has not slowed down the flow of undocumented workers. Undocumented workers are coming in just the same numbers. What the various U.S. law enforcement operations on the border have done is simply push undocumented migrants to more peripheral towns like Columbus, New Mexico. In 2004, U.S. agents made 1.1 million arrests, increasingly in more and more isolated areas, away from the well-guarded urban centers along the border. In effect, the squeeze on undocumented immigration at major cities and towns has only pushed the crossing routes into the dangerous desert.[6] This has brought about some ghastly consequences.

THE DEAD

The war on undocumented migration on the border is producing an increased number of casualties. As the U.S. government has escalated its efforts against undocumented migration on the border, the men and women who want to make it to the United States take greater and greater risks on their lives by trying to cross through the hostile deserts of Arizona and New Mexico. The hostility of the desert is causing more and more undocumented migrants to perish, as they lose their desperate gamble to make it into the United States under the very harsh conditions of the desert summer. In 2004, according to the Border Patrol, 464 undocumented workers perished in the desert.

The Pima County Medical Examiner's Office, in Arizona, receives the bodies of the hundreds of undocumented migrants who lose their own war against the desert to make it into the United States. The bodies are kept in the morgue for a certain period of time. If no one claims the body, the Medical Examiner sends the body to be buried, but keeps a small sample of the body's bone in order to conduct DNA tests, in case someone ever comes to claim the body. In fact, a man from Hidalgo came looking for his sister once. He gave a specific description of her to the Medical Examiner. The description matched the characteristics of a body found just a week before. The Mexican consulate paid for transporting her body back to her hometown so that at least this one young woman may rest closer to her family.[7]

The stories of the casualties of the war on undocumented migrants on the border can be found all along the border from the Pacific to the Gulf of Mexico as the number of undocumented workers perishing in the desert and dangerous mountains of the Southwest has increased to several hundred a year. In the town of Holtville, California, lies a cemetery where about 150 undocumented workers are buried. Their tombstones line a patch of land and read only "No Olvidado" (Not Forgotten). Such tombstones now dot the border counties of the Southwest and are a clear sign that stricter enforcement has not stopped the flow of undocumented workers, it has only made it more dangerous to cross, costing lives in addition to billions of dollars in enforcement. The balloon effect is at work. The squeeze in California and Texas has only pushed the flow to Arizona and New Mexico, and the more hostile conditions of the Southwest deserts only cause more people to perish.

BUILD IT AND THEY WILL COME

The border is a paradoxical place. It is at once a place of opportunity and entrapment. It is a place of wealth and poverty. It is a place of freedom and violence. And it is the opportunities it offers, the wealth it possesses, and the freedom it provides that have attracted millions of immigrants from all over Mexico to its border. The past three decades have witnessed fast population and economic growth in northern Mexico. The combined population of the U.S. and Mexico border counties is now nearing 14 million residents. The border has some of the fastest growing counties and cities in the United

States and in Mexico. The total projected combined population could grow to over 23 million by the year 2030.[8] The majority of this growth will be people of Mexican descent. (To some Mexicans, the Mexicanization of the border is part of the "reconquista" or reconquest of the Southwest— to which many Mexicans feel a sense of connectedness.[9]) But the images of the border that dominate the U.S. media are the stories of entrapment, poverty, and violence. With this terrible image of the border, it is a puzzle that so many people still want to come to the border. Why do they see opportunity, wealth, and freedom where the rest of America (and even many Mexicans) sees entrapment, poverty, and violence? This is a puzzle that needs explanation.

The Backside of Economic Development

The growth of the border to its current and projected dimensions was caused largely by a fundamental shift in the Mexican economic orientation that began with the establishment of a virtual free trade border zone in the 1970s. U.S. manufacturers were able to settle just across the border to take advantage of cheap Mexican labor, taking their own supply materials free of import duties into Mexico and then returning them as finished goods to the United States. These plants came to be known as "maquiladoras," which to this day dot the entire border on the Mexican side, and have expanded to all of Mexico since NAFTA entered into effect in 1994. This maquiladora program stimulated rapid population growth along the Mexican side of the border. The population in cities like Tijuana, Ciudad Juárez, and the cities by the Rio Grande Valley grew exponentially because the jobs generated by the maquiladora industry attracted hundreds of thousands of people to them. Ciudad Juárez, for example, went from 425,000 people in 1980 to 1.3 million in 2000. Tijuana went from 460,000 in 1980 to 1.2 million in 2000. This rapid growth did not permit local and state governments to keep up with the infrastructure needed to sustain those levels of population growth. This eventually would give the Mexican side of the border its chaotic, underdeveloped look and it would cause the creation of colonias, some of them veritable shantytowns. The growth of some Texas border counties, particularly in the lower valley of Texas was similarly fast and nearly equally chaotic causing some of these shantytowns to spring up along the Texas side of the border as well. It would surprise many a visitor to the border to see so many of these colonias without basic services, such as running water, sewage, garbage collection, or paved streets in the Texas counties abutting Mexico.

For many of these workers coming from the interior of Mexico to the border, it also became a goal to cross over into the United States where they knew wages and the quality of life was considerably much better than even in the better-off Mexican border towns where there were jobs to be had.

In fact, whereas the Bracero Program was composed of mostly poor, hard working peasants being pushed off the land by Mexico's rapid industrialization and urbanization, undocumented migration to the United States during this period of rapid growth (1970s to today) is increasingly composed of the urban poor, leaving behind the economic and social stress of the rapidly expanding Mexican cities. And not much has changed. A recently published Pew Hispanic Center poll found that this desire to migrate north has not waned. A full 43 percent of Mexicans would leave Mexico today for the United States if they could.[10]

It is hard then to believe that so many find the border attractive at all. And yet they do. In Mexico, border cities have some of the highest standards of living in the whole country. In Ciudad Juárez, for example, the income per capita reaches well above $10,000, as opposed to about $7,000 for the rest of the country. But still, what brings so many people to the border?

It's Economics, Stupid!

Mexican migration both to Northern Mexico and to the United States is almost entirely motivated by economics. Mexicans, like nationals of other countries, move mostly in search of economic improvement. Inside Mexico, one can detect a push force. But there is also, within the United States, a pull force. Together, these push and pull forces motivate hundreds of thousands to move toward the border every year. On the push side, undocumented workers leave Mexico, in part, pushed out by the depressed economic conditions of certain areas like Zacatecas, Oaxaca, Michoacán, and Chiapas.[11] On this, it is worth keeping in mind that Mexico creates just over half a million jobs a year, but over 1 million of its young people enter the job market every year.

There is also some evidence that Mexican undocumented migration has a lot more to do with the employment needs in the United States than with unemployment in Mexico—that is the pull force.[12] An enormous number of undocumented workers are pulled to the United States by their own migrant networks already existing in U.S. cities. Workers already in the United States inform people in their hometowns in Mexico (and increasingly, other countries) that there are jobs waiting for them. Those already here receive the new migrants and get them jobs in the industries where they work. This network theory of migration has been relatively well studied by sociologists and anthropologists. On account of these networks, some workers even leave their existing jobs in Mexico—it is not only the unemployed who migrate—and follow their networks in the United States. Thus, although there are criminals that migrate, the overwhelming majority of undocumented border crossers are economic refugees or economic migrants. Interestingly, the U.S. labor market seems to be able to absorb somewhere between 300,000 and 400,000 undocumented workers every year. A study in *The Economist* showed that even so, the U.S. market continues to have a shortage of labor. There are, the magazine argued, some 161 million employments in the United States and only about 156 million workers. The capacity of the U.S. economy to absorb large numbers of economic migrants, documented or undocumented, remains formidable. And the border is where all these forces come to a head. Everyday, bus terminals in Mexican towns all along the border receive busloads of men, women, and some children who are willing to risk life and limb to make a run into the United States for the sake of economic progress. Standing in any bus terminal in Nogales or Agua Prieta, I could easily identify these migrants because they carry little and know even less of the perils of the border towns they come to on their way to the United States. They often look disoriented and sometimes scared. Many refused to talk to me, nearly always a sure sign of distrust and fear of exploitation.

The Legal Side

But Mexican immigrants to the United States are not just undocumented immigrants. There are also many legal immigrants who come from Mexico every year. American consulate employees on Mexican border towns such as Tijuana and Ciudad Juárez process tens of thousands of permanent resident cards for Mexicans to move to the United States. The history of the United States shows that the motivations for allowing immigrants into the country have changed over time. In the latter part of the twentieth century, however, family reunification and skills became the primary criteria for allowing new legal immigrants to enter the United States. Family reunification is key to understanding Mexican legal migration not only to the United States, but also to the border counties. A quick but representative count of the reasons why Mexican legal entrants into the United States come is family reunification, although some entrants come in because of their professional or technical skills.[13] Cross-border social life also makes up an important component of Mexican legal migration. Many U.S. citizens marry Mexican citizens who eventually come to live with their spouses in the United States, many of them in border counties. These cross-border intimate networks are largely responsible for much of the growth of the Hispanic population in U.S. towns and cities along the border. The percentage of foreign-born residents in border counties is extraordinarily high due partly to these familial ties. Unless family reunification ceases to be a criterion in judging who enters the country, Mexican legal migration will continue at a healthy pace given that many Mexicans in the United States have family in Mexico. Some 55,000 Mexicans legally migrate to the United States every year.

The flow of goods and people across the border, except for a very brief hiatus during the days following September 11, keeps growing. Approximately 750,000 Mexicans cross the border every day at POEs, buying billions of dollars of goods every year and sustaining thousands of U.S. businesses all along the border. These crossers return home to Mexico every day as well. The border thrives with this flux of tourists, shoppers, workers, and other daily crossers. And all of these are legal border crossers. Compared with the roughly 1 million-plus yearly arrests by the Border Patrol and the estimated 400,000 Mexicans who make it across the border illegally every year, there are hundreds of millions of legal border crossers a year. The proportion of those adhering to the law is much greater than those trying to cross the border without documents. And yet, in the eyes of the media and the public, it is that small minority that gives the border its image of lawlessness and chaos.

MOTHERS AND THEIR BABIES

Alejandro is a student of mine. He spent his childhood in Ciudad Juárez and some years in the seminary, studying to be a priest for the Diocese of Ciudad Juárez. Alejandro left the seminary and moved to El Paso and now attends The University of Texas at El Paso. Alejandro is learning English as fast as he can even as he tries to study the subject matter of his core classes. Alejandro is a U.S. citizen. He was born in El Paso, even though his parents are Mexican, and still live in Ciudad Juárez. Alejandro is not a unique case.

Alejandro is an example of another form of legal migration phenomenon, largely hidden, in border counties. Many Mexican mothers prefer to come across the border to have their children born on U.S. soil and ensure them access to the "American dream." Many Mexican women take advantage of this unique opportunity to give their children the gift of dual citizenship. Universities along the Texas border, including my own, The University of Texas at El Paso, for example, have a considerable number of students who are Mexican in their cultural makeup and grew up in Mexico, but carry a U.S. passport by virtue of the fact that they were born in U.S. border towns. Few studies have been made of this phenomenon, but it is clear that Mexican mothers are increasingly taking advantage of this to ensure access to a "better future" through dual citizenship.

All along the border, hospitals and maternity houses aid this process by offering deals and plans to Mexican mothers who can pay the birth services fees in installments throughout their nine-month pregnancy period. Although this was a service mostly used by upper-middle and upper class families in the past, increasingly this opportunity is being taken advantage of by lower classes as well. For hospitals and maternity houses, these are business opportunities to make hundreds of thousands of dollars. For Mexican mothers, this is a way of ensuring access to the United States for their children.

HOW THEY COME

On March 13, 2005, *The New York Times* reported a harrowing story. A truck driver, Tyrone M. Williams, was carrying a cargo of seventy-four illegal immigrants hidden in the box of his 18-wheeler. Unable to breathe, nineteen of them died before Mr. Williams abandoned the truck in Victoria, Texas. He was paid a flat $7,500 fee for that fated trip. Mr. Williams had, 2 weeks earlier, carried another human cargo of sixty undocumented migrants to Houston.[14] Stories like this are unfortunately all too common on the U.S.-Mexico border. Hundreds of undocumented workers have lost their risky gamble to make it to the United States and die in the river, the desert, or caught in train cars, or cargo trucks, in the deadly heat of the Southwest summers. It is still hard to believe that such inhumanities happen on the soil of what is presumably the most advanced nation in the world. And yet, they do.

Reading this story, my mind zoomed into that 18-wheeler cargo box and went through the faces of each man, woman, and child, lethargic and fading out, unable to hold on to their lives. The question that came to me was: Who are they? Who comes? Why do they come? Why would they risk their lives like that? What do they want? What are the routes they follow? What are the contacts that help them cross? How much do they pay? These are the questions that, as simple as they may be, can shed light on the problem of undocumented migration on the border.

THE OLD CROSSERS: HOW TIMES CHANGE

In the 1980s, when I used to travel to El Paso, Texas, as a teenager to visit relatives, the sight of tire inner tubes floating on the Rio Grande carrying undocumented border crossers was quite common. Almost anyone could make a run and be in the United States in no time. Hapless Border Patrol agents would randomly chase one or another person on fields along the Rio Grande or on the downtown streets of El Paso on the suspicion that they had crossed the borderline illegally. Often they would be right because most undocumented border crossers used the major urban centers in Texas and California to come across the border. Most of them wanted work. Cities like Tijuana and Ciudad Juárez were growing fast and received hundreds of thousands of Mexicans from all over. Not every one of them could have a job. Conveniently, many of the undocumented border crossers were afforded the opportunity to come across as day laborers, return to Mexico at night, and come back the same way the next day. Some of these daily undocumented border crossers were agricultural workers, others were women who worked as maids and baby-sitters, others were construction workers, repairmen, gardeners and mechanics. All of them would come and go nearly as they pleased across the border. The moving force? Economics.

It was simple economics: they needed a job; the border was, for all practical purposes, a wide-open border; and the U.S. labor market craved (and still craves) the cheap labor undocumented border crossers provided. This breed of daily crossers who used the urban centers of the border to come across for daily employment is now pretty much extinct. As the U.S. government gradually closed the border around these urban centers, undocumented border crossers were forced to ever more rural, more hostile areas, often risking their lives. And many, once they crossed, stayed permanently because the risks of coming and going were increased considerably.

There were also those who came to the United States seasonally. They would make it well beyond the border and settle in cities and rural areas. Many were agricultural workers in the orchards and groves and fields of California, Arizona, Texas, and beyond. They would work for low wages and settle for living in rather squalid conditions. They were willing to move quickly from field to field as the harvests required it. These undocumented border workers would often go back to Mexico when the agricultural season was over. Many would return the following year. Other undocumented workers labored in the service industry, in construction, etc. What motivated every single one of them were the economic disparities between Mexico and the United States. Even the worst wages in the United States were much higher than what they could make in Mexico. In regard to undocumented migration, even more than in regard to illegal drugs, it is possible to say with certainty that it's economics, stupid!

It is very surprising that given this historical and current evidence of the fundamental economic motivation of undocumented migration to the United States, no American political leader has recognized this as another element of the economic interdependence between Mexican workers and the U.S. labor market and attempted to find a more permanent, mutually beneficial solution. The acknowledgement by President George W. Bush and by Senators Ted Kennedy and John McCain that a guest worker program might be a better, long-term solution is a step in the right direction, but it is a long shot, even within the President's own political party.

HUMPTY DUMPTY AND THE BORDER

The punitive, law enforcement approach to undocumented migration on the border is a typical American story. Let me illustrate. Nearly every American child is familiar with the story of Humpty Dumpty.

> Humpty Dumpty sat on a wall.
> Humpty Dumpty had a great fall.
> All the king's horses and all the king's men
> Couldn't put Humpty together again.

The approach of the U.S. government to Humpty Dumpty's problem would have been that putting Humpty Dumpty together again would have simply required more horses and more men. And so it is with the border. The approach of the U.S. government is that undocumented migration would be solved with more border patrolmen and more resources. More law enforcement has been the general answer to what is fundamentally an economic issue.

Thus, Congress and the American public have adopted an increasingly more punitive, law enforcement-oriented approach to the border. Throughout the 1980s, the border-patrolling bureaucracies became a "growth industry." The Border Patrol saw enormous quantitative and qualitative improvements. Between 1980 and 1988, the Border Patrol personnel nearly doubled, reaching 5,500 positions. Since then, it has doubled again. There are twice as many Border Patrol agents today, with about 80 percent of them assigned to the U.S.-Mexico border. And there are calls for another 10,000 agents. The hi-tech gadgets by the Border Patrol were also improved. There were sensors and night vision goggles and new, sturdier jeeps and other vehicles, and a much greater budget. Tougher sentences too have been created. The first arrest of an undocumented border crosser means deportation. By the second arrest, there are prison sentences. By the third arrest, there are stiffer prison sentences. In effect, this phenomenon has begun to fill American prisons with undocumented workers as well, placing an added burden on the American taxpayer. According to a study by the Urban Institute, the number of illegal aliens sentenced in federal courts rose by 167 percent, compared with 13 percent of the general population. Moreover, the number one crime these were charged with was unlawfully entering the United States.[15]

Interestingly, the statistics all around are not reliable. Looking at the number of undocumented border-crosser arrests, for example, does not make clear that all the additional efforts of the U.S. government to wage war on undocumented migration at the border have paid off at all. The number of arrests went up considerably in the early 1980s, peaking at 1.7 million in 1986, but dropping dramatically to less than 1 million after the 1986 Immigration Act legalized the status of nearly 3 million Mexicans living without documents inside the United States. Then it went back up somewhat to reach close to 1.2 million arrests in mid-2000. But the numbers are tricky. The number of arrests does not faithfully reflect the number of persons that crossed the border, given that a person can be arrested several times in a given year. Many workers caught and deported, simply turned around and tried to cross again. Moreover, it is difficult to calculate how many undocumented workers actually make it to the United States. A larger number of arrests could mean that there are more workers trying to make it across or it could mean that the Border Patrol's effectiveness has increased. Which is correct is nearly anybody's guess.

And yet, the 1980s failed law enforcement approach to the border did not deter Congress from trying more of the same on the border in the 1990s and the 2000s. Only this time, the Border Patrol became even more militarized in its approach and even implemented a series of military-style operations to "stem the illegal alien invasion" on the border.

THE MORE THINGS CHANGE, THE MORE THEY STAY THE SAME

By the early 1990s, Americans' attitudes toward undocumented immigration began to change rapidly once again. In 1992, 42 percent of Americans held a negative view toward foreign immigration in general. By 1993, two-thirds felt that immigration should be stopped altogether. There was particular outrage toward undocumented migration, although the reasons for opposing it had changed since the 1980s. Whereas in the 1970s and 1980s, undocumented workers were blamed for displacing American workers, in the 1990s and 2000s, the belief was that undocumented workers were placing an inordinate burden on the local taxpayers because of the services that they consumed. Everyone agrees in fact that many of the tax dollars coming from undocumented workers flow to the federal government but the costs of the services that they consume are paid by state and local taxes.[16] This localized outrage in the 1990s led to major efforts to prevent undocumented immigrants from coming across the border and some strong anti-immigrant movements in California, Arizona, and Texas. Some propositions on the ballot in California and Arizona have attempted to deny basic services to undocumented immigrants on account of the burden that they constitute to the local taxpayers.

All this attention to the issue gave the Border Patrol even more leverage in Washington and greater leeway to implement aggressive operations on the border. *Operation Hold the Line*, *Operation Gatekeeper*, and *Operation Safeguard* were three such efforts by the Border Patrol in Texas, California, and Arizona respectively. These operations marked a definite turn in the war against undocumented migration on the border and gave it its distinctive look today.

OPERATION HOLD THE LINE

In El Paso, Texas, by the mid-1990s, the head of the Border Patrol, Silvestre Reyes, had had enough. In 1994, *Operation Hold the Line* began in El Paso (soon followed by *Operation Gatekeeper* in California and *Operation Safeguard* in Arizona). *Operation Hold the Line* consisted in beefing up the Border Patrol and laying siege to the U.S.-Mexican border by posting Border Patrol agents every quarter mile, within sight of each other, for 20 miles east and west of El Paso, Texas. It was later extended into

New Mexico. Silvestre Reyes, chief of the Border Patrol at that time and now the Democratic Congressman for the sixteenth district of Texas (El Paso), thought that this would plug all the empty areas that the Border Patrol was unable to guard at all times. In San Diego country, *Operation Gatekeeper* also included building a wall between Tijuana and San Diego County. In Arizona, *Operation Safeguard* built a similar fence between Ambos Nogales (Sonora and Arizona).

This unprecedented law enforcement effort on the border led undocumented workers to move to more isolated areas and away from the urban centers, a situation that continues today and has made it increasingly dangerous to cross the border. None of these operations, which eventually became permanent fixtures of the border, actually decreased the number of crossers in the long run, although they did make the number of arrests drop dramatically in the urban areas they covered. Instead, these operations simply pushed undocumented border crossers to more remote, isolated areas, away from the cities. But clearly, the upto 12 million undocumented workers that today live in the United States, most of whom made it through the U.S.-Mexico border in the 1990s and 2000s, prove that these operations were largely unsuccessful except in confirming the balloon effect on the border: as they squeezed on certain areas, the flow would move to less guarded areas of the border.

The operations, however, represented an escalation of the war on undocumented migration across the U.S.-Mexico border. The personnel, the budgets, and the technology all escalated in an attempt to prevent these "economic invaders" from coming across the border. The unintended consequences of these operations reach beyond the increased number of deaths along the Southwest border. In fact, the tough approach to the border may be contributing to building strong criminal networks dedicated to the smuggling of humans across the U.S.-Mexico border.

GOOD FENCES MAKE GOOD NEIGHBORS

Robert Frost wrote his famous poem "Mending Wall" thinking perhaps about borders. As I walk along the steel wall that divides Naco, Arizona, and Naco, Sonora, I think of Robert Frost and recite his poem in my head: "Something there is that doesn't love a wall / Before I built a wall I'd ask to know / What I was walling in or walling out, / And to whom I was like to give offence / Something there is that doesn't love a wall, / That wants it down / And he likes having thought of it so well / He says again, 'Good fences make good neighbors.'"

A few days later, hiking on the rugged hills of north Tijuana, I can look down across the steel wall and see a Border Patrolman sitting inside a truck looking in my direction with his binoculars. I am talking to two men who are surveying the hills in search of an opportunity to make a run into the United States. It is a long shot for them. There is a steel wall, many Border Patrol jeeps, sensors, and the marshes between Tijuana and San Diego. It is nearly impossible to cross there today. And they know that. But they will try, nevertheless.

These miles of walls that now mark the U.S.-Mexico border in towns in Arizona and California were part of *Operations Safeguard* in Arizona and *Gatekeeper* in California. Steel plates that served as makeshift airport landing strips during the first Iraqi War were flown to the southwest and used to build walls along the borderline. The plates are rusty and unwelcoming. And they too have contributed to pushing undocumented crossers to more isolated and hostile areas of the Southwest desert. Whether they make good neighbors or whether they reinforce the separation between the two countries, even against all the economic forces that point to integration, is a matter for discussion. But the walls are there. They are a daily reminder to all that the U.S. government intends to fully enforce the border, even if they have yet to deter the determined workers bent on making it to the U.S. labor market. As with increased patrolling, the walls too have contributed to a perverse secondary effect: the creation of organized, strong networks of human smugglers.

Empowering the Coyotes

Walking down the Santa Fe Bridge between El Paso and Ciudad Juárez, one is struck by the number of idle men, hanging around the streets and corners of the main drag in Ciudad Juárez. My "guide," who met me at the end of the bridge, took me to one of these idle bystanders. He was leaning against a telephone booth. My guide told him that we had two "pollos" (persons hoping to cross the border illegally) in a hotel. The man promptly told us that he would charge $300 each to take them to El Paso. My guide then added that they were Cubans. The coyote said that he did not deal with Cubans at all. They were too difficult to cross. But he told us that he could take us to someone who would take that risk. However, it would cost a lot more to cross them into El Paso and probably about $6,000 each to take them all the way to Miami, Florida. The price to cross a Central American to El Paso was $600. An Asian or a Middle Easterner would be upwards of $1,000 to El Paso alone. It would cost much more if they wanted to go further up into the United States. Almost any immigrant today pays several thousand dollars to a coyote to smuggle him into the United States. If one is to multiply the hundreds of thousands of clients by the thousands of dollars that each is willing to pay, it becomes obvious that this is a multimillion dollar business every year. The rewards are obviously worth the risks and the forces of supply and demand impose themselves again.[17]

As the United States beefs up its law enforcement activities along the border and as more walls are built and more agents hired and more hi-tech gadgets employed to guard the border, its efforts seem to have contributed to empowering and enriching the coyotes or human smugglers. The undocumented workers who previously made runs across the border by themselves, with little or no guide, now have to rely on organized smugglers to help them across the border through more dangerous desert areas of the Southwest. This reliance on coyotes has in turn created well-greased networks of human smugglers (coyotes) and undocumented workers (pollos) that play a dangerous game of cat and mouse with U.S. law enforcement forces in some of the roughest terrain of the United States. Very few undocumented workers today make a run on their own anymore, empowering the coyotes and giving them the means to watch the moves of the U.S. government and to draw their own conclusions as to where are the best opportunities to smuggle undocumented workers. When the numbers reach the hundreds of thousands of workers and hundreds of millions of dollars, the game becomes one of risks and rewards, much like any other U.S. business makes its calculations.

In effect, it is very difficult to obtain data measuring the number of undocumented entrants. No one really knows how many make it across the border illegally. It is also very difficult to assess how many coyotes there are who help people cross the border and make it to U.S. cities for a fee. What we know for sure is that undocumented immigrants can no longer cross on their own. With the beefed-up law enforcement in areas along the border, the reliance on coyotes to cross them and guide them is greater than ever. Migrants rely on coyotes who have greater knowledge of the routes to take, can measure the probability of apprehension, etc. Coyotes demand more money, of course, if the risk of apprehension is greater. Throughout the 1990s, the coyote rates kept escalating, signaling the higher risk of crossing the border. Several factors influence the rates, but there is some evidence that the number of coyotes offering their services to smuggle people across the border has increased considerably. All this was evident in a study done by the Federal Reserve Bank, which also reads:

> . . . despite increasing coyote use rates, coyote prices were in steep decline until 1994. Median reported smugglers' fees fell from $941 in 1965 to $300 in 1994 (constant dollars), suggesting that increases in the supply of smugglers outpaced the increase in demand. Several factors contributed to the rise in smuggler supply. First, the border's improved accessibility through the building of roads and expansion of bus, rail and airway service significantly lowered transportation costs. Second, free entry into the industry by experienced migrants also increased supply. Third, the growth of the illicit drug trade during the 1980s attracted more smugglers as well.[18]

In all, the business of law enforcement on the border has created its own new enemy: the criminal organizations dedicated to beating the mechanisms for law enforcement on the border and to keeping the U.S. labor market duly supplied with cheap labor. In the process, hundreds of millions of dollars change hands from the undocumented workers and their families to the criminal organizations they hire, enhancing the ability of the coyotes to circumvent U.S. law enforcement. Thus, a new vicious cycle is now at work on the border.

The Crossing Card Trick

This same guide took me to a seedy hotel sitting in the middle of downtown Ciudad Juárez. In a dark upstairs room, we were shown a box containing perhaps 5,000 U.S. crossing cards. Crossing cards are given to residents of Mexico and allow them to come across for up to 72 hours—and now longer—but only within 25 miles of the border. To travel further up, border crossers holding a crossing card need to have an I-94 card to accompany the crossing card B1-B2 visa. The man we talked to in that hotel was told that I wanted to cross into the United States and I needed a crossing card. He had me sort out through the box to find a "look-alike." The process is fairly simple. I would find a card whose picture looks like me. I would pay $250 for the use of the card. I would cross the bridge into El Paso with that card. Someone from the criminal network would follow me and take the card from me once I was safely across the border in the streets of El Paso. Most of the cards in that box are stolen or lost cards. If I were to find a lost passport, I could also sell it to him. I would get $150 for it. If I lost a passport, however, and I found it in his box, he would sell it back to me for $500.

Such is the creativity of the human smuggling rings that have flourished as the U.S. government border enforcement efforts create a class of persons still desirous of entering the United States but who must now rely on "experts" to do so. Like drug lords, these criminal networks become ever more creative, but also take more risks on the lives of their "clients," resulting in an increased number of deaths.

NAFTA and Undocumented Immigration

As with drugs, the North American Free Trade Agreement has had an enormous impact on the U.S.-Mexico border. Again, truck traffic on the border has increased exponentially. Five to six million trucks cross the border in a given year. Millions more travel from and through the booming border towns north, east and west to the rest of the United States. The story of Mr. Tyrone Williams and his deadly cargo point to the primary way that undocumented workers, like illegal drugs, are transported into the United States today. Truck drivers are today responsible for carrying most of the undocumented workers deep into the United States where they meet friends or relatives and acquire the connections to begin working in the numerous industries that employ undocumented labor.

The networks are also very convoluted. There are individuals working with the coyotes who dedicate much of their time to recruiting truckers who are willing to hide their human cargo in their 18-wheelers. In El Paso, like in many other border towns, there are truck centrals, where drivers can get a hot meal, a shower, and some rest before continuing on their trips. On I-10, just east of El Paso, there is one such central. I saw many of them in Laredo and Nuevo Laredo, which together handle about 40 percent of all land trade between the United States and Mexico, overwhelmingly by truck. In those places, there are often recruiters who approach the drivers trying to gauge their vulnerability to the trade of both drugs and human beings. And many drivers often fall for it. It is a good deal for many of them to complement their income with a few thousand dollars for hiding a few persons in their truck box.

Trucks are the most convenient means of transporting smuggled undocumented workers to the urban centers of the country, not only because it is very hard to detect every person hiding in every box of every truck but also because at the internal checkpoint, usually between 50 and 80 miles from the border, the Border Patrol is looking closely at cars and vans but not necessarily inspecting the large trucks that come through. Even with all the new inspection gadgets, including the X-ray machines, it would still simply be a logistics nightmare and very expensive to open every one of the millions of 18-wheelers that travel the major highways along the border. Such exhaustive inspections are impossible, even at the international POEs between Mexico and the United States; it would be prohibitive to add yet more costs of inspecting trucks once they are circulating inside the United States. Generally, Border Patrol agents at the internal checkpoints use their intuition to pick the trucks they will inspect. A sign that something is wrong, for example, would be an exceedingly nervous driver.

OTM: Other than Mexicans

A colleague of mine at The University of Texas at El Paso, who travels to Poland frequently, mentioned to me that he had seen some posters outside travel agencies in that country announcing packages for travel to Ciudad Juárez, across from El Paso. He and I laughed at the idea that Ciudad Juárez would be such an attractive place for Poles to go to on vacation. We both suspected that there was something else to the poster. And yes there was. I discovered this standing on a field just east of Nogales, Arizona. There, a Border Patrol agent radios his colleagues telling them that he had detained some OTMs ("other than Mexicans"). He then explains that they are two Brazilian nationals. They will need translators. The agent will have to fill out an additional number of forms on that report. OTMs distract an agent from his daily work activities because they require much more paperwork than Mexicans. The whole process of detention and deportation is much more complicated for OTMs.

Walking into El Paso's Border Patrol detention center, the visitor is struck by the various languages other than English and Spanish spoken there. The number of nationals attempting to cross the border without documents and that come from countries other than Mexico is growing exponentially. Because so many Brazilians are coming to Mexico to make their way into the United States, the detention center in El Paso has a whole ministry in Portuguese for the detainees held there and they often ask for volunteers in the community who can translate between English and Portuguese.

The number of apprehensions of OTMs, particularly from Brazil and Central America, but also from Europe, the Middle East, and beyond, is growing at a fast pace. By the end of 2005, the estimated OTMs apprehended reached 150,000, up from 65,000 in 2004, and about 35,000 in 2002 and 2001. OTMs, however, though they make their way through Mexico, cannot be sent back to Mexico when they are apprehended. They are generally detained by the Border Patrol and then held in detention centers in the United States until they can be sent to their country of origin. Often, the detention centers are full and these OTMs are released on their own recognizance to report at a later date at an immigration center or in court. Most never do. In fact, an Inspector General report says that about 97 percent of all detainees released never come back to court. They disappear into the mass of the population and hide from U.S. law enforcement authorities in the crowds of undocumented workers everywhere. As many as 500,000 have taken advantage of this situation and stayed in the United States.

It is somewhat disconcerting that Mexico and the United States have not found a common agreement on how to deal with OTMs who break immigration laws in both countries. And yet, there is no real cooperation in dealing with this increasing problem between the two governments. Instead, Mexico becomes the passageway for these OTMs and the United States their final destination, exposing the flawed system of cooperation between the two countries and the increasing vulnerability of the Mexican law enforcement system itself, let alone the fact that there is a network of corruption that permits these OTMs to make it through Mexican territory to the U.S. border.

Other Modus Operandi

That many coyotes lead hundreds of thousands of undocumented workers through remote areas of desert land in Arizona and New Mexico does not mean that creative ways are not found to smuggle people at POEs. In El Paso is the National Border Patrol Museum. In it, there is a display of the many creative ways in which people attempt to cross right under the noses of the border inspectors. People are stuffed in second gas tanks; they are hidden in small compartments in vehicles; they are found inside washing machines; they are sewn inside the seat of a van; or they may use fake or stolen documents. Looking at the many different creative ways of smuggling persons across the border, the visitor to the museum gains insight into the desperation of the many that are willing to risk their freedom, and increasingly their lives, to seek better economic opportunities across the border.

THE MILITARIZATION OF THE BORDER

A book published in 2004 titled *Patrolling Chaos: The U.S. Border Patrol in South Texas* makes the argument that the border is chaotic and utterly poor.[19] Along these lines, other authors even speak of "loss of control over national borders." They sound as if the state were about to collapse under the weight of transnational crime. This is the dominant border narrative today in many quarters.[20] But even a war is not chaotic. And the border and the wars waged on it by the U.S. government are not chaotic. Border "illegal immigration" has its own logic—just like the drug war and homeland security do as well. The border in fact has a certain order. The armies of "criminals" and the armies of "government bureaucrats" are playing a strategic game in which they respond to each other with some degree of predictability. It is a cat and mouse game, not a free for all. Someone deeply ensconced in either the law enforcement or the "criminal" network who bothers to remove himself/herself sufficiently from his/her organization might just find that the cat and mouse border game on undocumented migration does have a certain logic: a logic of escalation *ad absurdum*. This logic becomes clear as one observes the Border Patrol do its work along the U.S.-Mexico divide.

Law Enforcement and Escalation

Along the U.S.-Mexico border the only consistent feature of the war on undocumented immigration, especially since 1986, has been escalation. Escalation of law enforcement activities, with no real thought to long-term solutions, or the market and labor forces that feed the movement across the border, has been the logic followed by the U.S. government responding to the so-called "crisis on the border." Even as the U.S. and the Mexican economy become more and more integrated and trade has quadrupled in the last 10 years, the physical border has become more and more tightly controlled. Almost any escalation on border enforcement is first followed by a wave of rhetoric about the chaotic nature of the border or about its lawlessness. Opponents of immigration began to speak of invasions, loss of sovereignty, devastation, vulnerability, etc. They use words that are sure to fire up fear and nationalism everywhere. The Federation for American

Immigration Reform is an anti-immigrant group whose Web page includes phrases such as "vulnerability of our borders," "border insecurity," and "terrorists will take advantage of the border."[21] With this kind of language, if it catches the attention of the national media, the border has become a matter of high politics, an issue of national security. The media's preference for "crises" and "conflict" and "scandal" and its herd mentality eventually engulf the entire debate and give it a national emergency outlook. This type of media frenzy is precisely what happened in the summer of 2005. The national debate was intensely focused on undocumented migration. There were thousands of stories about the loss of control on the border and the danger of this "alien invasion." Then hurricane Katrina struck New Orleans and the subject of undocumented migration was nearly entirely dropped from the airwaves. The media moved on to other issues relieving Congress and the President from having to tackle this "national emergency."

Nevertheless, with the rhetoric and media attention, nearly always also comes the attention of politicians. With political attention over the border, nearly always comes the escalation in resources, in personnel, and in border security technology. All law enforcement resources thrown at the border have increased considerably with every "border crisis." The Border Patrol is the preeminent agency on the border between POEs, to stem the flow of illegal immigration. The Border Patrol has a long history. It began as a mounted border patrol as early as 1904. On May 28, 1924, the Border Patrol was created as we know it today. By 1950, there were over 1,500 officers patrolling the Mexican, Canadian, and coastal borders of the United States. The Border Patrol has about 11,000 agents today, the overwhelming majority of them guarding the U.S.-Mexico border. Between 1994, the year when important law enforcement operations began in El Paso and San Diego, and 1999, the Border Patrol grew by anywhere between 1,000 and 1,900 agents per year. In 2005, some members of Congress proposed hiring 10,000 more border patrol agents to guard the U.S. borders.[22] President Bush cut that to about 200 more agents, but the number of Border Patrol officers is sure to increase considerably in the next few years, depending on the struggle between those who would "secure the nation" on the back of a huge budget deficit or those who would wait until all those agents can be paid for without incurring further national debt. Overall, by 2005, the U.S. government was spending about $7 billion a year on border security, including the Border Patrol budget, with at best mixed results overall.

Deterrence and Escalation

Such is the logic of escalation. The theory behind escalation is one natural to American society. Americans tend to assume that individuals are rational actors; that they make ends/means calculations; that everyone freely chooses his/her actions; and that these actions are directly related to the pleasure/pain calculations of hedonistic human beings or the costs/benefits that the action can cause. The natural follow-up to this nearly universal assumption behind U.S. policy is that the swiftness, severity, and certainty of the punishment will deter individuals from violating the law. To ensure compliance with immigration laws then, one must increase the swiftness, severity, and certainty of the punishment. The way to do it is to increase the possibility of getting caught; that is the reason for the law enforcement activities along the border.

Empirical evidence shows the failure of this cost/benefit or pain/pleasure theory to explain what is happening on the border. On the border such narrow logic is flawed—at least when applied strictly to the border alone. There are other considerations that defy the law enforcement escalation logic of the U.S. government at the borderline. The number of arrests and the number of undocumented workers in the United States keep growing in spite of the increased swiftness, severity, and certainty of the punishment if you get caught trying to enter the United States without documents. Why? The explanation to the presumed "choice" of the undocumented workers who attempt to cross into the United States at the border without documents must involve "rational calculations" that extend beyond what can happen to them on the U.S.-Mexico border as they try to cross—e.g., the probability of getting caught. The rewards once inside the United States must be greater than the risk taken by an undocumented worker on the borderline. And hundreds of thousands still choose to cross precisely because the rewards far surpass the risks, even as the risks keep escalating.

This kind of cost/benefit or pain/pleasure analysis, however, reveals another flaw in the U.S. strategy to contain undocumented migration at the border. The U.S. government's strategy focuses on the border nearly exclusively but its law enforcement against those who employ undocumented workers in the interior of the country is almost nonexistent. Undocumented immigration enforcement is a border phenomenon, not something that occurs inside the United States. American businesses and corporations who hire undocumented workers are seldom bothered or punished for their practices. The government is complicit because they implicitly allow thousands of businesses to operate by hiring undocumented workers. How else would 12 million workers have jobs without a social security card, a driver's license, or a working permit? The undocumented worker knows that once he has made it to Miami, Chicago, New York, or San Francisco, he is relatively safe from law enforcement efforts. All he has to do is keep a low profile, obey the rules, and say very little.

THE ILLEGAL DOCUMENT INDUSTRY

When I was living in Washington, DC, going to graduate school, I could count a Salvadoran family among my neighbors. At some point, a cousin, Isaias, came from El Salvador to join them in Washington. Isaias made the awful trek through Guatemala and Mexico, hiding wherever he could and guided by a coyote who would charge Isaias and his family $4,000 to get him to Washington, DC. When Isaias arrived in Washington, there were certain things that had to be taken care of first. The family first taught him how to dress, how to use the metro system, where to go and where not to go. They taught him some basic words of the English language. One other thing was to get him a driver's license, a social security card, and a working permit. After that, he would be introduced to a friend of a friend who would get him a job as a busboy in a restaurant in Arlington, Virginia. Curious about how this document industry worked, I asked to accompany some of the family members as a mere observer. We took the metro and got off at Mount Pleasant. We walked down Columbia Road until we came across a short, stocky, man. Very quickly, the family members accompanying him informed the man that Isaias needed a whole set of documents. The man promised the documents would be ready in 2 days. Isaias was given new first and last names. His new name was Martin Olivares and for $150, he received all the new documents, which were picked up at the same corner where they had been ordered. It was that easy.

The kind of border-oriented war that the U.S. government is waging against undocumented workers at the border allows these same workers to live and work in the United States unfettered once they have "made it" to a metropolitan area in the United States. The border focus of this war against undocumented migrants has, as a consequence, produced another phenomenon worth mentioning, the emergence of this formidable fake document industry. In fact, with fake social securities, undocumented workers function as legal residents. *The New York Times* reported on April 5, 2005, that the Social Security Administration receives nearly $7 billion a year from taxes withheld on fake social security cards.[23] That is because most undocumented workers hold jobs with these fake social security cards and pay taxes. Moreover, in the 1990s, the Social Security Administration received nearly $190 billion that it held in an account called "Earnings Suspense File." W-2s with incorrect social security numbers are now over 1.5 percent of all the reported forms. According to a study by the Government Accountability Office (GOA), of the bogus W-2s, 17 percent arrived from restaurants, 10 percent from construction companies, and 7 percent from farm operations, the kinds of industry well-known for the number of undocumented workers they hire.[24] Undocumented workers will never receive any of the benefits of Social Security that would accrue to a legal resident. Nor do they seem to want to claim such benefits.

THE ATTRITION ARGUMENT

There is an argument among government officials, conservative pundits and others who would advocate tough law enforcement measures called the "attrition" argument. They justify the increases in law enforcement resources and efforts along the border because, they argue, that the situation would be much worse if no measures were taken or no efforts were made to stop the "invasion" of undocumented workers. Somehow, they say, some must be deterred from making the trek to the United States by the sheer knowledge that it is increasingly difficult to cross and that the penalties are much higher.

Although this argument has some merit, the reader must be suspicious of the politicians, the bureaucrats, and even the groups of American civil society that present this argument. First, they do not really know if deterrence works. They simply assume that deterrence works, but no one has measured it yet. How many workers are prevented from trying to cross because law enforcement is tougher? That is a very difficult question to answer. Second, bureaucrats have their own organizational interests. I have yet to find a bureaucrat sitting atop an agency—or even a street-level bureaucrat—who will not say that "more is needed." A large agency means resources, prestige, perks, etc., for those who work for it. The unspoken agenda of every bureaucrat is to make his/her organization grow, not shrink it with "long-term" or "reasonable" solutions. At a Conference on Border Security that took place in El Paso, Texas, in August 2005, every government agent and Congress members Tommy Thompson and Silvestre Reyes spoke of the need for more resources, more agents, and more escalation. The Humpty Dumpty effect is everywhere, from the halls of Congress to the corridors of bureaucracy to the rugged terrain of the Southwest border. Finally, the logic behind this argument has been partially exposed by the fact that a cost/benefit or pain/pleasure analysis of a border-oriented deterrence strategy does not seem to work well. Not a single undocumented worker that I interviewed seems to have thought much beyond making it to Los Angeles, Denver, Chicago, or Houston.

THE U.S. MILITARY AND THE BORDER

The U.S. government has effectively increased the militarization of the border in two ways. First, the bureaucracies that work on the border are trained increasingly like a military body. They wear the uniform; they carry the hi-tech gadgets that include infrared goggles, spray, batons, etc.; they bear their firearms quite visibly; etc. The Border Patrol has installed ground sensors to detect movement along the border. It posted hundreds of cameras at various points along the international line. Each vehicle is equipped with hi-tech communications equipment. In terms of its personnel, it is now a force of some 11,000 agents of which about 80 percent work on the U.S.-Mexico border. There are also the vehicles that have gone from simple vans in the 1970s and 1980s to trucks with heavily welded steel cages. And of course, the Border Patrol is now within the Department of Homeland Security, not within the Justice Department. Their whole job has been redefined not as one of keeping "illegal aliens" out or enforcing the law but one of defending

America against would-be terrorists who might use the U.S.-Mexico border to harm the country.

Second, beyond militarizing the training, the look and the activities of the Border Patrol, Congress forced the military into the border by demanding that the Pentagon get involved in providing "support" to the law enforcement agencies operating along the border. The military was initially very reluctant to do it. Throughout the 1980s, they resisted getting involved. They alleged that the military under the Pose Comitatus law could not get involved in law enforcement activities. They were quite protective of this organizational tradition within the military. However, by 1989, they had to create an office for drug control support inside the Pentagon. They were also given a budget of roughly $1 billion for drug control support, mostly on the border.

The military, which could no longer avoid having to participate in border law enforcement, even if in a supporting role, decided to use that money differently or at least they viewed that money differently than law enforcement agencies did. The military began to pay for training for the military, although that training occurred along the U.S.-Mexico border. If any activity was detected along the border, it was reported to the Border Patrol, but in general the military was happy to have that money to get the soldiers "out there" in the wilderness to train all night using their hi-tech equipment. And this is not a secret at all. The March 3, 2005, issue of *The Monitor*, the military newspaper for Fort Bliss, Texas, ran an article in which they praised Alaska's 414th Cavalry, which was "preparing for deployment" by "assisting the Border Patrol." The unit, according to the paper, was concluding "a 60-day joint training mission in support of the El Paso sector of the U.S. Border Patrol" in New Mexico.[25]

Thus, in reality the military tends to use its participation in border law enforcement operations with an ulterior intent. They generally provide support for law enforcement agencies, but not with a view to the law enforcement work of these agencies, but with a view to give their own soldiers the opportunity to practice in rough terrain and use their hi-tech gadgets. If law enforcement is done on the border and they contribute, that is entirely coincidental. The military has long disagreed with using their own to enforce drug laws or immigration laws, etc. They would have preferred to stay away. Besides, the Marine Corps had already been stung by their participation on border law enforcement activities. A Marine training in the Texas borderlands killed a shepherd boy, Ezequiel Hernández, when he mistook him for a smuggler. This killing caused an uproar against the participation of the military in border enforcement operations and the Marines pulled out.

ALL THE BORDER'S A STAGE

Before Hurricane Katrina hit New Orleans, the undocumented immigration issue was picking up steam. A quick search for newspaper notes on the issue yielded hundreds of pieces in the months of July and August 2005 alone from newspapers and news broadcasts all over the country. The punch of the debate was sucked up by news of a devastated New Orleans. The most radically conservative newscasters would place the responsibility for undocumented immigration squarely on the backs of the workers attempting to cross the border and secondarily on the United States government. However, it is worth asking the question of whether most of the "problem" can be simply blamed on these two groups. In reality, this constitutes a more complex issue, if blame is to be assigned anywhere. Let us break down the responsibility for the "breakdown" of the border where it belongs, item by item, piece by piece.

The purpose of this section, however, is not to assign blame in any moral sense. I have consistently made the argument that these issues are motivated, at a very deep level, by economics. The purpose of assigning blame is simply to uncover the hypocrisy behind the undocumented workers debate and to answer the more neutral and eternal question: *cui bono* (who benefits)? And the answer is nearly everyone.

The American Public

Sometime in late 2003 and into 2004, a federal grand jury began an inquiry into the labor hiring practices of Wal-Mart. Wal-Mart executives were accused of knowing that their subcontracted janitorial services were using undocumented workers but ignored this because this was part of their strategy to lower the price of goods on its shelves. Wal-Mart, which is a major importer of cheap goods from China, has also been aggressive at cutting costs at home by paying low wages. This was all part of the bottom line for the company but extremely beneficial to Wal-Mart's customers who pay "Always Low Prices. Always."[26]

Walking up Wisconsin Avenue in Washington, DC, I visited a well-known Mexican restaurant where some of my Salvadoran friends worked. I walked up to the kitchen window and said "Hi" to several of them. I also know their personal stories. They had come from El Salvador in 1998, making a fear-inspiring trek through Mexico, squeezing through the border after paying thousands of dollars to a coyote in the Sonora-Arizona corridor, and then taking a flight to Washington National Airport, where a waiting relative received them, housed them for a few months, and then got them jobs in the restaurant in which they worked. After saying "Hi," I proceeded to sit down and enjoy a meal they had prepared in the kitchen.

In March 2002, Berta Trollinger, Robert Martinez, Doris Jewell, and Tabetha Eddings brought a lawsuit against Tyson Foods complaining that "all such persons have been victimized by a scheme perpetrated by Tyson to depress wages paid to its employees by knowingly hiring a workforce substantially comprised of undocumented illegal immigrants for the express purpose of depressing wages."[27]

These three stories have something in common. When I walk into a Wal-Mart or I sit down at a restaurant to enjoy a meal, I generally am surprised and even smile when I acquire a good or service at a relatively low price. Often, however, the prices are kept low by the low wages paid to the workers behind the scenes. In fact, new immigrants, including undocumented workers are overrepresented in the service industries (busboys and cooks, domestic help, janitorial services, and security guards, etc.), and the farm and forestry occupations. The construction industry is also heavily populated by undocumented workers. All of them contribute to competitive pricing of goods and services, which the American public enjoys at large.

Yet the same people sitting at a restaurant in Washington, DC, or eating *al fresco* in San Francisco, or buying cheap goods at a store in Little Rock, or hiring a day laborer in Newark, or having their grass cut inexpensively in Chicago or Dallas, are often the same people appalled at and angered by the debate on "illegal immigration." Few stop to think that undocumented workers often keep wages in check, thereby contributing to keeping inflation relatively low and the general goods and services consumed at relatively low prices. They also keep U.S. global competitiveness high. This might explain why law enforcement against undocumented workers is "thin," that is focused on the borderline but almost universally ignored inside the rest of the country, where undocumented workers feel safe and businesses thrive on their cheap labor.

Thus, the American public is largely complicit on the issue of undocumented immigration because they are mostly unwilling to pay higher prices for the goods and services they consume. Instead, the American public places enormous pressure on businesses to cut down their prices. Businesses are often obliged to do so upon the backs of undocumented workers who are generally loyal, hard working, and quiet employees. The American public contributes by its demands that shape the pull force that draws hundreds of thousands of undocumented workers to the border every year. The public would be enormously upset if they had to pay prices that reflected the wages that American workers demand when they work the jobs that undocumented workers take for so little.

The Minutemen

A few days into the month of October 2005, as I was driving my car about 30 miles east of El Paso, Texas, near Fabens, Texas, I came across a pair of men patrolling the Rio Grande river bank. I had been looking for them. These were, at last, the Minutemen, just the people I was looking for. They were the men "fed up" with the country being "overrun" by this illegal alien invasion. It was a veritable spectacle to observe these men scanning the border and the protesters watching them to ensure that they did not commit human rights violations on undocumented border crossers. It was also quite a sight to see the media give them so much coverage.

This operation east of El Paso was just like the operation in Sunland Park, Columbus, and Hachita, New Mexico, and elsewhere in some twenty-five spots along the border from California to Texas. It is not that civilian groups had not been unhappy before. They had. It is not that they had not patrolled the border before. They had. The reality, however, is that they were never more than a few hundred and, more often than not, just a couple of dozen men and women. But it was in 2005 that the Minutemen, led by Chris Simcox, decided to employ a different type of tactic to draw attention to the problem of undocumented migration and to "expose the incompetence of the federal government" to guard the border. They made an effort to recruit men and women angry at the "illegal alien invasion" across the border. They called them to arms in Tombstone, Arizona. They made a conscious effort to attract the attention of the media. And attention they got, even if the numbers failed to be what they had announced. They knew consciously that they were now shifting tactics, from simple patrol work along the border to a war for the perception of the general public. It was now a media war. Throughout the month of April, the Minutemen patrolled in Arizona. They left at the end of the month, but they kept relatively sustained media attention throughout the summer. They announced that they would come back to various points along the border in the month of October. And this they did. They recruited people to spread along the 2,100 miles along the U.S.-Mexico border.

The two men I spotted east of El Paso packed up and left at the end of October, with little more than having reported a handful of undocumented border crossers. They reported having been somewhat disappointed and even bored at the lack of activity on the sector they were patrolling. Similar operations had been conducted by civilians along the U.S.-Mexico border for quite some time.

The Minutemen project is not hard to assess materially. Even at the height of the media and public attention, they drew no more than a few hundred people and never really lived up to the numbers they announced. It is nearly impossible for a small number to guard a large, rugged, border through a civilian-funded and civilian-manned operation. They could not possibly make a real difference. If the Border Patrol, with about 11,000 members has been largely a failure in stopping the flow of undocumented workers and illegal drugs between POEs, it is not likely that the Minutemen Project will do so. It is also very expensive for a militia group to carry out sustained operations. For individual members and their families, it is simply too expensive. That it is materially impossible for the Minutemen to sustain an operation such as this one, has become clear over time. But the Minutemen understood that they were not going to make a difference on the ground. They did not seek to physically stem the flow of undocumented workers across the border. They sought instead to draw attention to the problem. And this they did.

The Minutemen have polarized the debate on undocumented immigration. Even if they were largely motivated by a sense of victimization and insecurity, they managed to expose the fact that the U.S. government had failed to stem the tide of both undocumented workers and illegal drugs. They showed that there was neither political will nor vision on the border. They showed the vacuum that is U.S. border policy. They exposed a broken system. As such, their effect is mostly symbolic, not material. They have drawn attention to the broken border system. That is perhaps their most important contribution to the debate on the future of the border. Still, as of mid 2006, they had not managed to move Congress to act on comprehensive immigration reform. Many of their efforts fell on deaf ears because they do not seem to have reached Washington, DC, in an effective way. Washington has its own eskewed logic for action.

Border Political Grandstanding

The politicians are another important group to consider in the border immigration debate. It is not only the national-level politicians that have entered the fray on this issue, but also the local politicians. To hear Washington politicians speak about the border is to hear people speak of complete chaos, absolute disorder. John McCain speaks of "the scourge of human trafficking and smuggling." Other Congress members have used similar rhetoric to draw attention to the issue.

State and local politicians have also taken advantage of the situation to carry out their own political grandstanding. Governor Bill Richardson of New Mexico declared a "state of emergency" over illegal immigration and stated that the federal government has been unable and unwilling to stop the crossing of undocumented workers. That was promptly followed by the Arizona Governor, Janet Napolitano, who also declared a state of emergency in her own state. She said that she would tap into an emergency fund of $1.5 million from the state disaster funds to pay for law enforcement on the border. The grandstanding by both Janet Napolitano and Bill Richardson did not lead to anything really substantial. Instead, it was much hot air to score points with their respective constituencies, and then the issue was dropped entirely. Congress is full of such opportunistic politicians.

A NEW APPROACH IS NEEDED

The problem with the bureaucratic restructuring that occurred after September 11 is that it was just that, a reshuffling of bureaucracies. There was no fundamental reform to the border immigration problem; there was no fundamental solution to the American businesses' unquenchable appetite for cheap labor; there was no long-term agreement to aid Mexico in its transition to a more prosperous and democratic society; there was no answer to the many questions on immigration that the American public had. The creation of the Homeland Security Department, which was supposed to offer an answer to the problem of undocumented migration turned out to be a dud. There are new requirements on the human mobility front. As of December 2007, Americans traveling even across the border will need a passport. The checks on immigration applicants are now deeper. Foreign students are more rigorously tracked. Penalties for visa overstays have been jacked up. And the US-Visit Program is supposed to track all border crossers not only when they come into the United States but also when they exit the country. These are all expensive measures that have increased the cost of immigration enforcement. In effect, separating immigration application adjudication and immigration enforcement may or may not have been a good idea. Perhaps the INS deserved to be split into the Bureau of Citizenship and Immigration Services (BCIS) and Immigration and Customs Enforcement (ICE), but neither this move nor the added requirements on border crossers or the additional layer of paperwork for all has resulted in a decrease in the number of undocumented workers employed in the United States or crossing the border every year.

CONCLUSION

The debate on immigration in the United States is not an easy debate. There are too many players, with too many ideologies and too many interests. Nevertheless, it is possible to make some generalizations regarding this debate because it is a phenomenon that occurs in a much greater context: the forces of globalization.

The U.S. society and economy are among the most open in the world. But its prosperity and competitiveness are increasingly dependent not only on the cross-border exchange of goods, services, and capital, but also on labor, particularly cheap labor. In other words, the forces of globalization are knocking hard at the gates of the U.S. economy and society, which have benefited enormously from the globalization processes of the last two to three decades—through the production of unprecedented wealth and the creation of a dynamic, ever-changing society. To the creation of this wealth and the maintenance of a vibrant society, undocumented migrants, with their labor, have contributed substantially. The heart of many an American city has revived with the influx of immigrants. Immigrants work hard; they abide by the rules and they hardly complain. Their contributions have hardly been measured because they get lost in the debate of how much they "burden" the American society.

And it is precisely because the debate on immigration focuses on the "burden" that immigrants represent to the American society and economy that the natural reaction by many in the media, in political circles, and in some conservative segments of society—and not just American society, because the problem is a European problem as well—has been to deny that globalization is both beneficial overall and inevitable in the long run and to denounce immigration as a major evil threatening the survival or the identity, or the whatever, of our society. This denouncement stems from a sustained focus on how painful the process is rather than its enormous benefits and the inevitability of immigration if the country is to remain competitive before the growing economies of Asia in what could become known as the "Asian Century."

The year 2005 saw the ideological resistance to globalization take the form of opposition to an important—and in the long run inevitable—component of globalization: human mobility. Clearly, there are push and pull forces at work in regard to undocumented migration. Traditionalist Americans tend to focus on the dilution of their identity and even on the local economic "costs" of undocumented workers. Seldom do they talk about the contributions of undocumented workers to the U.S. economy. But the debate should be couched in the language of globalization. Moreover, it should take place within the revival of the rhetoric regarding the North–South divide. Today no one talks about the North–South divide, that is, the discrepancy in wealth between the developed North and the underdeveloped South. This language died with the leftist movements inspired by communism. Yet, it is at these junctures (whether on the Mexico and the U.S. border, whether between Spain and Morocco, or whether between Italy and Libya) that we find the great human push from South to North. Undocumented migrants are pushed north to pursue opportunities and the wealthy North pulls them in so as to remain competitive, keep inflation in check, enjoy the fruits of cheap labor, etc.

In this regard, it will be painful and very difficult to achieve an immigration agreement that acknowledges the forces of globalization on human mobility and recognizes the de facto labor interdependence between Mexico and the United States. Such an agreement must acknowledge the existence of those already working in the United States—an amnesty of some kind to undocumented workers (yes, an amnesty program) even if disguised as something else—and the possibility of a guest worker program that will continue that supply of relatively inexpensive labor to U.S. businesses if they are to remain competitive in the twenty-first century. Compassion, and not just self-interest, also dictates the necessity of such an immigration accord, however painful it may be.

This is why the fact that in the year 2006 we saw the rise of huge marches in the country in favor of immigrants is important. From Los Angeles to Dallas to Chicago to New York to much smaller cities, we saw walkouts by workers, students, and citizens and protests that came out to the streets to demonstrate the enormous contributions of immigrants. If politicians do not have the courage to acknowledge these forces, immigrants and their advocates do. Their marches should force Congress to take a hard look at the last 20 years of ignoring the issue of undocumented migration while the U.S. economy and society benefit from it. It will force Congress to look into the future and see that if the United States is to remain competitive, immigration is an important component that demands being liberalized as much as capital, goods, and services.

CHAPTER 4

Homeland Security and the Border

THE WAR ON TERROR COMES TO THE BORDER

I arrived in El Paso, Texas, on August 22, 2001, from Washington, DC, I had just finished my Ph.D. at Georgetown University and I had been offered a position to teach at The University of Texas at El Paso. I was looking forward to living on the U.S.-Mexico border, a land of a thousand aspirations and social and economic ills. I was elated when I finally made it. But my elation was not to last long. Three weeks after I arrived, with most of my boxes still unpacked, two planes crashed into the New York World Trade Center, a third into the Pentagon, and a fourth went down in Pennsylvania. The entire nation was aghast and in pain. The world came to a standstill in New York and Washington, DC. We, in El Paso, saw the events unfold from afar. No one on the border would have thought that the border would be fundamentally changed after that attack.

In the early morning hours of September 11, 2001, the Border Patrol, U.S. Customs, and Immigration and Naturalization Service agents at the border ports were conducting their work business as usual. I saw these agents that morning as I crossed the Cordova Bridge from Ciudad Juárez into El Paso.

In this chapter, I will point out what September 11 did to American culture in its broadest sense and to some extent to the Mexican and Canadian cultures as well. I will look at the pre-September 11 history on the border to understand how previous border eras compare with the new security culture of the border. This analysis, as the entire book, attempts to enlighten the non-border resident to become aware of the impact of September 11 on the

U.S.-Mexico border. At the end, I will assess whether the border is anymore secure today than it was before the tragic events of September 11.

To examine these changes is important because every change in border security and its spillover effect into the country at large is the result of a decision made by elected officials and unelected bureaucrats. Such was the state of mind of those individuals in the aftermath of September 11 that, in my view, they reacted by acting in a way that can be compared to the impairments of rational processing of information by the mind. Their state of mind was such that imagination could be and was engaged so that any danger, even remotely similar to a terrorist attack, became real and immanent. This had led to confusion in Washington, compounded in the border region, producing much economic deterioration, pain, and personal suffering to both the decision makers but, above all, to those who are affected by their decisions.

These effects are analyzed next because it is important to sort out the decisions made out of rational choice and those made out of a psychological state of mind that has to do with the trauma of the attacks on New York and Washington, DC. In the nation's capital, for example, the attacks led to a groupthink mentality. Subjective judgments prevailed everywhere and objectivity had no effect on policymakers. This is understandable from the fact that the emotional shock of that day was enormous, but they also became obsessed by a foreign ideology to the extent that they were willing to transform the American way of life in exchange for what is increasingly clear are modest gains in security.

It was hard for politicians and policymakers and bureaucrats to distinguish why September 11th occurred from the debate on the long-standing ills of the border. Time and time again, though, government actors linked the U.S.-Mexico border security issues with the terrorist attacks. The national debate as to why the United States had failed to prevent the terrorist attacks began when the second plane struck the north tower in lower Manhattan. Watching the scenes on TV, many politicians and bureaucrats immediately began to assess what had happened. The question in order was: What failed inside the U.S. government? This was a difficult question to answer, however straightforward it was. Within a few hours the question was in the air as well. Politicians, media personalities, and talking heads all asked what had gone wrong. Although the answers varied, depending on whom you asked, a remarkable consensus emerged. Nearly everyone zoomed in on immigration enforcement and lax border security. Later intelligence would be added to the mix. As for the border, undocumented migration, illegal drugs, security, and economic integration and trade, became conflated with the war on terror.

The new war on terror produced a totalizing effect on the border. For too long after the terrorist attacks, there was a sense of vulnerability that could be assuaged only by protecting the U.S. periphery. All the language used to refer to the border indicated that many in Washington blamed lax border security for the terrorist attacks and desired to bring programs and practices of the war on terror to the border. A group of American nationalists, for example, wrote on their Web page,

> ... the ease with which the terrorists entered, and the bloodshed they have already perpetrated and may perpetrate in the future, the American people have to thank the open borders lobby – politicians who push for more immigration and fewer restrictions on entry, ideologues who insist that national borders and identities are obsolete, and Big Business, which demands a never ending flow of cheap labor, at the expense of American workers and the security of its own country.[1]

This linking of September 11 with the U.S.-Mexico border precipitated a massive mobilization by the U.S. government to "protect" the border. September 11 and the border would be inextricably linked for a very long time. Unfortunately, the advent of the war on terror to the border only complicated and obscured the region's problems and postponed the painful policy decisions required to establish a workable border arrangement between Mexico and the United States.

This mobilization and reorganization to "protect America's borders" was believed in Washington to be able to produce a more secure border. It has not. In fact, a central point of this book is to show the enormous failure of the border security regime, despite the enormity of resources thrown at "securing" the border. The new border security regime was powerful enough, however, to inaugurate a new era in the southwest: the "border security era."

THE BORDER AND THE IMMEDIATE AFTERMATH OF SEPTEMBER 11

This troubled reaction was not exclusive of Washington, DC. The border was also immediately affected. Within a few hours of that fated morning's attacks, as flames ballooned out from the windows of the Twin Towers in New York City and some of the walls of the Pentagon building lay in ruins, the first reaction of the street-level bureaucrats in San Diego, Nogales, El Paso, Laredo, McAllen, Brownsville, and elsewhere in the Southwest was to shut down the border. All persons, vehicles, and cargo were immediately brought to a halt. Gustavo A. Pérez, a resident of Ciudad Juárez and a student in El Paso at that time, recalls when officers came up the bridge and stopped the lines. All vehicles and pedestrians were prevented from crossing the bridge any longer. Many of them on their daily routines were forced to return to the Mexican side.

The effects of this irrational but understandable stoppage were immediate and devastating to the border—in the short run. Families were separated for days, unable to meet their loved ones across the border. Thousands of Mexican students could not attend classes at American schools and universities along the border. Shopping centers and malls all along the borderlands, from San Diego to Brownsville, showed a dramatic decrease in their daily business transactions as Mexicans could not easily come across the border to shop and do business. Tourism in the Mexican cities along the border collapsed, leaving hundreds of hotel rooms and restaurant seats empty. Tourism revenue on U.S. border towns also suffered.

Eventually, the border was reopened. But the world had fundamentally changed and, in many ways, the U.S.-Mexico border with it. Border crossers and borderlands residents were some of the first in the nation to appreciate the changes produced by September 11 in our new security conscious nation. Immediately, the treatment of crossers by border officers changed. Everyone and everything crossing the border was suspect. Everywhere along the nearly 2,100-mile international line, the inspections of vehicles and persons became very thorough and intense. The movement of trucks into the United States from manufacturing plants on the Mexican side became quite slow and cumbersome. It took many hours in inspection. Consequently, there was an enormous waste of fuel and human work hours. With the slow-down, pollution levels increased and productivity dropped as human-hours were wasted in lines and by trucks unable to meet their delivery deadlines. The entire move to just-in-time processes, which the maquiladora industry had been moving toward, came to a halt.

Those who were able to cross over the next few days found themselves under severe scrutiny and even questioning by border officials, sometimes under outright harassment and intimidation. Slowly all cross border activity eventually resumed its normal levels and even continued to grow but under a much stricter check system. The new system relied on fear as a deterrent to a large extent. Maria Rodríguez, who often comes across to clean houses in El Paso and to shop and to visit her relatives, remembers walking over the crest of the Santa Fe Bridge and thinking "the border will never be the same again." Her waiting times as a pedestrian increased considerably and she remembers being afraid of being harassed by the border officials. They could easily take away her border-crossing card just on their own very subjective judgment that she could represent a threat to America. This kind of fear was all around—although almost everyone understood and empathized with the United States given what had happened. Perhaps the uncertainty of what would happen next justified the action of shutting the border and intensifying all checks. That was a natural short-term solution palatable to everyone, but in the long-run it could contribute to building a fortress America that might not be healthy for anyone.

Interestingly enough, shutting the border temporarily, the new intensive check system, the fresh border procedures and the bureaucratic reorganization that was to come after September 11 would not affect cross border interaction in the long run. The crunch was felt only in the few weeks following the attack. As we will see, all statistics show that even through late 2001 cross-border transactions resumed their usual pace.

DIAGNOSING THE FAILURE OF SEPTEMBER 11

After the few nightmarish days at the border, politicians and policymakers in Washington, DC, were to drive their attention to what had gone wrong. They began combing the bureaucracy for failures but often their thoughts would come to the border. They settled on immigration failure, border-trade procedures, bureaucratic processes, and eventually on intelligence failure. These were the four great culprits, as Washington, DC, viewed them.

Immigration Failure

To many in Washington, DC, immigration procedures and immigration enforcement were evident culprits. The Immigration and Naturalization Service (INS) had spun out of control, they argued. It had failed to detect the terrorists who entered the United States on student visas because immigration enforcement had been thoroughly neglected. The INS, they said, had focused on visa adjudication and forgot immigration law enforcement altogether. INS bureaucrats were accused of having forgotten that they were also law enforcers, not merely employees pushing paper.[2] This conclusion was arrived at even though many argued that September 11 was not about immigration failure, but about intelligence failure.[3]

From this conclusion, it was not too long after the powers that be in Washington, DC, determined that border openness was an element that contributed to failure in deterring the attacks. Border openness had reached unprecedented levels, according to many. They of course ignored the fact that the border has been closing over decades not opening and it was in fact "more closed" than ever before in its history. Nevertheless, they alleged that people could come into the United States easily and stay as long as they wanted. There was no systematic tracking, for example, of those who overstayed their visas. (Two of the attackers had expired visas while in the United States). Strangely enough, when pointing to the failure of the INS to stop the terrorists, all of whom entered the country legally, many would wander off in the direction of the debate on undocumented migration as a failure of law enforcement by both the INS and the Border Patrol. The 1990s were labeled a decade of wanton neglect in regard to border openness, with little distinction made between legal and illegal entries. In the same sentence, talking heads would mention overstayed visas, undocumented migration, legal migration, and open borders in an effort to blame the bureaucrats for failing to stop the terrorist attacks.

The new ideology of North American integration, which emerged out of the North American Free Agreement (NAFTA) in the 1990s, was blamed for the openness of the border. NAFTA and all this talk about North American integration, some argued, was the culprit because it has caused immigration authorities to lower their guard with a consequent lack of vigilance on the border. The 1990s, as an "era of good feelings" about North American integration, would fall victim to the post-September 11 war on terror. Mexicans crossing the border were now viewed with heightened suspicion.

Moreover, U.S. immigration bureaucracies were also charged with a failure to share information with the State Department and other law enforcement agencies necessary to detect undesirables applying to enter the United States, or anyone over-staying his/her visa once inside the United States. This lack of information sharing by the INS with the State Department and with other law enforcement agencies was strongly held against it. The INS was held largely responsible for the ability of the September 11 terrorists to enter the United States, move about freely, and then carry out the activities they had in mind. The INS was blamed to the point of extinction. In effect, with the Homeland Security Act, the INS ceased to exist.[4]

Economic Integration, Trade, and Border Security

When it comes to the border, it is very hard to disentangle one issue from the other when it comes to finding culprits for September 11. The rhetoric on the openness of the border became furious. Border openness became the buzzword. Those searching for what had gone wrong went from faulting immigration law enforcement practices to focus on the trade practices of the border. NAFTA had propelled trade between Mexico and the United States to unprecedented levels. Trade between Mexico and the United States increased from some $80 billion in 1993 to $250 billion in 2001.[5] Most trade crossed the U.S.-Mexico border by land, in trucks and in trains. With the substantial increase in cross border trade, it became nearly impossible to inspect every truck. As already mentioned, anywhere between 4 and 5 million 18-wheeler trucks cross the U.S.-Mexico border every year.[6] The capacity of the ports of entry (POEs) to handle the volume of trucking that NAFTA produced was overwhelmed. Inspection was almost necessarily done randomly and only on a very small percentage of the trucks coming across. Both the infrastructure and the number of inspectors were insufficient to do any more than that. When Congress passed NAFTA, they did not necessarily provide for the infrastructure to secure the volume of trade expected from the new agreement.[7]

After September 11, however, these "lax" trade inspection practices were blamed for the "porousness" of the border.[8] The media ran various random stories about how trucks were being used to smuggle undocumented workers and illegal drugs.[9] Moreover, many speculated that these same trucks and vehicles and even undocumented workers could cross a "dirty bomb" or a "briefcase bomb" into the United States.[10] These hypothetical border-jumping terrorists could conceal weapons of mass destruction or materials useful to terrorists once inside the United States.

The rhetoric of the war on terror warped even the way border trade was viewed. Every truck driver was a potential terrorist and every truck became a potential terrorist weapon trying to penetrate into the United States and "harm America." The totalizing war on terror rhetoric had swallowed the debate on border trade as it had swallowed the immigration debate. From there, it was just a leap before politicians in Congress concluded that something had to be done about lax border-trade inspection practices. As with immigration, a series of new trade-related measures and programs were implemented to "secure the border" and prevent future terrorists attacks while "allowing the binational trade to flow freely." Interestingly, there was little talk about raising trade barriers or stopping the flow of trade, as in immigration. Immigrants are a vulnerable constituency, easy prey for politicians. Businessmen are not. Thus, the debate did not center on stopping trade altogether. Trade had to be allowed to flow. Congress was not about to hurt trade between Mexico and the United States because $1 trillion of trade every 4 years touches many interests, which in turn touch many members of Congress. Thus, Congress was unwilling to harm such powerful economic interests that ride on U.S.-Mexican trade. There were no rumblings against NAFTA; only against the lack of vigilance it had presumably produced along the border.

Arizona and New Mexico

Other analysts focused on border openness in Arizona and New Mexico as a fundamental problem that contributed to September 11, in spite of the fact that the border had hardly anything to do with the terrorist attacks. Various quasi-military operations to seal the border around urban areas in the 1990s had succeeded in pushing undocumented workers to seek crossing points in those two states, particularly in Arizona, which saw its number of Border Patrol arrests soar. Arizona alone still accounts for about half of the undocumented migrant detentions on the border. This was perceived as a serious gap in border security, a gap through which terrorists could sneak into the country.

The media contributed to this hysteria by covering stories that showed the presumed ability of terrorists and other undesirables to enter the country illegally by crossing the desert in Arizona. The *Arizona Daily Star*, for example, published a note stating that the American Border Patrol, a vigilante group, had conducted a "weapons of mass destruction smuggling test" successfully in the Arizona desert by sneaking a fake WMD and making it to a house in Sierra Vista without being caught.[11] Thus, the backpacks of undocumented workers walking the Arizona desert were transmogrified into weapons of mass destruction and undocumented workers into potential terrorists ready to attack America. These speculations further conflated the problem of undocumented migration with the issue of national security with the attacks on New York and Washington, DC. They made no distinction between one or the other or the other. The state of the border was viewed as a national security threat. From there, the natural follow up was a generalized discourse about "controlling" the border or "regaining control" of the border, as if the border had ever been under control in the past.

Damn Those Bureaucrats!

Eventually, analysts and politicians asking what had gone wrong focused on what they labeled outdated bureaucratic structures, the supposed backwardness of the technology used by U.S. officials on the border, and general bureaucratic inefficiency and incompetence, all of which translated into a "porous" border that represented a national security threat. The bureaucratic organizations of the U.S. government in charge of managing the border were blamed for contributing to a lawless, chaotic border that now threatened the very survival of the nation. All the agencies working on the border, from U.S. Customs to the Border Patrol to the Drug Enforcement Administration to the Immigration and Naturalization Service, were scrutinized and made part of the failure of September 11. The paranoia inside these bureaucratic organizations spread like gunpowder because no one was certain on what was going to happen to them. As the hearings of September 11 proceeded in Congress, these border agencies were accused of being insular in their missions and tasks. They were to blame for their inability to work together and the gradual collapse of communication among them. Eventually, the discourse became so intense that no agency was safe. In all, they were somehow held responsible for the attacks. The result was that they all were reorganized into a single department in order to have them "work together." Whether they have achieved that level of coordinated efficiency by being placed under a single roof is something that has yet to be demonstrated. Early evidence shows that they have not.[12]

Intelligence Failure and the Border

Unfortunately, though the terrorist attacks were later fully acknowledged by the *9/11 Commission Report* to be a consequence of intelligence failure, initially, a hard look at the intelligence structures took a back seat to immigration, trade, and border security legislation. And I use the world "legislation" deliberately. I use it instead of the word "reform" because there has been no reform in either the immigration or the trade or the anti-illegal drug policy regimes that prevail on the U.S.-Mexico borderlands. In fact, there has not been even superficial reform to any of these regimes as a consequence of September 11. Trade is still a priority on the border. Immigration, both legal and illegal, continues apace and follows along the same principles as before. Illegal drugs are just as abundant as before and their price has decreased. The strategy to combat them is still a largely unilateral, supply side strategy that has produced no results before or after September 11. If anything, the fundamental immigration and trade and anti-drug problems and policies remain essentially the same. The only thing that has changed is the structure of the bureaucracies that deal with these policy problems.

Still, curiously enough, after information sharing ("intelligence failure") inside the U.S. government was identified as a serious problem that contributed to September 11, President George W. Bush himself was reputed to have resisted intelligence reform and was unwilling to even fire George Tenet, the Director of Central Intelligence, for the intelligence failures related to the terrorist attacks. President Bush was also reputed to have resisted the creation of a Director of National Intelligence to coordinate all intelligence activities of the United States government. His legislative proposal focused instead on reorganizing the bureaucracies that dealt with immigration and trade on the border. The reorganization, however, was somewhat superficial, however massive it may have been. It had no substantial effect on the philosophy that underlay U.S. policy toward these fundamental issues. By 2006, it seems that the creation of the Homeland Security Department has, at best, created only a new layer of requirements for border crossers and a new layer of paperwork for the corresponding bureaucracies.

Eventually but somewhat reluctantly, the Bush administration and Congress would acknowledge intelligence failure as a major cause of September 11, and only then did President Bush add it to the mix of proposed legislation. Still intelligence reform continued to be resisted in Washington, DC. The politician-favored suspects for failing to deter the terrorist attacks were: (1) immigration, (2) border openness (largely due to economic integration and trade), and (3) an ineffective bureaucratic organization. And both the President and Congress stuck to their guns. The creation of the Homeland Security Department reflected their preoccupation with these three issues, not with intelligence. Sure, some members of Congress called for a serious restructuring of the intelligence system. These members of Congress felt vindicated by the *9/11 Commission Report*, which would agree that intelligence failure was a major cause of the attacks. In the end, however, the White House and Congress responded by passing intelligence legislation but not until 2005. For the first 4 years, their efforts went into legislating and implementing changes on immigration and trade practices. Illegal drugs seemed to have fallen out of the political agenda altogether. The Drug Enforcement Administration was not touched in the reorganization of border bureaucracies. Thus, through 2002, various acts of Congress focused on tightening border control and making changes to the immigration adjudication and enforcement and the trade control bureaucracies through the Homeland Security Act of 2002.

CONFLATING THE ISSUES

The matter of conflating the terrorist attacks with border issues deserves further attention because it has been very damaging to the border and a potential border agenda for the future. As late as March 2, 2005, Peter Gadiel, who testified in Congress, before the Subcommittee on Immigration, Border and Security, still sounded the same trumpet declaring that:

> We know there were intelligence failures leading up to 9/11. We know that complacent government officials simply refused to believe that something like 9/11 could happen here. More than anything else, though, we know that our government failed to maintain control of our borders leading up to 9/11. Those 19 murderers counted on lax scrutiny of their visa applications and overwhelmed inspectors at our ports of entry. Once here, the terrorists counted on being able to hide in plain sight in the ocean of 10 million or more illegal aliens living in the United States. They benefited from the fact that enforcement of immigration laws inside the United States is virtually nonexistent and that Americans are so inured to this fact that no one – civilian or law officer – would notice them or interfere as they planned, rehearsed, financed, and then carried out their conspiracy to commit mass murder.[13]

This testimony before Congress shows the carelessness with which experts, politicians, talking heads, and others viewed September 11 through one single lens: border control. All issues were conflated: immigration adjudication and enforcement, border security, trade and economic integration, border openness and control, etc. They were all "bad" and the bureaucrats that handled them "incompetent." In Gadiel's statement there was hardly any attempt to carefully sort out the failures. Others were even more radical than Gadiel. There were even some attempts to relate al-Qaeda directly to the border! At a hearing before the Senate Select Committee on Intelligence on February 16, 2005, Adm. James Loy, Deputy DHS Secretary, testified that:

> ... entrenched human smuggling networks and corruption in areas beyond our borders can be exploited by terrorist organizations. Recent information ... strongly suggests that al-Qaeda has considered using

the Southwest Border to infiltrate the United States. Several al-Qaeda leaders believe operatives can pay their way into the country through Mexico and also believe illegal entry is more advantageous for operational security reasons. However, there is no conclusive evidence that indicates... operatives have made successful penetrations... via this method.[14]

This is the same kind of paranoia about the border that prevails among radical anti-immigrant groups in the United States, but also in certain segments of the American public. And this image of the border may be spreading even further in the American public. A November 2005, Rasmussen Report survey found that "sixty percent of Americans say they favor building a barrier along the border between the United States and Mexico." Only 26 percent were opposed to this approach.[15]

There is a serious problem with this sort of carelessness, however. The United States and Mexico are neighbors. Neither of them is going to go away. And yet, both countries relate to each other in a schizoid manner. Their border problems are very serious: Human smuggling, illegal drugs, the transit of Central and South American undocumented workers through Mexico, poverty, economic and human development issues, and economic integration. Mexico and the United States must deal with these problems together. It is insufficient to build a wall along the border and pretend that the other side is nonexistent. A comprehensive, bilateral approach is required to deal with each of these issues under a single border regime that will benefit both countries. But this is not happening. There is almost no contact between the officials on one side and the other. Each country operates under its own rules, with its own psychological barriers to openness with each other. The sort of conflation of the issues that is present in the rhetoric cannot help. Labeling the border a dangerous place that must be sealed off is a recipe for a continuation of what has been happening on the border for the past 40 years. And 40 years of efforts to seal the border have only deepened the problem. This "closing of the border" mind-set has created better and more efficient illegal drug criminal organizations; forced undocumented workers to rely on emerging human smuggling networks; weakened cross border social ties; and built a sense of separation that is detrimental to cross border cooperation. Lumping all border issues together into a single, large crisis is counterproductive. A wall along the border is not just a wall; it impedes a serious look at the border and its dilemmas in order to find workable solutions for both Mexico and the United States.

REORGANIZING FOR BORDER SECURITY

With every border regime (frontier, customs, law enforcement, and now security) came the creation of new laws and new bureaucracies to "secure" the border. And perhaps they have only gotten worse. Still, the U.S. government's response to the border is explained by a logic of escalation. With every "border crisis," Congress has passed new legislation and has continually reorganized and increased the number of bureaucrats operating on the border.

The advent of the security era of the U.S.-Mexican border, which resulted from the war on terror, could not be the exception to this historical trend. As a response to the 9/11, Congress passed the Patriot Act, a law designed to enhance the authority of law enforcement agencies to fight terrorism.[16] In 2002, Congress moved on to reorganize the border bureaucracies. It passed the Homeland Security Act of 2002, which effectively established the Homeland Security Department pooling together twenty-two different agencies from various departments into a single unit with a workforce of some 180,000 bureaucrats and a budget of over $40 billion in FY2005.[17] In regard to borders, Title IV of the Homeland Security Act explicitly created the Office of the Undersecretary for Border and Transportation Security grouping all agencies responsible for border security under him.[18] A shrewd observer of border affairs could have predicted this response. Starting a few weeks after September 11, some of the most important security initiatives coming out of Congress and the White House were escalating the penalties against terrorists and those who could help them; increasing the budgets to secure the border; and reorganizing the bureaucrats that work on the region. These new laws and the bureaucratic reorganization they implied were supposed to make U.S. borders more secure.

The border security initiative of the new Department broke down into programs. The three most important of these programs were, first, the Customs Trade Partnership against Terrorism (C-TPAT) began in November 2001. C-TPAT was designed to secure the supply chain—from the factory plant on Mexican maquiladora plants to the transportation companies to the U.S. importer. All producers, importers, and carriers were to register with Customs and Border Protection (CBP) in order to receive preclearance before their merchandise and personnel gets to the border. This would presumably expedite their crossing at the POE. New technology was introduced to scan the trucks in order to detect any specific loads that were not consistent with the declaration of the importer/exporter or the trucking company.

Another initiative is the National Targeting Center, which gathers statistics on all border crossers (people, vehicles, and transactions) for the purposes of detecting higher risk crossers and targeting inspections on those that have a higher probability of being associated with criminal or terrorist elements. It integrates government, commercial, and law enforcement databases into an evolving, statistics-producing mechanism to make the latest criminal trends on the border available to law enforcement officers on the ground. The targets identified as higher risk are screened upon arrival at the POE, while the less risky crossers are only randomly checked. This was once again an example of the heavy reliance on technology to screen the considerable volume of traffic across the border.

A third effort was the US-VISIT Program (United States Visitor and Immigrant Status Indicator Technology Program). It is a system initiated at airports and seaports and being tested on land POEs on the U.S.-Mexico border. The system scans travel documents and takes fingerprints and pictures of the border crosser. The data is then run through databases to determine whether the individual is a presumed criminal or terrorist. This system also keeps track of all border-crossing information of any one individual over time. US-VISIT has not been fully implemented because the infrastructure is not there to conduct the same kind of inspections upon exit that there are upon entry. This would require many more agents and gadgets and a very high investment by the United States government to control those who are exiting the country. While it may be possible at international airports, the hundreds of millions of passengers and travelers that come in by land would have to be screened also upon exit, a mathematical nightmare onto itself.

There were, of course, many other programs introduced to gain further "control" of the border. American citizens, for example, are slated to be required passports to cross the border. The times when American citizens could simply jump the border and return by simply declaring their citizenship would be over. Anyone traveling across the border will be required to carry a passport. In reality, this is a response to the unwillingness of the American public to support a national identification card. A national ID is unpalatable but a passport can be required in its stead. With the kind of technology available today, all passports need is a sufficiently powerful chip to carry vast amounts of information on that person in the passport booklet. Similarly, MANTIS was a program introduced to keep track of foreign students who must now register their moves. These and other initiatives are all supposed to contribute to border security and control.

A NAGGING QUESTION

The efforts of the U.S. government to control the border, with all the programs that they bring, are not the real issue in any event. Programs come and go. The U.S. government is entitled to invent programs and fund them. The vital question that must be asked is: Are the policies and programs paying off? Is the game worth the candle? Have all these programs and additional resources resulted in a more secure border? Are we now finally in control of the border? Is the war on terror on the border giving an acceptable return on investment? About 5 years after the disaster of September 11 and the U.S. efforts to wage a war on terror, we have had enough time and sufficient evidence exists to judge whether the Bush administration got a reasonable bang for its buck.

Given the initial diagnosis and the eventual response of the United States government, it is probably accurate to say that no other geographical area of the country underwent the intensive and extensive changes that the U.S.-Mexico border did. Speaking with some Canadian scholars in Victoria, Vancouver, in December 2005, it became evident that they too worry about U.S. unilateral action on the Canadian border. But in the end, the Canadian border was not as deeply affected as the U.S.-Mexico border. In light of the bureaucratic restructuring in the areas of immigration, trade and governmental organization on the border, it is reasonable to ask two important questions related to homeland security, specifically to border control. First, do the new practices and structures of homeland security place an undue burden on the border and its border residents? Second, do these burdens increase security?

To answer these two important questions is pivotal in order to understand what the border is today and what it may become tomorrow. The answer must be the result of a detailed before-and-after analysis of border practices and a careful cost-benefit analysis of the price paid by border residents and the added national security obtained in exchange for that price. The intuitive answers to these questions is that border residents bore the brunt of the U.S. government's response to September 11, perhaps more than any other area of the country, and that the added national security after the bureaucratic reorganization of 2002 is negligible and perhaps even negative in terms of an ineffective, irrelevant, but expensive regime that has been detrimental to border relations and seriously affected the U.S.-Mexican relationship.

NEW IMMIGRATION PROCEDURES

The more abstract effect of September 11 on the border was the redefinition of immigration as a national security issue. Immigration has been a malleable issue in U.S. history. The very location within the national bureaucratic framework illustrates how policymakers defined the issue of immigration over time.

For a long time, immigration services were located in the Labor and Commerce Department. This clearly framed the whole issue of immigration as one of labor and economic development. Migrants were seen as workers. After the Department was split into the Labor Department and the Commerce Department, immigration services continued to be located in the Labor Department. This indicates that immigration continued to be looked at through the labor needs of a fast-developing economy. Immigration quotas were largely assigned on the basis of the labor needs of American businesses across the country. From time to time, there was some discomfort with open immigration and was accompanied by deep anti-immigrant sentiments. These were particularly virulent around the turn of the twentieth century. But immigration continued to be looked at as a matter of economic development well into the twentieth century.

Eventually, immigration services came to be perceived differently. The U.S. government began to shift its conception of the issue of immigration. It finally was defined as a matter of law enforcement. This paradigmatic shift in the way immigration was viewed culminated in 1940 when the Immigration and Naturalization Service moved from the Department of Labor to the Department of Justice. Moreover, the Border Patrol, charged with preventing undocumented immigration, was also lodged in the Department of Justice.

September 11 would redefine the issue of immigration from a matter of law enforcement to a subject of national security. The INS was broken up into two different branches, the Bureau of Citizenship and Immigration Services (BCIS), in charge of immigration applications adjudication, and the Immigration and Customs Enforcement (ICE) bureau, in charge of immigration enforcement. The idea was to ensure that immigration law enforcement would never be neglected again. In addition, both of these new agencies were placed under the Homeland Security Department, effectively redefining the issue of immigration as a matter of national security. Immigration had gone from a purely economic issue to a matter of law enforcement and now to a concern of national security.

Several immigration-related programs were also changed. To a visa application there were new forms added to determine visa eligibility. These forms were to provide the consular officers with more information to conduct clearance and background checks in order to deny visas to those petitioners who might constitute a threat to the national security of the United States. Moreover, nonimmigrant visa holders could no longer stay in the United States for periods longer than 30 days, compared to the previous stay of 6 months. B1/B2 Visa holders, most of whom are residents of Mexican border towns, however, were now able to extend their stay beyond 72 hours. Foreign students were also affected. The Interim Exchange Authentication Program (ISEAS) was implemented to ensure that students were who they claimed to be and to ensure that the government could keep track of those students wherever they went once inside the United States. This required foreign students to register with the government and notify any change of address within 10 days. It also required schools to "authenticate" the student by providing law enforcement with information regarding that student—a move fought by U.S. universities for privacy and bureaucratic reasons. Finally, the government stopped granting J-1 visas for agricultural workers placing the farming sector of the economy in a bind across the southwestern Border States and beyond. In addition, U.S. citizens could be required to carry passports, even if they are just crossing the Canadian or Mexican border for a few hours. There is a possibility that this passport requirement may still be waived, but the White House has so far not acted on this.

CONSEQUENCES OF THE NEW IMMIGRATION PROCEDURES

The consequences of these changes were felt readily and heavily on the border. The J-1 visa stoppage left employers without workers on the United States side and labor without jobs on the Mexican side. There were no consultations with Mexico on this matter, a fact that further cooled off the already chilly relationship between the two neighbors. Finally, the federal government attempted to deputize state and local police forces to perform immigration and customs enforcement, a move opposed by these entities as an unfunded mandate. The non-visible consequences were even greater. There were fewer opportunities for border residents on either side of the border to interact with each other. Business people and tourists saw their ability to interact across the border increasingly difficult on account of the time it took the border inspectors to go through each vehicle and person. In this regard, the most important impact is that the new immigration practices and the immigration procedures on the ground constitute today a further severance in the community ties between border towns, a shift bound to decrease the level of intimacy between twin-city populations. This severance of cross-border social interaction cannot be underestimated. It is more difficult now to interact across the border and increasing numbers of residents are choosing not to cross the border at all. This can only alienate both nations further, rather than build more bridges between them.

NEW TRADE PROCEDURES

The new security procedures in cross border trade were presumably designed to prevent terrorists or anyone who would "wish America harm"[19] from entering the United States by utilizing the intense commercial links between Mexico, Canada, and the United States. Indeed, these commercial links are substantial. Trade over the 1990s had grown enormously, reaching totals in the hundreds of billions of dollars between the two borders. In FY2002, customs inspectors processed information of cargo valued at $1,183 billion, most of it (some $800 billion) coming from Mexico and Canada. Much of this trade arrives by truck, with railcars in second place. According to the former Customs and Border Protection Commissioner Robert Bonner only about 10.3 percent of trucks and 9 percent of railcars were inspected intrusively or non-intrusively.[20] Laredo, Texas, proved to be the busiest POE for trucks on the U.S.-Mexico border, with 1.4 million trucks in 2003 alone. Trade between the United States and Mexico reached $235.5 billion in 2003 and is now estimated to hover around $250 billion a year.

Unfortunately, NAFTA did not provide for serious infrastructure improvements necessary to accommodate the growth in trade. The stress on infrastructure from the sheer volume of trade, i.e., 4.5 million trucks, has become evident. But the transportation infrastructure is of less concern here than the inspection infrastructure. Trade liberalization under NAFTA was particularly broad. Federal and local governments on both sides of the border placed some emphasis on improving capabilities and efficiencies in transportation across the border but they neglected serious investment required to ensure that drug traffickers, human smugglers, and even terrorists would not use the intense trade between the two countries as a conveyor belt for their contraband. As it became clear in our chapter on illegal drugs, NAFTA has been quite a blessing for drug traffickers. They take full advantage of the inability of U.S. bureaucrats to inspect every truck in order to smuggle their cargo. The new X-ray-scanning machines that are used still may or may not detect illegal cargo, depending on how well hidden or camouflaged it may be. All in all, the capacity of CBP to make sure that contraband, both drugs and human, is not yet up to the security needs of the United States. This, however, may say more about the U.S. government as a whole than the valiant efforts of bureaucrats working along the border.

Nevertheless, after September 11, the U.S. government woke up to the fact that security on the border needed to be revamped. Steady improvements began on the POE lanes dedicated to handling the millions of trucks that cross the border. New technology was introduced to scan the trucks carrying cargo. New and more intense checks were conducted on the drivers of those trucks in the hope of preventing that a terrorist might one day take advantage of the border openness to conduct an attack on the United States.

There were specific adjustments to trade programs implemented such as the C-TPAT (Customs Trade Partnership against Terrorism) and the 24-Hour Rule on international textiles. Along the Canadian border the FAST (free and secure trade) program was put into effect.

The C-TPAT program was designed to ensure that all the players of the supply chain (exporters, importers, and transporters) "know" and "trust" each other. The importer is obliged to develop and implement a plan to enhance security throughout the supply chain. When an importer does not control the facilities, he is to follow a series of recommendations by Customs and Border Protection to ensure that every responsible party along the supply chain complies with U.S. government rules. C-TPAT involves a series of rules pertaining to procedural and physical control of the product and to ensure that the personnel that works along the supply chain is properly trained so as to ensure the total security of the goods traded. The burden falls on the importer to comply with these rules and file the required C-TPAT documentation with CBP. Of course, this largely means that the U.S. government has shifted the costs of security to the cross-border businesses. They have to pay the price of "securing" the supply chain. In effect, the U.S.

government has made it more expensive to operate across the border for everyone in the import/export business.

The 24-Hour Rule required carriers to file a cargo declaration 24 hours before the cargo is laden aboard the vessel at a foreign port. The 24-Hour Rule, however, did not significantly impact the border, given that it applied mostly to sea vessels abroad, although it did impact some of the cargo moving from Mexico to the United States by vessel.

An additional trade security measure was the Container Security Initiative (CSI). This program was implemented to identify and target high-risk containers coming into the United States; to prescreen the containers identified as high-risk; to use high technology to scan these containers; and to replace old containers for smart or secure containers. Although this initiative affected the U.S.-Canadian border and not necessarily the U.S.-Mexican border, it represented, along with C-TPAT and the 24-Hour Rule, a new need to balance security and trade. There were a whole new series of programs that also affected the U.S.-Canada border but have not yet arrived at the U.S.-Mexico border, including the Free and Secure Trade (FAST); the Pre-Arrival Processing System (PAPS); the National Customs Automation Program (NCAP); as well as the Smart and Secure Trade Lanes Initiative (SST).

THE CONSEQUENCES OF THE NEW SECURITY TRADE SYSTEM

The New Homeland Security department understood that its solutions had to be designed to close the border even further, with the hope of detecting the undesirables that might want to exploit the openness of the border. There was no effort to create a truly U.S.-Mexico binational trade inspection regime where the Mexican government played a role to ensure that all trade was safe and secure. The U.S. government decided to work instead with the importers/exporters and the trucking companies to secure the supply chain.

The cost of the new measures, particularly C-TPAT, on the U.S.-Mexico border is bound to be considerable. The costs associated with compliance with the new measures include training and registering truck drivers, making the trucks and equipment comply with U.S. requirements, filing paperwork in advance for the cargo hauled by a given truck, etc. Most of these costs have been borne by the Maquiladora and the trucking industries on the border. Few have protested these costs, however, because the U.S. government has portrayed these measures as a must or the cargo will be subjected to intrusive inspections or outright delays upon arrival at the POE.

Some of the secure trade programs implemented after September 11 represent a burden to the international supply chains located at border POEs. The new requirements and their costs can also decrease some of the gains made by the companies in increases in productivity and the use of technology. Over time, however, these new programs seem to have made trade flows somewhat more efficient by the use of technology and the use of lanes exclusive for trade trucks. Suppliers and importers scrambled to figure out all the rules of the new security measures and tried to integrate them into their cost transaction. But nothing guarantees that the trucks are any more secure. Clearly, drugs and sometimes humans are smuggled routinely in those same trucks.

This has increased the amount of time and resources spent complying with the new rules. Sometimes, there are additional delays at the POEs because trucks and vehicles carrying cargo must comply with the added security measures. Membership in C-TPAT requires, however, that those participating in the program be able to certify, to the satisfaction of the government, that their shipments come from the right suppliers and that the cargo is secure. The added delays are costing maquiladoras and other businesses considerably more.

There are also costs associated with implementing C-TPAT for businesses. Those who wish to participate will have to implement security policies and procedures as advised by the government; conduct periodic self-assessments to insure that their supply chains have not been infiltrated; submit additional paperwork to Customs and Border Protection; train their employees and personnel in the new security procedures and policies; and guarantee that their cargo is not compromised. All these costs represent an added burden to those doing business along the border in twin plants. In addition to the costs directly related to the new security measures, there is lost production time, higher transportation costs, and lost business opportunities.

The inevitable consequences is that the border trade regime is still largely run unilaterally by the United States, much of the cost for securing the supply chain has shifted to the business community; and the Mexican bureaucracy that sits largely idle on the border does not bear any burden in ensuring that trade going to the United States is safe and secure. The new patchwork of programs created by Homeland Security bear the burden of ensuring that the conveyor belt that are the 4.5 million trucks crossing the border every year are not used by drug smugglers, human smugglers, and terrorists.

THE VALUE ADDED BY THE NEW TRADE PROCEDURES

The U.S. government has yet to demonstrate that the new procedures regarding trade, particularly along the border, have resulted in a substantial increase in the security of the nation. Stephen Flynn has made it clear that there are still many patches to fill in, particularly at ports.[21] However, along the U.S.-Mexico border the major effect has been the added burden and costs on importers and exporters rather than an increase in the security of the merchandise that crosses the border. This is in addition to the added burden to the American taxpayer who has to foot the bill for the added personnel and technology along the nearly 2,100-mile border. Nevertheless, illegal drugs still "contaminate" the cargo of many of these vehicles that cross the border and go undetected. A Ciudad Juárez businessman recently complained that they still had no control over the trucks once these left the warehouse and drug traffickers sometimes bribed the drivers to hide illegal drugs in the cargo.

The real problem here, therefore, is only remotely a potential terrorist but more likely the "contamination" of the truck cargo by drug traffickers. That security problem continues unabated in light of the fact that drug trafficking has not ceased in spite of the added inspection activities. Illegal drugs continue to represent a substantial business activity of the Mexican cartels. It may be illegal drugs, in fact, that actually proves whether the added inspection measures on the border add a measure of security above and beyond the inspections that had already been conducted before the Homeland Security Department was created. There were voices inside the United States government who argued for plugging the holes in the government activities along the border, rather than creating a whole new Department of Homeland Security.

THE INORDINATE BURDEN ON BORDER RESIDENTS

Border residents bear the brunt of the new United States government measures on the Southwestern border. No area of the country has been as affected as the U.S.-Mexico border after September 11. Even as New York City and other areas of the country recovered a sense of normalcy for the most part, the border continued to be affected and is still subjected to a series of security experiments.

In addition to the immediate effects felt by border residents in the days after September 11, there were other more permanent effects. The first is the increased militarization of the border, where fences, border patrols, aerostats, military personnel, intrusive evening lights, infrared technology, motion detectors, and other gadgets, give the sense that the U.S.-Mexico border is a border at war, a border under siege. Instead of an increasingly integrated border, the Southwest has seen the worst type of separation of any other time in the history of U.S.-Mexican relations.

A second cost to border residents has to do with the added time and resources that it takes to do business on the border. It is increasingly more difficult to move across the international boundary to conduct daily activities, including academic, business, leisure, and family activities. The only people that take the border more casually today are the teenagers that live, for example, in El Paso, Texas, and wish to party across the border where the drinking age is eighteen, instead of twenty-one.

Some residents, for example, in El Paso, who benefited from the cheaper labor of Mexican maids, day laborers, and gardeners are now finding it increasingly difficult to get a hold of that labor.

Although the Designated Commuter Lanes (DCL) between San Diego and Tijuana and El Paso and Ciudad Juárez make it easier for American workers to cross to work in Mexico and come back and for Mexican students to cross to study in the United States, the DCL is expensive and not available to everyone. Most others have to suffer the exceedingly long lines on the regular lanes to come across, with the consequent pollution, man-hours lost, and resources up in smoke from the exhaust pipes of the thousands of vehicles crossing the border everyday.

With the increasingly exhaustive checks on pedestrians, there is an increasing number of border residents that are prevented from going shopping or to enjoy leisure activities on the other side of the border. Businesses on both sides of the border reported that they have not yet recovered fully from the slowdown of the border retail economy after September 11. Tourism is yet to reach the normal levels of the pre-September 11 period.

THE COSTS OF HOMELAND SECURITY AT THE BORDER TO THE TAXPAYER

The actual costs to the government in increased Full Time Employment (FTE) personnel and in inspections budget has also increased considerably. However, the figures are not comparable across time given the bureaucratic reorganization of twenty-two federal agencies into a new Homeland Security Department. The following tables show the total inspections staff for all locations at borders, including immigration and customs commercial inspections.

Fiscal Year	Immigration	Customs	Agriculture	CBP
2001	4,717	8,184	n/a	
2002	5,422	9,008	n/a	
2003	6,741	10,538	1,480	
2004			1,446	17,784

Source: CRS Report for Congress. *Border Security: Inspections, Practices, Policies and Issues* (May 26, 2004).

Fiscal Year	Immigration Inspection (Millions of Dollars)	Staffing (FTEs)
1998	168	n/a
1999	481	5,199
2000	475	5,123
2001	1,494	5,472
2002	2,440	n/a

Source: CRS Report for Congress. Border Security: Inspections, Practices, Policies and Issues (May 26, 2004).

Fiscal Year	Commercial Activities	Staffing (Commercial Activities FTEs)
1998	853	9,295
1999	886	9,363
2000	922	9,070
2001	1,085	9,256
2002	1,173	9,728

Source: CRS Report for Congress. Border Security: Inspections, Practices, Policies and Issues (May 26, 2004).

In addition to the budgetary costs of the new security regime, the learning curve of the various new agencies is still working itself out. There are some problems of cooperation among agencies as they readjust to the new security regulations and share what is essentially a shared mandate on the area of national security. The Customs and Border Protection agency, for example, must work closely with the Food and Drug Administration and other agencies to synchronize their rules and procedures in order that businesses and corporations do not face delays or contradictory action upon their arrival at the border POE.

BACK TO NORMALCY?

The initial reaction to the terrorist attacks of September 11 affected the border quite deeply and continues to do so. There has been no deep reform to solve any of the border's problems. In other words, the border is still the border.

Take immigration, for example. There has been no considerable reduction in the number of undocumented workers crossing the border between POEs. Although no one really knows how many Mexicans cross the border without documents every year, the numbers vary from 300,000 to 500,000.

The number of OTMs (other than Mexicans) crossing the border without documents is still on the rise. The issue of immigration has undergone no real reform in order to deal with both the demand for cheap labor in the United States and the supply of this labor from Mexico, Central America, and other parts of the world. In other words, what the war on terror has left is a reorganized immigration bureaucracy, with no real reform or solution to the permanent problem of undocumented or documented migration. This reorganization constitutes perhaps no more than a slightly more sophisticated layer of requirements for border crossers and paperwork for the bureaucracies working on immigration issues. In that sense, the border is still the border.

Nearly the same thing can be said about illegal drugs. The U.S. drug war on the border has forced the cartels to consolidate their operations; to make their practices more efficient; and to take advantage of the economies of scale. Cartels have become flexible hierarchies, ready to respond to the contingencies of the drug war. And they generally succeed in doing so. It would appear that the border drug war waged by the United States has consolidated drug smuggling into four large oligopolies that continue to send massive supplies of illegal drugs to the country. There are no strategic successes in the drug war, and the tactical successes of the drug war appear to have the ability to squeeze the small-time smugglers out and make it easier for the large, consolidated drug smuggling organizations to operate. Illegal drugs are just as abundant as ever. There is also evidence that their price is going down and that the quality of the drugs is on an upward trend, both signs that on the issue of illegal drugs, the border is still the border.

But still, not everything is the same.

THE TREATMENT OF BORDER CROSSERS

Teresa Ibarra is a woman from a town in the southern part of the state of Chihuahua, across from El Paso and New Mexico. On a day before Christmas, she made her way to the border by bus. Her intention was to spend some time with her sister who lives in Albuquerque, New Mexico, and is married to an American citizen. Teresa holds a B1-B2 visa crossing card, much like the hundreds of thousands of crossing cards that allow Mexicans to cross the border into the United States to shop, visit relatives, etc. When Teresa got to the border inspection point, the agent treated her with great suspicion. He asked her a series of questions that she did not refuse to answer but which prompted only greater hostility by the border agent. Eventually, Teresa was taken to the "interrogation room" inside the POE building. Teresa was questioned for nearly 4 hours on her status, her activities, and contacts, the reasons for her visit, etc. Her version of the story was checked and doubled-checked against the version of her sister and her sister's husband who were traveling with her. Teresa was eventually let go, but she had felt humiliated, harassed, embarrassed, ill-treated, and her spirit was nearly broken.

Legal border crossers, like Teresa, are a diverse lot: American workers who commute into Mexico for managerial jobs in the manufacturing sector; Mexican students who study in schools and universities in the United States; American tourists who cross to shop, eat, or be entertained; Mexican shoppers who consume nearly $7 billion a year in retail goods on the U.S. side of the border; families crossing back and forth to visit their loved ones; investors, truckers, taxi drivers, maids, and gardeners.

Yet, since the war on terror began, every one of these border crossers has had to undergo a closer scrutiny by border inspectors. And almost no one minds the closer scrutiny. There is an understanding that after September 11, things are not the same and that closer inspection for the sake of national security is required. All Mexican border crossers would readily acknowledge that. What everyone minds is the harassing attitude of the Customs and Border Protection officials who increasingly make people feel unwelcome. A quick interview with border crossers at various points of the border revealed that they are generally afraid of the arbitrariness with which an inspector often decides to pick on a given person. They also believe that they pick on a border crosser based on "the way he dresses," or "the way he looks," or "the way he moves," etc. Very often, border crossers are not given reasons for their detention and questioning. They are kept in the dark. They are often kept for hours. They are accused of having this or that intention. In Teresa's words: "They make you feel like you are worth nothing, like you are a criminal."

The story of Teresa is somewhat similar to the story of Megan, a University of Texas at El Paso student, who is an American but lives in Ciudad Juárez and commutes to El Paso every day to go to school. She believes that the border inspectors exercise the most arbitrary reasons for questioning people and that the treatment they give border crossers today, particularly those on foot, is that of criminal suspects. Everyone, she says, is guilty until proven innocent. Such is the new, post-September 11 attitude along the border, to go with the new homeland security regime.

CONCLUSION

Five years after September 11, we have seen unimaginable consequences on the U.S. border system. It is true that the border was already closing, albeit slowly. The aftermath of September 11, however, fell strongly on the U.S.-Mexico border. The initial burden on border residents was quite large: long lines on the bridges, more exhaustive inspections, a harsher treatment of legitimate border crossers, a drop on retail sales all along the border, and a deeper culture of suspicion overall.

Elsewhere, I have demonstrated that much of the border is back to its normal levels of cross-border traffic, waiting lines, and shopping—even drugs and other contraband, including human smuggling, are back to normal. However, the culture of suspicion is not gone. Those that would close the border are here to stay. And the problems of the border continue unabated. The only move has been toward greater and greater enforcement of border laws, without regard to the fact that it means nearly more of the same, that is, the same as before September 11.

Someone once said that human beings are the only animal that keeps doing the same thing over and over again expecting different results. This may be true of the U.S. border security policy. The border security policy has been a largely unilateral approach by the United States. It has hardly engaged Mexico. It has hardly accounted for the globalization forces that come knocking on the U.S.-Mexico border. Instead, the U.S. border policy has been one of escalation: more cops, more guns, more gadgets, more vehicles, more technology, etc. It is as if the U.S. government thought that the only route to go was to increase all of these and as if all of these were sufficient to stem the tide of labor moving toward the border by the millions.

A new approach to security is needed, an approach that will be a North American approach, with a comprehensive solution that takes into consideration the tension between globalization and security. The ultimate goal should not be to close the border but to keep it open, while keeping it secure. Until now, closing it has been the equivalent to securing it, clearly a mistake that swims against the tide of history.

CHAPTER 5

The Panopticon Border

THE PANOPTICON BORDER

Jeremy Bentham, an English philosopher born in 1748, is the author of a concept that best captures what is happening at the U.S.-Mexico border. Among his works is the design of a *panopticon* penitentiary where the prison layout had rows of single cells arranged in tiers and running down long halls radiating from a central vestibule. It was designed much like the spokes of a wheel. Each cell, small and narrow, made for a single prisoner, had a tiny back-window to the outside world. The front wall of the cell was all bars and looked into the narrow landings of the prison galleries. This layout, known as a panopticon, was labeled so because a single guard could watch an entire row of prisoners from a central position. In effect, he could see everything.[1]

Michel Foucault would later expand the concept of a panopticon prison in his work *Discipline and Punish: the Birth of the Prison*.[2] In *Discipline and Punish*, Foucault traces the history of the contemporary penal system. He sought to analyze the social and political context of the development of punishment and to examine how power relations among the various actors in a penal system affected punishment. Foucault correctly perceived that the powers of the state (government) had grown considerably. He sensed that its reach had become totalizing. Government, he argued, was systematizing their grip on the lives of every lawbreaker—a short step from controlling the lives of everyone else. Indeed, the new forms of punishment that the state planned were not necessarily created to rehabilitate the prisoners but to exercise the power of the state to control society. The new modes of penality were designed to deter those who would be lawbreakers. In the end, the result of this process has been a slow but steady movement toward a society largely under surveillance and control by the state.

Bentham's concept of a panopticon prison and Foucault's analysis of the surveillance and control powers of the state are particularly relevant to the border. At the border, the U. S. government has undertaken the colossal task of increasing its surveillance and control over it by exercising the powers of the police state. In the borderlands, the U.S. government is waging a war to surveil and control all border crossers. It has fallen on law enforcement organizations, the primary agents of the U.S. government at the border to wage this war. They have continuously over the twentieth century and into our century escalated their efforts to create a system of total surveillance and complete control along the boundary line. The final draft of the Homeland Security Department's Strategic Plan outlines just that goal.

> The Department will enforce border security in an integrated fashion at ports of entry, on the borders, on the seas and before potential threats can reach out borders. Through the continued deployment of the appropriate balance of personnel, equipment and technology we will create "smart borders."[3]

The international boundary line between Mexico and the United States has turned into a virtual Maginot line, including, as we have seen, the stalemate between the "enemy" and the United States.

Unfortunately, the strategy of surveillance and control along the border-line is a sure sign that the U.S. government is thus far not interested in a long-term solution to the issues plaguing the border. Neither the White House nor Congress has provided the leadership to conceptualize and tackle the problems of the border from a broader perspective. Instead, the force of the state, with all its resources, quasi-military operations, timetables, and drills, and so on, has come down on the border to "regain control" of it. Any visitor to the border can see the new technologies being deployed on the border, including cameras, sensors, night goggles, X-ray machines, helicopters, Humvee-style vehicles, etc. The increase in the number of Border Patrol agents, the watchful human eyes, is also quite evident. All of these are at the disposal of the state to create the panopticon border of the twenty-first century, where everyone is under surveillance at all times, where everyone is tracked in every move, where everyone can be brought under the swift control of the government. Surveillance alone is supposed to deter any potential law-breaking border crossers—even though it has hardly done so. On this new border, everyone is suspect of wanting to harm America. In this process, unfortunately, human rights take a back seat.

The ultimate goal of this panoptic strategy is to shut down the border and, myopically, define the world of the United States as an entity that ends at the border. In this view, there is little thought given to the forces that brew beyond the boundary line and eventually impact right up against it. On the border, the worst of nightmares of George Orwell's *1984*, with an ubiquitous Big Brother, are already a near reality.[4]

TECHNOLOGY AND THE PANOPTICON BORDER

What has facilitated the creation of a panopticon border is the progressive introduction of one important element to the border: high surveillance and tracking technology. This is a natural product of American faith in technology as a panacea. The U.S. government has continually sought to introduce new technological developments into the activities of those in charge of sealing the Southern border. This trend toward the use of technology to close the border has been gradual through the customs and law enforcement eras of the borderlands, but accelerated after the terrorist attacks of September 11. The result has been the effective implementation of a panopticon border. Just a few instances will demonstrate how quickly this trend toward hi-tech gadgets is developing.

In October 2005, a group of students from a Texas university went to Monterrey, Mexico, to attend a parliamentary procedures workshop. The same bus took them from San Antonio to Monterrey and back. On their return, when they arrived at the inspection point, they were asked to get off the bus. The empty bus was taken to a driveway where a moving X-ray device (which looked like a small mobile home) with a long arm extending over the bus scanned the vehicle back and forth. These X-ray devices are now quite visible in nearly every relatively large POE along the border. They are even more common in the yards where semi-trucks and even some smaller vehicles arrive with import cargo. They are one of the latest weapons with powerful new technology designed to detect illegal drugs, weapons, and human cargo.

If these students want to go back to Monterrey after December 2007, each of them would have to carry a U.S. passport. As per the Intelligence Reform and Terrorism Prevention Act of 2004, the United States intends to require all citizens to carry a passport if they cross the border and reenter the country, beginning on January 1, 2008.[5] Even casual tourists who cross for a day or local border residents who cross to visit family or to shop will have to carry a passport. This of course makes it even harder for border residents to go across the border. Many may not even be able to afford to get a passport, given that many of those who have relatives across the border are relatively poor and have large families. A foreseeable secondary effect of this new rule would be the dissolution of familial and social ties between border twin cities and their residents even more than they have already been dissolved over the last four decades.

An issue of greater concern is the fact that such a move would grant the U.S. government the ability to track people who use the border all the time because all new passports would be equipped with a chip—at least that is the hope of law enforcement agencies. The chip could contain enormous amounts of data on an individual, data that would be easily accessible to any law enforcement official. Moreover, in an extreme case, these chips could even serve as a homing device. Privacy advocates, business travel groups, and some security experts are opposing both the passport chip and the new passports requirements that the U.S. government wants in place by the beginning of 2008.[6]

Driving along the border in Naco, Arizona, I saw a helicopter hovering along the steel wall that separates it from Naco, Sonora. The helicopter was hovering looking for undocumented border crossers trying to make their way through the many walk paths weaving through the thorny bushes in the rugged desert. As of 2002, the Border Patrol employed fifty-eight helicopters, most of them deployed on the U.S.-Mexico border: eleven MD 600Ns; four MD 500Es; one MD 500C; three UH-1H Hueys; four Aerospatiale AS-350s; and thirty-five Hughes OH-s. That year, the Attorney General was lobbying to increase the Border Patrol budget for aviation assets.[7]

In addition to the manned aircraft, such as the helicopters used by the Border Patrol, a Congressional Research Service Report in 2005 explored the introduction of Unmanned Aerial Vehicles (UAV) as a method to improve border security. Such drones were tested at Fort Huachuca and Gila Bend in Arizona for use along the U.S.-Mexico border. The Department of Homeland Security, through Customs and Border Protection, intends to make such drones part of their equipment to conduct missions on the border. Ten million dollars were budgeted to acquire this technology, along with more sensors and video technology for border surveillance.[8]

While in Naco, looking up at the helicopter, which appeared to be looking down at my activities right up against the steel wall, I was struck by a row of tall posts with mounted cameras looking out in every direction. Such cameras are increasingly a common sight along the border, particularly near urban centers but also in certain more rural areas. Hundreds of cameras now beam images of what is happening on the ground to a central location where the images are scrutinized. If any activity is detected by these cameras, it is immediately relayed to the Border Patrol agents on the field. Of course, cameras have been a permanent feature of every POE for a very long time. At a POE it is harder and harder not to be under the view of a camera. This trend is now being extended to many other parts of the border where powerful cameras can record what is happening 5 miles around. Many of these cameras have night vision capabilities as well.

Along the New Mexico, Arizona, and West Texas borders, it is also easy to run into high intensity lights mounted on a permanent electricity generator.

These high intensity lights are portable; they can be easily hitched to a vehicle and moved to other areas. The idea behind these high-density lights is to produce sufficient illumination in order to deter undocumented border crossers from using certain passageways in the wilderness and to facilitate the job of the Border Patrol agents at night. There are, of course, rows of these lights in urban areas as well, although most of those are permanently fixed on lampposts. These lights facilitate the detection of any activity along the borderline.

Driving along a ditch that runs parallel to the Rio Grande in West Texas, about 25 miles west of El Paso, I ran into a Border Patrol agent. He and I engaged in a very brief conversation. I asked him about the sensors buried under ground. The officer mentioned briefly that indeed the U.S. government was making increasing use of these underground sensors to detect any movement across the border. These sensors tend to be located in the more transited parts of the border, where undocumented crossers are known to journey. This information too is related to a central location and piped live to the Border Patrol agents on the field.

A Border Patrol vehicle is also equipped with hi-tech gadgets, including equipment to receive in-time information of what is going on around them from other sources. The border agents carry powerful weapons, including M16 rifles and other handguns. They also have infrared goggles, such as those that the U.S. military uses, to detect body heat. This enables the agents to detect human bodies hiding in the bushes, ditches, etc. Night vision capability by the agents guarding the border makes it increasingly difficult for border crossers to come in undetected.

Iris recognition technology—in addition to thumbprints—is now widely used at U.S. airports and also along the border when Mexican border crossers request an I-94 permit to travel into the United States further than 25 miles. Iris technology is also used at American consulates and there are plans to use it when the US-Visit program is fully implemented, intended to check everyone who exits the country.

Statistical tools are also being used to track cross-border movement of persons and vehicles. A new system implemented along the U.S.-Mexico border gathers and patterns information accumulated at every POE. If the system detects that a certain type of vehicle has been "busted" with drugs at several parts along the border, a "memorandum" goes out urging agents to "watch out" for that type of vehicle because it might be likely that the drug traffickers are using such vehicles for their drug smuggling. If there is a spike in drug busts at a particular POE, inspection activity is ratcheted up because the spike indicates that that POE is being used more frequently. And so forth. The statistical database accumulates information on a permanent basis and relays it in real time to all agents working along the border. Moreover, a researcher at New Mexico State University, Stefan Schmidt, has come up with a mathematical model that will presumably predict where smugglers are likely to cross.[9]

These are among the multiple technological devices being used today to gain control of the border. The overall result has been that the technology that the U.S. government uses on the border is increasingly more sophisticated. There is a much larger investment now in the use of high technology, turning the border into a veritable panopticon border where soon no one will be able to move without being seen or heard or noticed. Technology continues to change at a heady pace and will enable the U.S. government even more to acquire further operational capabilities on the border. There is indeed a race to close the border definitely and technology will probably accomplish this. George Orwell should have titled his novel *1984*, as *The Border 2020*.

MILITARIZATION OF THE BORDER

The use of technology to guard the border came accompanied with the increased use of quasi-military operations on the border. Dunn has successfully shown that low-intensity conflict precepts have been adopted by U.S. law enforcement agencies to conduct their operations along the border. In his study, he concludes that "Overall, it seems clear that immigration and drug enforcement efforts in the U.S.-Mexico border region during the 1978–1992 period coincided to a significant extent with the precepts of the LIC [Low-Intensity Conflict] doctrine."[10] As previously discussed, Congressman Silvestre Reyes' *Operation Hold the Line* in the El Paso area in 1994 took the militarization of the border even further. His efforts were an all-out assault on undocumented migration with an unprecedented strategy. Before *Operation Hold the Line*, some attempts had been made at using the military to guard the border and there have been renewed calls for the use of the National Guard to patrol the border. The military got involved in operations along the border, which they mostly took on as part of their training, as early as 1981–1982. Still, it was Mr. Reyes who first implemented a massive border control operation with a distinct paramilitary feel to it. It was a blockade strategy taken right out of military manuals. In fact, the operation was originally titled *Operation Blockade*, but the name irked many groups inside the United States and upset the Mexican government. The name was then changed to *Operation Hold the Line*, which intended to choke the border and close it completely by positioning an agent every quarter of a mile, within sight distance of each other. This formation, stretching for about 25 miles along the Rio Grande, would make guarding the border a totalizing activity. Reyes also began to talk about interoperability among the various agencies working on the border. He personally briefed border agents on the newest trends and what was happening on the ground. He personally debriefed them when they came off the field. In the absence of a national strategy, Reyes implemented an operation designed to use all the personnel and assets available to draft a blueprint of substantial deterrence on the border.[11]

Congressman Reyes' operation succeeded in sealing the border at El Paso. Arrests of undocumented workers dropped considerably in the sector. Of course, undocumented border crossers simply moved away from the urban areas into more rural and even more rugged, empty areas of the border, with many more deaths as a result. It was at this time that the number of undocumented migrant deaths in the Arizona desert began to climb. By some estimates there have been over 3,000 undocumented migrant deaths in the Arizona desert since these operations began; as many persons died on September 11 in the terrorist attacks. According to the Border Patrol, there were 1,954 casualties of the war on undocumented immigration between 1998 and 2004 alone, with anywhere between 300 and 500 dying every year. Most die of dehydration, hypothermia, heart attacks, and car accidents.[12] Doris Meissner, former chief of the then Immigration and Naturalization Service (INS) acknowledged that the multiplication of deaths on the southwest border was an "unintended consequence" of the new aggressiveness of U.S. strategies on the border. If the United States managed to seal the urban centers, the rugged geography of the rest of the border, they said, would be the deterrent.[13] It has not been so. The balloon effect was at work. Reyes' success was success but only where he was operating. The rest of the border was ready to receive the migrants who would not cease the pursuit of their "American dream."

Reyes' operation was so successful in El Paso that it was imitated also elsewhere, in California (Operation Gatekeeper) and in Arizona (Operation Safeguard) and in the Lower Rio Grande Valley of Texas (Operation Rio Grande). In California, Border Patrol Chief Gus de la Viña argued that such physical blockades did not fit the problems endemic to his San Diego sector. Instead, he argued for high steel walls to be built along the borderline. And he got them. The physical blockage of the border in the urban centers between California and Baja California now include steel walls that a visitor can see running right into the sea. Such fences exist in other places along the borderline in Arizona as well. In Calexico-Mexicali, there are also water canals, dug like trenches and filled with water to serve as a deterrent for border crossers. Such canals are a common sight in various parts of Texas, along the Rio Grande.

The training of the Border Patrol has also become more and more military-like. Although their job remains a law enforcement effort, it has now a distinct military feel to it. In Arizona, they train with heavily armed Marines; in California they get help from the National Guard in inspecting vehicles at POEs; in the Imperial Valley, they hunker down with soldiers using night vision equipment to detect stealthy border crossers. Their vehicles used to be open vans and SUV-style vehicles. Today, they are trucks with steel cages welded on the platform that resemble military jeeps. Their weapons are also becoming more sophisticated and military technology has been adapted for use on border operations. Driving along the Rio Grande riverbank in Fabens, Texas, I was stopped by a Border Patrol agent who wanted to check on my activity along the river. I was surprised at the number of gadgets at his disposal around his waist belt, besides his handgun. Within 3 minutes of his stopping me, several other Border Patrol vehicles were speeding toward us. Communication between patrols is now swift and support can be at hand within a couple of minutes. Somewhat upset at my use of their exclusive road along the Rio Grande, they escorted me out to the main highway in the town of Fabens and asked me not to use their road, newly improved by the military, again. Along the U.S.-Mexico border there is a push to build a law enforcement military infrastructure in an effort to control the border.

These physical blockade strategies of the Border Patrol in El Paso during *Operation Hold the Line* have been imitated extensively along other sectors of the border since 1994. The logic of escalation at the border continues apace. The consequence, of course, has been even more deaths along the border, but not a fundamental, long-term solution to the border's undocumented migration issue. Consider, for example, that since 1994, the number of undocumented workers in the United States has gone from 3 million to as many as 12 million. The steel fences, the cameras, the Humvees, the helicopters, the hovercrafts, the ATVs, and fixed-winged aircraft, etc., have not stopped the flood of undocumented workers—or illegal drugs.

THE BORDER AS A SYMBOL OF A RELUCTANT PARTNERSHIP

Mexico and the United States are not friends. They may be friendly, but they are not friends. At least, they are not friends in the sense that Canada and the United States are friends. And yet, both countries understand that they are bound by destiny. Their geographical proximity makes them associates in a reluctant partnership. Both Washington and Mexico City like to stress the importance of their relationship, but there are really few real institutionalized mechanisms of cooperation between the two countries, even in the face of deepening economic integration under NAFTA. Under the George W. Bush administration there have been even fewer contacts between Washington and Mexico City than under the Bill Clinton administration, when there were periodic cabinet-level meetings between the two nations. Americans often perceive Mexico as a source of trouble. Mexicans are preoccupied with the United States, but feel between abused and neglected by their neighbor. Across the border, Mexicans and Americans eye each other with deep suspicion. Americans overestimate their generosity to Mexico and Mexicans view Americans as self-centered and demanding. The mutual distrust runs very deep. Mexico feels dominated by the United States; the United States seldom views the relationship as one of domination. It is possible to go on specifying the many divides between Mexico and the United States, but they have been plentifully explained elsewhere. Here, suffice it to say that they are engaged in a reluctant partnership.

More crucial to us here is that nowhere is this reluctance of both Mexico and the United States to be partners more manifest than on their borderlands. The millions of Americans who reside in the Southwest borderlands of the United States know the importance of Mexico. Mexico is an increasingly essential part of their lives. Their lives are closely intertwined with the lives of Mexicans living on the border. The economic, social, and cultural ties are ever stronger but under threat of extinction by U.S. border policies. Yet there is a veritable convergence at the borderlands. Most U.S. counties along the border, some twenty-six of them, are nearly solidly Mexican and Mexican–American now. Spanish is a dominant language in the region. Family bloodlines cross the border millions of times. Jobs on one side generate additional jobs on the other side. Put together the economy of the border counties and border municipios (equivalent to counties in Mexico) would constitute a formidable manufacturing powerhouse.

The problem is not in the understanding of those of us who have to live on the border. The problem is with those who live away from the border in the United States Their perceptions are distorted by the media and the political rhetoric that is heard loud and clear in their living rooms. Their perceptions are heavily influenced by the media's attention to the negative news coming from the border and their neglect of the many positive things that happen on the borderlands. To a housewife in St. Louis, or a student in Portland, or a blue-collar worker in Sioux Falls, the border is a dangerous place. To a border resident, the border is home and he/she makes the best of it, much as everyone else in their community.

AGENT GONZÁLEZ AND THE PROBLEM WITH THE PROBLEM

Peering through a hole in the steel wall that divides a small California border town from a tiny settlement on the Baja California side of the border, a Border Patrol agent sitting in his truck became aware that I was studying the borderline. Trained to be suspicious of every activity occurring anywhere near the wall, the agent sped toward me. Agent González came out of the truck and walked toward me. He asked me what I was doing. I said I was studying the fence. He was not happy about it at all. He said that I should not be there because it was dangerous, because it was a liability for the federal government, because I should have gotten permission to be there, etc. He was behaving considerably more zealously than the other Border Patrol agents I had encountered in New Mexico and Arizona. He ordered me to report to the nearest Border Patrol station and to ask for permission if I wanted to study the fence.

The barrage of questions that he shot at me prompted me to come up with some of my own. "Why is there no port of entry between these two towns?" I asked. "Is the settlement on the other side just a ranch? Or is it a full township? When people want to cross, where do they go?" He was visibly annoyed by my questions and said, pointing toward Mexico, "I don't know. That is Mexico on the other side. I don't know anything about it."

It dawned on me that this answer was quite revealing of the whole "problem of the border." Agent González's answer expressed several realities regarding the border. The other side is their problem. My problem begins here, with this fence. My job is not to view the problem of immigration comprehensively, but to view each person crossing the fence as a transgressor and anyone moving along it as a potential criminal. My job is not to know what is on the other side and how it relates to my job. My job is to prevent border jumpers from coming through. I do not care about what is on the other side. My care begins at this point and from here northward. Agent González epitomized the reality of the border. It is a dividing line. It separates. It determines our concerns. It determines what we care about. It shapes out views of what it means. It limits our vision of the problem. It focuses the wars of the border on the dividing line. It prevents a global view of the matter. It gives meaning to our jobs and our careers. What the relationship between our "immigration problem" and what may motivate it on the other side of the borderline is, we do not care. On the other side of the fence, regardless of how strong the sun shines there too, there is only darkness. It is an abyss. It is the unknown. Existence drops, ceases to be for a Border Patrol agent at the borderline. And perhaps he, the border-level bureaucrat, is not to blame. He is paid to guard the border. Period. His commands come from above. His orders are clear. The policy itself is someone else's matter.

Unfortunately, it is not any different for our politicians and the public, than it is for Agent González in the field. Politicians in particular seem to be trapped in a myopic view of the border that forbids us from conceiving it as a North American problem. This is worse than good fences making good neighbors. Good fences make the neighbor disappear until the neighbor's problem lands on "our" side of the fence. Then the solution becomes more guards, more walls, taller walls, more agents, more vehicles, more lighting and sensor systems, and binoculars. Success is measured in terms of the number of arrests, jail time, deportations, etc., with little thought to whether the strategy overall is paying off. For 12 years, the United States has pumped billions of dollars into fortifying the border, with little success so far, in spite of the many tactical successes here and there.

As far as Agent González was concerned, there is a border war going on. He is just a foot soldier in it. His job is to stop the invasion of human smugglers who lead over 1 million undocumented workers, the enemy, across the borderline. He patrols the trenches. He watches the battle line. He detains the prisoners of the war on immigration. As far as the politicians are concerned, Agent González is a hero in action because the border is to be "protected," the "invasion" is to be stopped, "border security must be ensured," and so on. The strategy is a war of attrition, a continual grinding down of the border with more and more resources, even as drugs flow just as freely and human smuggling rings prosper. Agent González's myopia extends from the borderlands to Washington, DC.

THE DEFINITION OF BORDER SECURITY

Agent González's perspective is important because it reveals that the two countries do not coincide on the definition of the border. In effect, Mexico's border is an open border. Americans can go into Mexico without a visa; they can travel at will inside Mexico and they can even reside in that country without much hassle. One and a quarter million American citizens living and working in Mexico can testify to that. Moreover, since NAFTA entered into effect, Mexico has practically become a nation open to trade and investment at unprecedented levels in its history. Americans benefit handsomely from this openness. Contrastingly, the U.S. border is a closed border, or more specifically, it is a border wide open to trade and investment, but closed to labor. Labor is a fundamental component of any economy. Yet, the United States has been very slow to acknowledge that Mexico has a comparative advantage in the labor that it can provide to a humming American economy. This discrepancy has been explored by Peter Laufer in *Wetback Nation: The Case for Opening the Mexican-American Border*.[14] Still, Mexicans are required to have a visa to enter the United States. They cannot easily obtain a permit to either work temporarily or to migrate to the United States. This creates an enormous pressure to move without a visa and risk death at the border and living in the shadows of the American society once inside the country.

More important here is the fact that if they do not share a common definition of the border, it becomes obvious why they do not share a common definition of security. Not having a common definition of border security is a fact that in and of itself should impede any serious cooperation between the two on "securing the border." Since September 11, it has become even more palpable that Mexico and the United States do not see eye to eye on the very definition of security. This disagreement weighs heavily on the border.

Thus, it is important to examine the definition of security and what the security goals of each country are and how they rub at the border. There are two definitions of security. First, there is national security. Second there is public security. National security refers to the threats coming from outside and which jeopardize the safety of the nation as a whole. Public security refers to the safety of the citizens from each other, e.g., criminal activity by citizens on other citizens or their property. The United States definition of security focuses on the concept of national security, external threats. The State Department is quite clear on what security means to the United States today:

> But new deadly challenges have emerged from rogue states and terrorists. None of these contemporary threats rival the sheer destructive power that was arrayed against us by the Soviet Union. However, the nature and motivations of these new adversaries, their determination to obtain destructive powers hitherto available only to the world's strongest states, and the greater likelihood that they will use weapons of mass destruction against us, make today's security environment more complex and dangerous.[15]

There is evidence that in the United States, national security and public security are increasingly becoming confused—at least in the law enforcement community. Since September 11, the two concepts have become merged and citizens and aliens are often seen as threatening national security in both senses. A passenger in a domestic flight who might be perceived as behaving erratically may be shot to death by the Air Marshals because he/she poses a "national security threat," which is in such a case nearly indistinguishable from a crime. In fact, the Patriot Act seems to conflate the two types of security definitions—a considerable departure from the past. The February 2005 conviction of Lynne F. Stewart, a lawyer for "smuggling messages out of jail from a terrorist client," is an example that U.S. citizens can today be seen as a threat to national security.[16] The detention of U.S. citizens, such as José Padilla, without due process by the Justice Department under the George W. Bush Administration is another example that the distinction between national security and public security is increasingly blurred. Thus the new concept of "security" in the United States is primarily a "national security" concept, but combines some elements of the concept of public security. The fundamental assumption, however, is that, even if the national security threat may be found in a domestic context, the threat is to the national security, in effect, the very survival and way of life, of the United States. The survival and well being of the nation are primordial in this narrower understanding of security.

Mexico views these two terms quite separately and quite distinct from one another. And national security is not Mexico's main concern. Foreign threats to Mexican sovereignty are not a reality that Mexicans consider important today, even if they did in the past. Public security however is a big concern for Mexico.

> Inadequate public security presently ranks near the top of Mexico's political agenda and has become central in shaping U.S.-Mexico relations. There is much debate about the meaning of 'public security'... The debate concerns the boundaries of the concept and whether and how to include such issues as income inequality, poverty, education, popular culture, morality, and the like.[17]

The threat of organized crime, for example, is a serious worry to the Mexican government. The Mexican government increasingly worries about drug cartels and the effects that they have on the country's economy and society. Mexicans worry also about the safety of Mexican undocumented workers traveling to the United States and their human rights once inside the United States. Mexico has even declared that poverty and environmental degradation are in and of themselves threats to the security of the country. Mexico understands security to be a much broader concept than a terrorist threat coming from abroad.

But there are points of coincidence nevertheless, where the two countries could conceivably cooperate to make the border safer. If public security, say in regard to organized crime, specifically drug trafficking, is a preoccupation of both nations, then there is an overlap in their definitions of security and this constitutes an opportunity for cooperation. That such coincidences exist with minimal mechanisms of cooperation is a glaring example of how the political will of both governments has failed to produce sustained, effective collaboration on one of the most serious problems of the border and beyond. Unfortunately, the U.S. government does not trust the Mexican government and the Mexican government is still highly suspicious of U.S. intentions. U.S. anti-drug bureaucrats, for example, can cite many examples of intelligence sharing where the information has been compromised by a corrupt Mexican official leaking it out to criminal organizations. Mexico still suffers from a historical paranoia regarding U.S. violations of its sovereignty in the past. This mutual discomfort does not allow the two countries to work together fully in fighting drug-trafficking at the border from the same stand. Each tackles the problem differently and separately, which enables the drug-trafficking organizations to operate between the cracks.

The blurring of the distinction of the definitions of national security and public security in the United States affects the border in yet another way. If the border is not viewed as a matter of public security but it is perceived as a matter of national security instead, this image justifies the increased militarization of the border. Such militarization is no longer seen as an anomaly but rather as a natural response to the presumed threats that the border represents. All such threats on the border have now been welded into a single department, Homeland Security. Moreover, because it is the survival or welfare of the country that is at stake, a unilateral response is perceived as appropriate by the United States. Such approach, however, irks Mexico considerably because that definition of security has a lot to do with the threats the United States faces but not the threats that Mexico faces. In fact, it appears that the United States does not take Mexico's definition seriously at all. Thus, instead of focusing on the points of coincidence, the two countries go their separate ways and the border lacks a coherent, binational approach to ensure that it is a safe and prosperous place for the many millions of Mexican and American citizens that live and work and study in the borderlands. Criminals and other undesirables find a wedge of safe haven in the gray area where joint solutions do not exist.

THE CONSTRUCTION OF SECURITY

That Mexico and the United States cannot agree on a common definition of security is testimony to the fact that security on the U.S.-Mexico border is a constructed concept. Politicians, policymakers, and the media choose to portray the three great issues of the borderlands—drugs, immigration, and homeland security—as threats to the nation as a whole. The way issues are perceived is not a trivial matter because changing the discourse around them may help find broader, more successful solutions. For example, undocumented immigration from Mexico to the United States is an economic phenomenon spurred by the economic asymmetries between the two. If Mexico cannot generate enough jobs to absorb its unemployed, these will tend to flow to the United States in search of work. If Mexico's wages are significantly lower than those in the United States, labor will go where higher wages can be had. Moreover, the labor needs of the United States are also a significant pull. Labor demand in the United States makes it possible for an undocumented worker to imagine himself working in the United States. It has been sufficiently shown that undocumented immigration has a lot to do with the networks that already exist between certain communities in Mexico and specific U.S. metropolitan areas. Those already in the United States inform those at home that there is a job to be had. They are further encouraged to make the trek to the border and beyond because they also know that once they reach a U.S. metropolitan area, they will not be caught.

Yet, officials and the media in the United States have chosen to view undocumented migration not as an economic issue but as a security issue. They seldom talk about the economic forces that constitute the push and pull forces for migrants. In effect, the U.S. law enforcement community has chosen to "construct" its own definition of security by referring to migrants as a national security threat and using language that includes the words "invasion," "war," "threat," "crisis," "disorder," "chaos," "frontlines," etc. Security concepts arise "out of discursive practices within states."[18] Since

September 11 this kind of rhetoric has only increased exponentially. And language does matter in the construction of an environment and the creation of solutions to a given problem. Whereas under the Clinton administration the concern was with "managing the border," today the concern is with "controlling the border."[19] Whereas immigration was then a law enforcement issue, it is labeled a national security issue today. Each of these labels imply different solutions, even if there is remarkable continuity between them. Political discourse is being captured by a new rhetoric that necessarily leads to quasi-militarized techniques of responding to border issues. In a previous section, we have also explored how there is a strong tendency to conflate the issues by labeling every one of them a matter of national security.

UNHELPFUL RHETORIC

Although one would like to think that the American public has all the information it needs at its disposal to make appropriate judgments about the border, the views of the majority are largely shaped by the media and those who would be news makers, more specifically politicians. How the media frames the issues and the rhetoric that politicians use in their border narratives heavily weighs on the perceptions of the border among Americans. This was obvious through 2005.

On August 17, 2005, a *New York Times* headline read "Citing Border Violence, Two States Declare a Crisis." On August 20, 2005, the headlines read, referring to the same border states, Arizona and New Mexico, "United States of Emergency." On August 23, 2005, the same paper's headlines read "For One Family, Front Row Seats to Border Crisis" On August 24, 2005, it read "Homeland Security Chief, With Nod to Public Discontent, Tells of Plan to Stabilize the Border." On December 3, a *Baltimore Sun* editorial called to "Regain Control of Our Borders." On December 4, 2005, they read "Rival Drug Gangs Turn the Streets of Nuevo Laredo into War Zone." Similar headlines could be found across the country in large papers, like the *Washington Post*, the *LA Times*, the *Dallas Morning News*, the *Houston Chronicle*, etc. The broadcast media has employed the same kind of rhetoric. Some national anchors and TV show hosts have chosen to talk about the border as a lawless, chaotic place where violence and illegality reign. Fox News has contributed to this kind of rhetoric perhaps more than any other network. In all, the rhetoric keeps growing more alarming. All these stories portray the border as being under siege by all kinds of criminal organizations. In addition to the many articles in the print media and the hundreds of reportages on the border in the broadcast media, several books have come out as well detailing what is happening at the border as a disaster, as a national security threat, etc.[20] This sense of urgency is found nearly everywhere in the national debate regarding the border.

Politicians too entered the fray, mostly to profit from it, as politicians are wont to do. John Kerry himself, well before he ran for president wrote a book, *The New War: The Web of Crime that Threatens America's Security* in which he said that a new war had to be waged against criminal organizations that flouted the border continuously smuggling both drugs and human beings.[21] For Kerry, the border was seen as practically governed by criminal organizations. Patrick Buchanan, who also ran for president in 1996, advocated the construction of a border wall that would be patrolled by the military.[22] The idea was eventually dismissed as too controversial. Nevertheless, more recently Representative Duncan Hunter of California, who chairs the House Armed Services Committee, insisted on his presumed necessity of building two parallel steel and wire fences with a lighted strip from the Gulf of Mexico to the Pacific Coast.[23] Mexico's Foreign Ministry immediately released a communiqué arguing against the construction of this wall. But border walls have been going up nevertheless and are now nearing a 100 miles total along the border between El Paso and San Diego. Others have been quite vocal, like Congressman Tom Tancredo (R-CO), who on December 12, 2005 said that fifty-one terrorists had been arrested crossing the border illegally. Congressman Tancredo never really defined what the definition of a terrorist crossing the border illegally is.[24] Citations by politicians regarding the lack of control along the border can be found by the thousands. Of course, they forget that the border has never really been under control. It has always been out of the total control of the U.S. government. Moreover, those who would speak of border control hide the fact that as the current border strategies of the United States to control the border have escalated, the same problems have only gotten worse and the consequences more deadly.

The words used to describe the border kept escalating the tone of the debate regarding the border throughout 2005. This flurry of alarming notes regarding the border was stopped cold by the media's attention to the Katrina Hurricane disaster in New Orleans. Not much was said until the end of the year, when President Bush took a tour of the southwest promising to make border security a priority in his legislative agenda. Although President Bush sounded like a man trying to find a workable solution, many in Washington, DC, would likely be unhappy with a solution that would grant undocumented workers amnesty. Many politicians responded to the President's message in a manner equally unhelpful in the search for creative, long-term, binational solutions to a common border. The same politicians and policymakers that contribute heavily to the "securitization" of the border by using language that resembles the media's and certain vigilante groups that patrol the border from time to time rejected the idea of any kind of amnesty for undocumented workers.

It is lamentable that the media and politicians often feed off the same cycle of news and create a border crisis by the images and representation of border problems. Obviously, the issues of the border are serious. They need to be dealt with seriously. But the rhetoric of those who do not reside on the border is very often unhelpful in finding good solutions to these problems.

TALKING PAST EACH OTHER AT THE BORDER

Leaving aside the fact that there is no agreement on the definition of security between Mexico and the United States, the political leaders seem to be talking past each other—when they talk to each other at all. Although some assessments say that the U.S.-Mexico relationship is advancing and security cooperation is overall better today than ever, there are two fundamental items missing from the relationship today. First, there is little political will in either country to take a serious look at the border and how to solve common problems together. Second, there is little vision among the leaders of both sides in regard to the future of the border. Even the mechanisms for cooperation at the ministerial level that had been created under the Clinton Administration seem to have disappeared under the Bush Administration. The consequence is that, if the relationship is altogether on hold, the border there is nearly a total abandonment. Indeed, a striking feature of the border is that sometimes bureaucrats look at each other in the eye from across the fences but seldom do they talk to each other at all. There is very little contact on the ground among officials of agencies whose mission is to guard the border on either side.

As a sign of the fact that the two nations are talking past each other is the fact that Mexico tried to reach out to the United States early in the Fox administration by creating a "border czar" position within the Mexican government. And although the position did not come with real resources and jurisdictional power, one of the important elements of its undoing was the fact that the titular of that post in the Mexican government, Ernesto Ruffo Appel, could not find a counterpart in the United States government to talk to. In general, there is very little dialogue between the two nations to solve their common problems. And NAFTA has not produced any other inter-governmental institutions that could help take a serious look at the border with an eye to finding common solutions.

A NEW APPROACH IS NEEDED

The 1990s were an odd time for the border. It would seem almost as if the border suffered from the schizophrenia of both Washington, DC, and Mexico City. The 1990s saw some of the strongest movement to "militarize" the border on the part of the United States government. Yet, the North American Free Trade Agreement (NAFTA) brought about all sorts of speculations about North American integration and the birth of a North American community. There was enormous optimism around in the air.

Finally, it was thought, Mexico and the United States would break decades of mutual suspicion and begin a long-term process of integration. This was manifest in the visit that President George W. Bush paid President Vicente Fox in his ranch in the state of Guanajuato. September 11, however, brought about the "securitization" of the border, with "security" being defined in very narrow and conventional terms as a threat to the survival and welfare of the country. The catastrophic events made the U.S. government retreat from its orientation toward North American integration. Yet, the integration, at least the economic integration, of North American continues apace, a fact that both the Mexican and the United States government have failed to understand. There is clearly also a cultural convergence in the Southwest, where Mexicans and Mexican-Americans are beginning to constitute important majorities in border states and many counties. Yet the two governments have failed to build any credible institutions that can effectively systematize the future of the relationship and the future of the border. Border issues are resolved one at a time, with great difficulty, often too late and sometimes not at all. Both countries generally react to border troubles and recriminations about each other's behavior along the boundary line are plentiful. A narrow definition of security by the United States and a perceived lack of cooperation from Mexico around U.S. concerns is slowing the process of cross-border cooperation even further.

It is therefore unfortunate that the war on terror has come to the border because the economic opportunities and the market forces as well as the cultural convergence at work in the borderlands could help push forward toward a binational agreement on how to deal with the border. The political will and the political vision of leaders in Washington, DC, and Mexico City, however, lag well behind. Everyone, it seems, is thinking very small. A new approach to North American security is needed, one that will ensure the periphery well beyond the border.

THE NORTH AMERICAN FREE TRADE AGREEMENT AND THE BORDER

On January 1, 1994, the North American Free Trade Agreement entered into effect. At that time, and in spite of the Zapatista rebellion in southern Mexico and a peso devaluation, with a corresponding financial crisis at the end of 1994, there was enormous optimism about the integration of North America. Finally, Mexico and the United States, along with Canada, had recognized their common destiny—at a minimum, their geographical ties—and come together to formalize their economic integration. There was considerable talk about the North American continent comparing it with the European Union.

And NAFTA has been very successful. Since it entered into effect, it has propelled trade among the three to unprecedented levels. Financial flows among the three countries also multiplied. Travel among the three countries also grew dramatically. The opportunities for interaction among Mexicans, Canadians, and Americans burgeoned. North America was becoming an integrated region. Most trade barriers between the three countries were eliminated.

But NAFTA was not altogether good. And its effects along the border can be easily intuited. First, there was very little in the NAFTA negotiations that dealt with the possibility that in some sectors in Mexico, the gap between the haves and the have-nots would actually grow, compelling many of them to leave their home in search of a better life in the United States. The development gap between Mexico and the United States has widened and the United States never made provisions for the possibility of increased migration. The number of undocumented workers after NAFTA entered into effect grew from 3 to 12 million in the United States. Curiously enough, NAFTA did not plan either for the increase in traffic between Mexico and the United States. Trade tripled and the infrastructure for receiving and inspecting the increased trade along the border lagged. The inability to inspect every truck, for example, did mean that they would eventually serve as a conveyor belt for illegal drugs, as we explored in Chapter 3.

There is a theory known as functionalism. It is a favorite of those who study the European Union. They claim that if two distrusting partners begin cooperating on a small issue, they might just build the trust to cooperate on a slightly more important issue, and so forth. By the time they realize it, they have built lots of trust and solid mechanisms of cooperation. If these mechanisms are then institutionalized, soon they will have strong links with each other and their partnership will not easily be destroyed. The favorite example of functionalists is Germany and France, which, after warring each other unceasingly, managed to serve as the two engines of the European Union by moving from a single issue (coal and steel) to forming a solid confederation today. In North America, NAFTA, as broad as it is, had not produced any new mechanisms for cooperation on other issues, and certainly none for cooperation on the problems that plague the U.S.-Mexico border. NAFTA in effect did not address the creation of credible institutions to coordinate border policy. And it certainly never addressed the issue of security. Even if it was not meant to do so, it has now spilt over into any other areas than trade and investment flows. September 11 only drove a deeper wedge between Mexico and the United States. Hardly anyone stopped to consider that the border is where NAFTA would have some of its most negative effects: an overburdened infrastructure; the more efficient flow of drugs; the congregation of undocumented migrants pushed by the development gap between the two countries and pulled by the opportunities for employment in the United States. NAFTA would address none of these "security" problems.

In other words, NAFTA has been a blessing for the economies of the two countries, but it has been a curse to the border. The social and economic dislocations in Mexico have turned to security problems on the border for the United States. There was an evident lack of foresight among the drafters of NAFTA.

THE NORTH AMERICAN SOLUTION

On March 23, 2005, President George W. Bush, President Vicente Fox, and Prime Minister Paul Martin met. The background was West Texas. In that meeting, they announced the "Security and Prosperity Partnership of North America." This document was based on the idea that security and economic integration go hand in hand. The reality before and after, however, has been that no progress has been made in setting up any kind of bilateral or trilateral institutional mechanisms to deal with security for North America, much less with border security.

President George W. Bush's concept of security, a unilateral definition with a unilateral solution largely based on force, has been laid waste in Iraq. The concept of border security that he outlined on November 29, 2005, in Tucson and El Paso is no different. It means more of the same. Thus, the responsibility of both politicians and policy makers is to begin to look to the post-Bush era and create a new approach to the border. I want to suggest that this approach must be a North American approach. In addressing immigration, it is probably convenient to address the development gap between Mexico and the United States. In addressing drug trafficking, it is probably important to find ways to build reliable cross-border mechanisms of cooperation to disintegrate the powerful drug cartels that operate in the vacuum of inter-governmental cooperation between the two countries. In addressing the potential of terrorists infiltrating the border, it is probably important to address an integrated travel system in the whole of North America where clearance checks are coordinated and standardized among all three. Doing so would take enormous pressure off the border law enforcement community and, above all, the burden of suspicion that all border residents must live with day to day. The problems of the border are more a symptom of larger forces than a cause of those problems. They must be looked at as such.

Even important initiatives like the "smart border" approach, essentially more technology underlain by strong networks of prechecks and preclearances, are not enough. The problems of North America must be addressed together, just as the problems of the border must be addressed comprehensively. Forty years of a single-track solution on the border have only made the border worse, cost hundreds of billions of dollars and now thousands of lives. Ignoring the forces of globalization in North America has been costly and deadly. And it is clear that the border is not more secure now than before. As Chapters 2, 3, and 4, have shown, the drug trade continues to flourish with organizations better equipped to handle new law enforcement efforts; undocumented workers continue to flow just as much as before; and the possibility of a terrorist coming through the border was low in the first place but may still happen, reason enough to cooperate across North America.

Everything points to a North America solution. But there are two elements lacking in the American leadership: political vision and political will. That vision was actually beginning to flicker early in the Bush and Fox administrations. In Guanajuato, Mexico, both presidents endorsed a North American vision in February 2001. However, September 11, like a flash of light on an open pupil, shut all possibility of a broader vision. President Bush's reaction was first to retreat the concept of North America back to within the borders of the United States and then to fall into the unilateral temptation of finding a U.S.-based solution to national security threats. Iraq only retrenched this approach.

The North American solution calls for a Council or a Commission similar to the European Commission to begin to identify and define common North American problems. This Commission should be trilateral and should both prepare the common agenda for executives and legislative bodies and give these issues continuity after the persons occupying those posts are long gone. Their studies, conclusions, and recommendations should facilitate further integration and cross-border cooperation on economic, social, diplomatic, and law enforcement efforts. They should also seek to standardize policy across North America—in the longer term, that is. Such commission would embody a forward-looking approach to border problems. This is quite a different approach than being stuck in the same reactive approach, always lagging behind the problems of the border.

The biannual meetings of Cabinet Members that took place under the Clinton Administration should be restored. Top-level officials should convey to their underlings the importance of dealing with the issues from top to bottom, in a comprehensive way. Congress members should probably institute an inter-legislative group, with permanent membership. The purpose of this group should be to gather the feedback from the Commission and introduce it in the legislative agenda of each country. The most painful change will have to occur in the United States, which is largely used to wielding power that enables it to act unilaterally or multilaterally. Canada and Mexico are already quite conscious of the importance of their relationship with the United States and may be better prepared psychologically to make the leap into a trilateral framework than is the United States. It is also very likely that Canada and the United States will have to take some responsibility for closing the development gap between them and Mexico. People from Mexico cross the border because they are aware of the wage levels that can be had in the United States and because of what that money represents to their families back home. At the bottom, it is that simple. A slate of policies and sufficient aid designed to close that gap should do the job. Europe demonstrated that with Spain, Portugal, and Greece and is still doing so with other newly integrated nations.

DEFINING A NORTH AMERICAN COMMUNITY

The vision of a North American community can come from the top to the bottom or from the bottom to the top. It is not likely after September 11 that the creation of a North American community will come from the bottom, even though it is at the grassroots, particularly along the border that most interaction occurs and where integration is most visible. It is also at the grassroots level, though, that several loud groups are organizing and lobbying the media, the public, and the politicians to "close the border." The most prominent group is, of course, the Minutemen, that occasionally patrols along the border.

Instead, the initiative to create a North American community that might take some of the pressure off the border will have to be based on political leadership. Astute political leadership might be able to accomplish it given that over the past 20 years there has been a convergence of values in North America. Although some argue that the values of Latin Americans are fundamentally different than the values of Anglo-America, more and more Mexicans hold the same values for personal freedom and democracy that Americans do. There is also a convergence on public policy, particularly with Mexico's turn to the right by opening its economy to market forces and inserting it in the process of globalization. Political leadership can shift the discourse on the border to the need for creating a larger trilateral community to propel an integrated economy to eliminate border problems. A guest worker program would probably go a long way toward that. Creating a common database to detect suspects in all three countries is another step. Issuing Mexicans and Canadians a universal ID card to travel to the United States on a preclearance basis, such as the SENTRI card that already exists for commuters along the U.S.-Mexico border would also help. Legitimate travelers, workers, students, etc., could be more easily tracked and encourage trust-building as well we further integration.

THE NORTH AMERICAN SECURITY BUBBLE

For a long time, Canada and the United States have defined a continental perimeter for the purposes of defense that ended at the U.S.-Mexico border. NORAD is largely in charge of this continental defense within that perimeter. During the attacks of September 11, it was a Canadian in Cheyenne Mountain who was in charge at the moment of the attack. The Department of Defense did not replace him. They trusted a Canadian to be able to respond appropriately in defense of North America in case of an attack. This trust was built over time between the two countries, but also out of the determination that there was a North American perimeter that could be capsuled and defended as a unit.

No such conception links Mexico and the United States, in spite of the increasing economic integration and cultural convergence, particularly in the Southwest. Law enforcement and military coordination could help both countries go a long way in building that trust required for the solution of common problems. All three countries must redefine their security perimeter as a North American, three-country perimeter. Immigration and Customs in all three countries must work together to stave off terrorist threats and to ensure that cross-border interaction among all three is safe. But Mexico must be carefully dealt with, given that it is still dealing with the historical scars of American nineteenth-century expansionism.

BUREAUCRATIC POLITICS AND THE BORDER

In the early 1970s, Graham T. Allison published his book *Essence of Decision: The Cuban Missile Crisis*. In that book, Allison argued that bureaucracies build stakes in what they do. Various studies after that have tested his theory and concluded that there is a lot of powerful evidence to show that bureaucrats tend to build stakes around what they do because enhancing the budgets and the prestige of what they do redounds in various perquisites and privileges for themselves. In other words, bureaucrats have a stake in preserving and enhancing the organizations they work for and portraying their mission as indispensable. Consequently, they develop a stake in exaggerating the threat they face because they can make the argument that their organization needs even more moral and financial support. Now, put together Allison's theory of bureaucratic politics with the idea that institutions are harder to dismantle or destroy than they are to create, and it becomes clear that creating enormous law enforcement bureaucracies to "secure" the border is equivalent to generating a momentum around the law enforcement approach to the border. Undoing this approach, given that most of the investment in gaining control of the border is going to law enforcement, will be even harder in the future. The momentum of thousands of bureaucrats conceiving their mission as shutting the border and receiving nearly $7 billion for it will be very hard to undo. This is important to point out because it may in the future preclude the possibility of reversing that trend toward a North American solution to the U.S.-Mexico border problems.

THE BORDER REINSTATED

The U.S.-Mexico border is a region in constant transition. It has had periods of stability, but the historical trend has been toward closing it. The twentieth century saw a dramatic escalation of law enforcement efforts and, in the 1980s and 1990s, an appeal to the military to "defend the border." Border policy in the United States has been quite linear: increased efforts to seal the border, but very little thought to the unintended consequences. NAFTA has created a new conveyor belt for drugs; sealing urban center to undocumented migration has increased the number of deaths in Arizona; the use of better technology to detect drugs has given the large cartels a comparative advantage; and so on. U.S. policy on the border has a lot of symbolic content useful to politicians and bureaucrats who want to portray an image of control. Yet, the border has never been under control. In fact, the law enforcement escalation has coincided with a rise of both powerful drug cartels and now powerful smuggling organizations. Yet, the persistent failures of the U.S. government's border policies do not seem to face anyone in Washington, DC. Underlying this, there is a denial that the United States and Mexico's economies are increasingly interdependent and are likely to become even more so in the future. Mexico and Canada are the two natural economic partners of America, given their proximity and the comparative advantages that they hold vis-à-vis the United States.

This observation points to a paradox. The fortification of the U.S.-Mexico border has come on the heels of an unprecedented economic, cultural, and political convergence. As Mexico has embraced the liberalization paradigm promoted aggressively by the United States, North America is practically a border-free economy, except for certain sectors such as the energy sector in Mexico, which remains largely closed. And of course, except for labor, a main reason for the immigration disaster on the border. Sooner or later, NAFTA will have to be renegotiated in order to further integrate the North American economies, simply because it pays off. Labor will have to be part of that agreement, if there is to be a solution to the undocumented immigration issue.

North America is also increasingly alike in its values. The growth of Hispanics in the United States has also spurred a surge in the cultural influences that Mexico exerts in the American society. The Hispanic media, for example, is today the fastest growing media sector in the United States. According to a Pew Hispanic Center report, half of the Hispanic population prefers to speak Spanish and 28 percent are bilingual.[25] Other forms of cultural convergence are very obvious throughout the southwest and increasingly beyond.

There is also an increased political convergence in North America. Although Canada and the United States have shared their democratic values for a long time, Mexico is fast moving in their direction. Under the Vicente Fox administration in Mexico, the country has become more democratic and it is presently going through the pains of creating institutions with true checks and balances to complement its already largely free and fair elections. Mexicans enjoy today unprecedented levels of freedom, even if public security remains a very serious concern. The media is freer than ever, though problems remain given killings of some journalists. But more and more Mexicans, 59 percent, say today that a democratic government is better than any other form of government. Only 13 percent would trade democracy for a prosperous economy.[26]

It is interesting then that as borders are lowered by these globalizing trends, while politicians and bureaucrats roll in the U.S. police apparatus along the U.S.-Mexico borderlands. Hence the paradox, the economic, cultural, and political convergence of North America is denied in U.S. policy by an unprecedented effort to police the border. There is little understanding of how these two great waves clash against each other on the borderlands producing the kinds of undesirable border trends that are so widely talked about. It is at this juncture that the state should not retreat from tackling the larger problems of North American integration, because they hold the key to the great pressures of the border, much as they do in Ceuta and Melilla between Africa and Spain or between Poland the far eastern Europe.

And there is something even more ominous about the cultural convergence along the U.S.-Mexico borderlands. As the face of America changes, its future can be seen emerging right along the southwest.

THE BORDER IS THE FUTURE OF AMERICA

There is a vital reason why the border requires a new look, and it has to do with the future of America. For the observant eye, driving down the Texas border counties, this becomes all too obvious. Any visitor to West Texas and South Texas Rio Grande Valley should be struck by the nearly solid nature of their Hispanic population in those counties. In effect, cities like Brownsville, Laredo, Eagle Pass, Del Rio, and El Paso are now anywhere between 80 and 95 percent Mexican-American and Mexican. The same trends hold state by state. Texas is now 38 percent Hispanic; New Mexico is 43 percent Hispanic; Arizona is 30 percent Hispanic; and California is 35 percent Hispanic. Nevada and Colorado now have large Hispanic populations as well.[27] Hispanics are projected to total about 103 million Americans in the year 2050, or roughly 25 percent of the population of the country.

Yet, Hispanics tend to have some of the lowest socioeconomic indicators in the country. As the country becomes more Hispanic, this does not bode well for the border states—or for the nation as a whole. Hispanic median income is well below the rest of the nation, at $32,997. The poverty rate among Hispanics is 22 percent, compared to 12 percent for the nation as a whole. Only 52 percent of Hispanics have a high school education, revealing that a high percentage do not reach that education level. Only 11 percent of Hispanics aged twenty-five and over have college degrees. The border already sees many of these symptoms, particularly in the

Texas borderlands. If the forty-three counties of Texas that constitute the borderlands were a separate state, they would rank first on poverty rates (23 percent); first on school children in poverty (38 percent); first in unemployment rate (8 percent); first in the percentage of adult population without a high school diploma; first in birth rate; third in death rate for diabetes; fifty-first in per capita income; forty-ninth in households with telephones; fifty-first in annual average wage in construction.[28] In all, these statistics show that the border is a largely impoverished area, with many infrastructure and socio-economic deficiencies and an enormous income inequality. It resembles Mexico much more than it resembles the United States.

These trends are detrimental to the country as a whole because Hispanics are likely to constitute the most important minority in the nation today and may be a quarter of the population in the next decades. Their low averages will certainly drag all national averages down if they do not catch up with the population as a whole. This will place the United States in a comparative disadvantage vis-à-vis other countries. If the border can serve as a crystal ball to the future of the country, the numbers do not bode well for anyone. Only a well devised, binational plan to tackle the issues of the border can help both sides catch up much faster to the rest of the United States, a fact that in and of itself would ease a lot of the pressures that collide on it and make the border look like a third world nation, rather than the thriving area that it is caught between the lack of political will and the dearth of political vision of the leaders of both countries.

The border is nevertheless young. And it should resent the old established centers of power in Washington, DC, and Mexico City in any event. Both areas are largely centers of neglect. Border residents have felt the neglect from Washington. They also feel a common bond with Mexico in their history and their geography. There is also an acknowledgement that there is a high degree of economic interdependence. Multiple studies by the Federal Reserve Bank, El Paso Branch, show time and again that there is already a high degree of economic interdependence between border cities. The Mexican maquiladora industry has spurred a good deal of economic growth in U.S. border counties.

NO END IN SIGHT

Unfortunately, as the three border wars grind on, on a quasi-mechanical, monotonous and dehumanizing routine, there is little hope that the United States government, its growing border bureaucracy or the American public will come to a permanent, long-term solution to these border wars. If anything, the idea of sealing the border enjoys enormous support, inspite of the fact that occasionally someone may acknowledge that thus far the same approach has not worked at all. But the country has gone conservative. Everyone is ready to be "tough on crime," a stand that translates into unwavering support for current U.S. policies of escalation in policing the border. Few would even speak of a longer term solution to border issues, much less of a North American solution. The political cost of this kind of rhetoric could be too high.

Similarly, agencies working on the border have developed their own interests in maintaining current policy. If a whole new approach to the border were adopted, they would be out of a job. Bureaucracies become addicted to the dollars, the jobs and the careers that are made in these border wars. More technology, more buildings, more equipment, and larger budgets mean greater prestige and lifelong careers for many agents on the border. That is how they make their living. Why would they advocate a different approach? In fact, nearly every bureaucrat, appointed or civil service, who testifies in Congress argues for more resources. And everyone is unwilling to publicly acknowledge the futility of his battles.

Most Americans are oblivious to the costs of these border wars. Most Americans do not live on the border. But millions of them benefit from the undocumented labor they hire to trim their lawns, clip their bushes, clean their houses, prepare their meals, and raise their children. Americans are addicted to the availability of cheap labor and cheap goods and services, the prices of which are kept low in many places by the labor of those who live in the shadows, always afraid of being caught, deported, and separated from their families. Moreover, millions of Americans are addicted to illegal drugs, drawing many to the business of drugs with deadly consequences for many, not just along the border. Cocaine, heroin, marijuana, and methamphetamine addicts represent a huge market whose horrifying effects are lived day to day at the border, though most consumers live away from the border. They have no incentive to reach into their consciences and consider the motivations of the drug lords and dealers or the cost of the drug war on the American taxpayer. They are not in the trenches of the border; they cannot see; they cannot care.

There is therefore a huge coalition of politicians, bureaucrats, and the American public that have a stake in keeping the borders open, even if the rhetoric is fiery when it comes to the "insecurity" of the border. Nevertheless, there is some hope that the U.S. Congress will address the issue in 2006, but perhaps not before the Congressional elections of November 2006. The Democrats are largely unable to bring about their preferences in Congress, so it will all depend on what the Republicans want to do. And the Republicans are divided. The coalition that supports President Bush, on one hand and Christian conservatives and the business interests of America on the other, are on opposite sides of the spectrum. President Bush will need to be a magician to find a solution that is acceptable to both of these groups. If he cannot find the right proposal, his coalition may come undone and his ability to be more than a lame duck president will be crippled. He will then sit at the Oval for the remainder of his term, watching the border burn.

CONCLUSION

Winston Churchill said that Americans could always be trusted to do the right thing, after they have tried everything else. There is no doubt that the American public is, at heart, a generous public. There is little doubt that most Americans are by and large good people. But when it comes to the border, almost all reason is lost. September 11 spurred just such loss of reasonableness by Congress, politicians, and a large segment of the general public. The border is viewed as a chaotic, violent, and lawless land, whereas it actually is a place of great human struggles and epic lives. Although there is crime, violence, drug trafficking, human tragedy, and dire poverty along the border, the borderlands are also a place of wealth production, rich family interactions, and daily interaction among people from both Mexico and the United States.

Not to acknowledge that the destinies of the two nations are tied is to be nearly blind. Not to understand that the prosperity of both countries is increasingly dependent on one another is absurd. Not to recognize that the security of the United States depends on the actions and the needs and the future of its neighbors is incongruous with current trends. Nowhere is this more clearly outlined than on the border counties of the United States and the border municipalities of Mexico. Drugs flow north; human smugglers carry people north; and undocumented workers flow north. Guns flow south; financial capital and direct investments flow south; but, goods and services flow both ways. Millions of Mexican citizens live in the United States. Well over 1 million Americans live in Mexico. Over $1 trillion in goods and services are exchanged every four years in binational trade between Mexico and the United States. If all these figures do not imply the necessity of a North American security regime where everyone participates in building a safer North America (including Canada, of course), then there is no argument to be made but one for isolation and crude nationalism.

The mutual interdependence of the two countries dictates a new vision of security. It also exposes the weaknesses of the current security regime: unilateral, enforcement-based, with a logic of escalation, and ultimately unsuccessful. It is clear that the problem of security at the border needs to be grown to be a much larger problem so that solutions may also be larger and the North American security regime be stronger. Canada and Mexico are indispensable partners in this security perimeter. And the United States already trusts Canada with its own security, given the close cooperation that exists between these two countries. It is time now to bring Mexico into that circle of trust, perhaps with a plan that will slowly integrate Mexico further into North America, as Mexico fights corruption and becomes a reliable democracy and economy. A safer, stronger, and democratic Mexico is good for the United States and is good for American security. Mexico is about at the same place where Spain was in 1975. Perhaps in 30 years, the United States can bring Mexico up to par and create, finally, a prosperous continent around it, one with stability and security for all. To postpone this is simply to postpone the inevitable and to make it even more painful to have to acknowledge this mutual interdependence in the future.

NOTES

CHAPTER 1

1. Danna Harman, "Mexican Drug Cartels' Wars Move Closer to the U.S. Border," *USA Today*. Note found at http://www.usatoday.com/news/world/2005-08-17-mexican-cartels_x.htm (Accessed on October 30, 2005).

2. Paul Strand, "Border Invasion: Stemming the Illegal Flood," in *CBN News*. News note found at http://www.cbn.com/cbnnews/news/050414a.asp (Accessed on November 23, 2005).

3. Jon E. Dougherty, "Lawmaker: Terror War Spilling Across Border: Concern Rising Following Arrest of al-Qaeda Suspect in Mexico," *WorldNetDaily* http://www.wnd.com/news/article.asp?ARTICLE_ID=47401 (Accessed on November 27, 2005).

4. See Hobbes "The Leviathan" at http://oregonstate.edu/instruct/phl302/texts/hobbes/leviathan-c.html (Accessed on November 25, 2005).

5. See Census Data at http://www.census.gov/ (Accessed on November 26, 2005).

6. Border line data at http://us-mex.irc-online.org/borderlines/PDFs/bl79.pdf (Accessed on November 26, 2005).

7. At http://www.scerp.org/population.htm (Accessed on January 27, 2005).

8. The 1853 Gadsden Purchase Treaty at http://www.yale.edu/lawweb/avalon/diplomacy/mexico/mx1853.htm (Accessed on December 10, 2005).

9. Juan Mora-Torres, *The Making of the Mexican Border* (Austin, TX: University of Texas Press, 2000) 6.

10. The Act of February 26, 1885; the Act of February 23, 1887; the Act of March 3, 1887; and the Act of March 19, 1888.

11. At http://uscis.gov/graphics/shared/aboutus/statistics/legishist/456.htm (Accessed on January 27, 2005).

12. George T. Kurian, ed., *A Historical Guide to the U.S. Government* (New York: Oxford University Press, 1998).

13. At http://www.archives.gov/research_room/genealogy/immigrant_arrivals/mexican_border_crossings.html#special (Accessed on February 1, 2005).

14. Américo Paredes, *A Texas-Mexican Cancionero: Folksongs of the Lower Border* (Urbana, IL: University of Illinois Press, 1976) 1.

15. "US Border a 'Safety Valve' for Latin Poor." *Providence Journal* (Rhode Island), May 11, 2005, at http://www.commondreams.org/views05/0511-26.htm (Accessed on November 27, 2005).

16. President Discusses Border Security and Immigration Reform in Arizona. Available at http://www.whitehouse.gov/news/releases/2005/11/20051128-7.html (Accessed on November 29, 2005).

17. "Bush Vows to Harden Border Policy." In his speech, he focuses on crime, danger, and high costs linked with illegal crossings. Available at http://www.chron.com/disp/story.mpl/metropolitan/3489624.html.

18. "Governor Schwarzenegger Delivers a Speech on Closing Borders." Available at http://www.foxnews.com/story/0,2933,153988,00.html (Accessed on November 28, 2005).

19. Jurisdiction Boundary Marking Act. Available at http://www.constitution.org/pol/us/jbma.htm (Accessed on November 29, 2005).

20. President Discusses War on Terror at National Endowment for Democracy. Available at http://www.whitehouse.gov/news/releases/2005/10/20051006-3.html (Accessed on November 29, 2005).

21. Michael Hedges, "Bush Budget Scraps 9, 790 Border Patrol Agents: President Uses Law's Escape Clause to Drop Funding for New Homeland Security Force," *The San Francisco Chronicle*, February 9, 2005, 8-A.

22. President Bush Signs Homeland Security Act. Available at http://www.whitehouse.gov/news/releases/2002/11/20021125-6.html (Accessed on November 29, 2005).

23. Timothy J. Dunn, *The Militarization of the U.S.-Mexico Border 1978–1992: Low-Intensity Conflict Comes Home* (Austin, TX: The University of Texas at Austin Press, 1996).

24. Secure Border Initiative, Customs and Border Protection. Full document found in CBP's Web page http://www.cbp.gov/xp/cgov/newsroom/fact_sheets/secure_border_initiative/secure_ border.xml (Accessed on December 5, 2005).

25. Peter Andreas, *Border Games: Policing the U.S.-Mexico Divide* (Ithaca, NY: Cornell University Press, 2000).

26. Scott Rogerson, *Weekly Alibi*, Albuquerque, NM.

27. "Rethinking the Role of the U.S. Mexican Border in the Post-9/11 World." Available at http://www.cfr.org/publication/6906/rethinking_the_role_of_the_us_mexican_border_ in_the_post911_world.html (Accessed on December 3, 2005).

28. A Secure Europe in a Better World. "Europe Deals with Its Borders," at http://ue.eu.int/uedocs/cmsUpload/78367.pdf (Accessed on December 5, 2005).

29. "Department of Homeland Security," Office of Management and Budget at http://www.whitehouse.gov/omb/budget/fy2006/dhs.html (Accessed on December 8, 2005).

30. "Militarizing the Border," at http://mediafilter.org/CAQ/CAQ56border.html (Accessed on December 10, 2005).

31. "The War on Drugs," at http://www.pbs.org/wgbh/pages/frontline/shows/drugs/cron/ (Accessed on December 9, 2005).

32. "Illegal Immigration & Enforcement Along the U.S.-Mexico Border: An Overview," at http://www.dallasfed.org/research/efr/2001/efr0101a.pdf (Accessed on December 9, 2005).

CHAPTER 2

1. See "Pot-Laden Truck Creates Armed Standoff," *El Paso Times*, November 19, 2005.

2. See "Former EP Border Agent Sentenced for Letting Drug Couriers Pass," *El Paso Times*, September 23, 2005.

3. See Michael Marizco, "Smugglers Getting Sneakier," in *Arizona Daily Star*, December 26, 2004.

4. See "Portrait of a Mexican Drug Lord," in CBS News, Mexico City, October 24, 2003. Note found at http://www.cbsnews.com/stories/2003/10/24/world/main579960.shtml (Accessed on October 10, 2005).

5. "Survey: Illegal Drugs: Stumbling in the Dark," *The Economist*, July 28, 2001.

6. See http://laborsta.ilo.org/cgi-bin/brokerv8.exe#261 (Accessed on June 20, 2005).

7. David J. Pyle analyzed various theories examining the economics of crime and establishing a strong, but not absolute relationship between crime and unemployment and low incomes. See David J. Pyle, *The Economics of Crime and Law Enforcement* (New York, NY: St. Martin's Press, 1983).

8. U.S. Department of Labor, Bureau of Transportation Statistics. See http://www.bts.gov/programs/international/border_crossing_entry_data/us_mexico/pdf/entire.pdf. (Accessed on June 21, 2005).

9. See Peter Braunstein and Michael William Doyle, *Imagine Nation: The American Counterculture of the 1960s and '70s* (New York, NY: Routledge, 2002). See also *Pulse Check: Drug Markets and Chronic Users in 25 of America's Largest Cities* (Washington, DC: Executive Office of the President, Office of National Drug Control Policy, January 2004). The current issue of the publication and previous *Pulse Check* issues can be found at http://www.whitehousedrugpolicy.gov/drugfact/pulsecheck.html (Accessed on September 28, 2005).

10. Several books that analyze the relationship between an illegal product and the consumer market for it—essentially black market economics—are: Lawrence J. Kaplan and Dennis Kessler, eds., *An Economic Analysis of Crime* (Chicago, IL: Charles C. Thomas Publisher, 1976); Annelise Graebner Anderson, *The Business of Organized Crime: A Cosa Nostra Family* (Stanford, CA: Hoover Institution Press, 1979); David J. Pyle, *The Economics of Crime and Law Enforcement* (New York, NY: St. Martin's Press, 1983); André Bossard, *Transnational Crime and Criminal Law* (Chicago, IL: The University of Illinois at Chicago, 1990); Susan Pozo, ed., *Exploring the Underground Economy* (Kalamazoo, MI: W. E. Upjohn Institute for Employment Research, 1996); and R. T. Naylor, *Wages of Crime: Black Markets, Illegal Finance, and the Underworld Economy* (Ithaca, NY: Cornell University Press, 2002).

11. For a recounting of these efforts in the Caribbean, see Charles M. Fuss, *Sea of Grass: The Maritime Drug War, 1970–1990* (Annapolis, MD: Naval Institute Press, 1996).

12. See various chapters in Bruce M. Bagley and William O. Walker III, eds., *Drug Trafficking in the Americas* (Miami, FL: University of Miami North-South Center, 1994).

13. See some of these accounts in Elaine Shannon, *Desperados: Latin Drug Lords, U.S.A. Lawmen and the War America Can't Win* (New York, NY: Viking Press, 1988).

14. This story is told at length and quite eloquently by one of the greatest chroniclers of the Mexican illegal drug business: Jesús Blancornelas in his book *El Cártel: Los Arellano Félix: La Mafia Más Poderosa en la Historia de América Latina* (México: Plaza Janés, 2002) 46–52.

15. This game of escalation and the logic behind it is explained in Peter Andreas' *Border Games: Policing the U.S.-Mexico Divide* (Ithaca, NY: Cornell University Press, 2000) 3–14.

16. *Illegal Drug Price and Purity Report* (Washington, DC: Drug Enforcement Administration, April 2003). Publication found at http://www.usdoj.gov/dea/pubs/intel/02058/02058.html#2 (Accessed on September 28, 2005).

17. Witness, for example, how quickly the warring factions of the Sinaloa and the Gulf Cartels responded to the new Chief of Police of Nuevo Laredo, Alejandro Domínguez and his strong language against the drug cartels. Within eight hours of his swearing in, on June 8, 2005, they gunned him down summarily to avoid further complications in the ongoing drug war in Nuevo Laredo.

18. Interview with a former member of the Juárez Cartel, who wished to remain anonymous. Interview conducted in Ciudad Juárez, Chihuahua, on August 3, 2005.

19. Hear the story of drug smuggling through the Tohona O'odham Reservation on National Public Radio's Web site http://www.npr.org/templates/story/story.php?storyId=1125387 (Accessed on November 20, 2005).

20. Interview with a federal court employee in El Paso, Texas, who wished to remain anonymous. Interview conducted on August 18, 2005.

21. John Burnett, "Corruption at the Gates: Series Explores Lure of Money, Prestige Among U.S. Border Agents," *National Public Radio*, September 12–13, 2002. Entire report found at the Web page of NPR: http://www.npr.org/programs/atc/features/2002/sept/border_corruption/ (Accessed on October 2, 2005).

22. Bureau of Justice Statistics, *National Transportation Statistics 2005* (Washington, DC: Department of Transportation, 2005). Tables at http://www.bts.gov/publications/national_transportation_statistics/2005 (Accessed on October 5, 2005).

23. "Securing the Global Supply Chain" (Washington, DC: U.S. Customs and Border Protection, November 2004).

24. Interview in San Antonio, Texas, with "James," a trucking company operator who asked to remain anonymous. Interview conducted on August 5, 2005.

25. Interview with "James" in San Antonio, Texas, August 5, 2005.

26. Pablo Bachelet, "Tucson a Hub for Mexicans' Drug Trade," *The Arizona Daily Star*, August 1, 2005.

27. At http://www.cbp.gov/linkhandler/cgov/careers/customs_careers/border_careers/border_patrol_factsheet.ctt/careers_bpa_fact.doc (Accessed on September 7, 2005).

28. Interview with a member of the Juárez Cartel in Ciudad Juárez, Chihuahua. Interview conducted on August 4, 2005.

29. Rubén Ruiz, "Ejecutan a Tres Ex Policías," *El Imparcial*, June 7, 2005.

30. Interview with a member of the Juárez Cartel in Ciudad Juárez, Chihuahua, August 4, 2005.

31. See Ambassador Antonio O. Garza's Press Release at the U.S. Embassy on Mexico City's Web site http://mexico.usembassy.gov/mexico/ep050610violence. html (Accessed on October 30, 2005).

32. L. D. Johnston, P. M. O'Malley, J. G. Bachman, & J. E. Schulenberg, *Monitoring the Future National Survey Results on Drug Use, 1975–2004, Vol. I: Secondary School Students* (NIH Publication No. 05-5727) (Bethesda, MD: National Institute on Drug Abuse, 2005) and L. D. Johnston, P. M. O'Malley, J. G. Bachman, & J. E. Schulenberg, *Monitoring the Future National Survey Results on Drug Use, 1975–2003, Vol. II: College Students and Adults Ages 19–45* (NIH Publication No. 04-5508) (Bethesda, MD: National Institute on Drug Abuse, 2004).

33. Interview with a federal court employee in El Paso, Texas, who wished to remain anonymous. Interview conducted on August 18, 2005.

CHAPTER 3

1. *El Paso Herald Post*, April 28, 1956.

2. At http://www.fas.org/sgp/crs/homesec/RL32562.pdf (Accessed on September 7, 2005).

3. *The New York Times*, November 29, 2004.

4. See "American Immigration: An Overview," by the U.S. English Foundation. Document found at http://www.us-english.org/foundation/research/amimmigr/Chapter3.PDF (Accessed on November 20, 2005).

5. At http://www.customs.gov/linkhandler/cgov/border_security/border_patrol/national_bp_strategy.ctt/national_bp_strategy.pdf (Accessed on September 7, 2005).

6. *The Washington Post*, March 7, 2005.

7. Ted Robbins, "Illegal Immigrant Deaths Burden Border Towns," on *National Public Radio*, October 6, 2005. Story found at http://www.npr.org/templates/story/story.php?storyId=4948382 (Accessed on November 19, 2005).

8. At http://www.scerp.org/population.htm (Accessed on September 7, 2005).

9. "Americans for Immigration Control and Zogby Poll" (Released on June 11, 2002). The article on the results of this poll can be found at http://www.immigrationcontrol.com/AIC_Zogby_Mexican_Poll.htm (Accessed on September 10, 2005).

10. The Prew Hispanic Center, Roberto Ruso, Director, "Attitudes Toward Immigrants and Immigration Policy: Surveys among Latinos in the U.S. and Mexico," August 16, 2005. See entire report at http://pewhispanic.org/files/reports/52.pdf (Accessed on November 15, 2005).

11. An excellent collection of essays that explores this push force is *Border Crossings: Mexican and Mexican American Workers*, Jason Mason Hart, editor (Wilmington, DE: SR Books, 1998).

12. This is a perennial argument in regard to U.S. documented and undocumented immigration. For interesting arguments on this, see John McAuley, "Immigrants Keep U.S. Economy Supple," *Minnesota Star Tribune*, September 4, 2002.

13. "Survey of Recent Immigrants at the U.S. Consulate in Ciudad Juárez," conducted by Brenda Thomas and Tony Payan, 2003–2004.

14. *The New York Times*, March 13, 2005.

15. Rebecca L. Clark and Scott A. Anderson, "Illegal Aliens in Federal, State, and Local Criminal Justice Systems," *The Urban Institute*, June 30, 2000. Entire text found at the Web page of The Urban Institute http://www.urban.org/url.cfm?ID= 410366 (Accessed on October 15, 2005).

16. "Illegal Immigration," in *Migration News*. Full text found at http://migration. ucdavis.edu/mn (Accessed on November 24, 2005).

17. Even the most modest numbers can be staggering. If 300,000 migrants make it to the United States every year and each pays $2,500, the total amounts to $750,000,000. This is not counting those that do not make it but pay anyway or those that pay more than once or those that pay more.

18. Pia M. Orrenius, "Illegal Immigration and Enforcement along the Southwest Border," Federal Reserve Bank of Dallas (June 2001) *The New York Times*, March 13, 2005. At http://www.dallasfed.org/research/border/tbe_orrenius.html (Accessed on September 15, 2005).

19. Robert Lee Maril, *Patrolling Chaos: The U.S. Border Patrol in Deep South Texas* (Lubbock, TX: Texas Tech University, 2004).

20. For one such example, see Susan Strange and Claire Sterling, *Crime Without Frontiers* (London: Warner, 1995).

21. At http://www.fairus.org/site/PageServer.

22. The advocates of such an increase ignore the considerable problems in finding and recruiting qualified people and then hiring and training these potential new hires. See General Accounting Office, *Border Patrol Hiring: Despite Recent Initiatives, Fiscal Year 1999 Hiring Goal Was Not Met* (Washington, DC: GAO, December 1999).

23. "Illegal Immigrants are Bolstering Social Security with Billions," *The New York Times*, April 5, 2005.

24. "Tax Administration: IRS Needs to Consider Options for Revising Regulations to Increase the Accuracy of Social Security Numbers on Wage Statements," *General Accounting Office*, GAO-04-712, August 2004. See also "Social Security: Better Coordination Among Federal Agencies Could Reduce Unidentified Earnings Reports," *General Accounting Office*, GAO-05-154, February 2005.

25. "Stryker Training," *The Monitor*, March 3, 2005, 30–31.

26. Cynthia Green, "Federal Grand Jury Investigating Wal-Mart's Use of Undocumented Migrants." Story found at http://www.laborresearch.org/story.php?id=332 (Accessed on September 18, 2005).

27. Text of the lawsuit found at http://www.vdare.com/misc/tyson_complaint.htm (Accessed on September 18, 2005).

CHAPTER 4

1. See http://www.vdare.com/francis/open_borders.htm (Accessed on November 1, 2005).

2. See Government Accountability Office Report, "Immigration Enforcement: DHS has Incorporated Immigration Enforcement Objectives and is Addressing Future Planning Requirements," GAO-05-66, October 2004.

3. Margaret D. Stock and Benjamin Johnson, "The Lessons of 9/11: A Failure of Intelligence, Not Immigration Law," *Immigration Policy Focus*, 2 (3), December 2003.

4. See Press Release of the Department of Justice, "Department of Justice Announces INS Restructuring Plan Splitting Service and Enforcement Functions," November 14, 2004. At www.usdoj.gov. See also Doris Meissner, "Two Jobs for One INS," *The Washington Post* (March 18, 2002), A29; Cheryl Thompson, "INS Tightens Rules for Visitors," *The Washington Post* (April 9, 2002), A01; Cheryl Thompson, "INS Role for the Police Considered," *The Washington Post* (April 4, 2002), A15; Dana Milbank, "Bush Poised to Back New Border Agency," *The Washington Post* (March 19, 2002), A01; and Dana Milbank and Cheryl Thompson, "House Panel Agrees on Plan to Split INS," *The Washington Post* (March 22, 2002), A08.

5. U.S. Census Bureau, Foreign Trade Division, Data Dissemination Branch, Washington, DC 20233, http://www.census.gov/foreign-trade/balance/c2010.html#2001 and http://www.census.gov/foreign-trade/balance/c2010.html#199 (Accessed on November 5, 2005).

6. See Bureau of Transportation Statistics at http://www.bts.gov/publications/transportation_statistics_annual_report/2001/html/chapter_07_table_01_219.html (Accessed on November 5, 2005).

7. See Construcción de una Communidad de América del Norte, by The Council on Foreign Relations at http://www.cfr.org/content/publications/attachments/NorthAmerica_TF_final_esp.pdf

8. Congressional Research Service Report, "Border Security: Inspections, Practices, Policies, Issues," May 26, 2004.

9. See U.S. Info State. United States Department of State at http://usinfo.state.gov/eap/east_asia_pacific/chinese_human_smuggling/smuggling_in_the_press/crime.html (Accessed on November 4, 2005).

10. See "A Case of Selective Enforcement," at http://www.townhall.com/opinion/columns/terencejeffrey/2003/07/02/170036.html (Accessed on November 4, 2005).

11. Ignacio Ibarra, "Border Group claims WMD Test," *Arizona Daily Star*, July 22, 2004.

12. "Testimony by Secretary Michael Chertoff Before the House Homeland Security Committee," April 13, 2005. Entire text found at http://www.dhs.gov/dhspublic/display?theme=45=4460 (Accessed on December 1, 2005).

13. Testimony of Peter Gadiel. U.S. House of Representatives. Committee on the Judiciary. Text found at the Committee on the Judiciary's Web page http://judiciary.house.gov/OversightTestimony.aspx?ID=289 (Accessed on November 5, 2005).

14. U.S. Department on Homeland Security, "Testimony by Deputy Secretary of Homeland Security Admiral James Loy Before the Senate Select Committee on Intelligence." Text found at http://www.iwar.org.uk/homesec/resources/natsec2005/loy.htm (Accessed on November 5, 2005).

15. See http://www.rasmussenreports.com/2005/Immigration% 20November% 207.htm (Accessed on November 15, 2005).

16. Patriot Act. Text found at http://www.epic.org/privacy/terrorism/hr3162.html.

17. *Homeland Security: Overview of Homeland Security Management Challenges* (Washington, DC: General Accounting Office, April 20, 2005) 2–4. See also

the Homeland Security Budget Sheet for FY 2005 at http://www.dhs.gov/ dhspublic/interapp/press_release/press_release_0541.xml (Accessed on October 19, 2005).

18. Congress Homeland Security Act Title IV. Entire Text of the Homeland Security Act found at http://www.dhs.gov/dhspublic/interweb/assetlibrary/hr_5005 _enr.pdf (Accessed on October 20, 2005).

19. See Department of Homeland Security at http://www.dhs.gov/dhspublic/ (Accessed on November 21, 2005).

20. See remarks from former Customs and Border Protection Commissioner Robert Bonner at http://permanent.access.gpo.gov/websites/www.cbp.gov/xp/cgov/ newsroom/commissioner/speeches_statements/archives/2003/sept092003_2.xml.htm (Accessed on November 30, 2005).

21. Stephen Flynn, "The Neglected Home Front," *Foreign Affairs*, 83(5), September/October 2004, 20–33.

CHAPTER 5

1. Jeremy Bentham, *Panopticon*, in Miran Bozovic, ed., *The Panopticon Writings* (London: Verso, 1995) 29–95.

2. Michel Foucault, *Discipline and Punish: The Birth of the Prison* (New York: Vintage Books, 1995).

3. "Securing Our Homeland," Department of Homeland Security, Washington, DC, 2004, 14.

4. See George Orwell's "Nineteen Eighty-Four," Part I, at http://orwell.ru/ library/novels/1984/english/en_p_1 (Accessed on December 5, 2005).

5. See "New Requirements for Travelers Between the United States and the Western Hemisphere," at http://travel.state.gov/travel/cbpmc/cbpmc_2223.html (Accessed on December 5, 2005).

6. Ryan Singel, "Passport Chip Criticism Grows," in *Wired News*. Full text of the news note can be found at http://www.wired.com/news/privacy/0,1848,67066,00. html?tw=wn_story_related (Accessed on November 1, 2005).

7. "Attorney General Wants More Border Patrol Helicopters," *Aviation Today*, January 1, 2002. Web page at http://www.aviationtoday.com/cgi/rw/show_mag. cgi?pub=rw&mon=0102&file=0102civup.htm (Accessed on December 5, 2005).

8. Christopher Bolkcom, Congressional Research Service Report, "Homeland Security: Unmanned Aerial Vehicles and Border Surveillance," February 7, 2005.

9. Louie Gilot, "Researcher Says Math Can Protect Border," *El Paso Times*, December 12, 2005, A-1.

10. Timothy Dunn, *The Militarization of the U.S.-Mexico Border 1978–1992: Low-Intensity Conflict Doctrine Comes Home* (Austin, TX: The University of Texas at Austin Press, 1996) 149.

11. Ellwyn R. Stoddard, "U.S.-Mexico Borderlands Issues: The Binational Boundary, Immigration and Economic Policies," from *Borderlands Trilogy*, Vol. I (El Paso, TX: The Promontory, 2001) 42–45.

12. See http://www.signonsandiego.com/news/reports/gatekeeper/20040801-9999-1n1econ.html.

13. Marc Cooper, "On the Border of Hypocrisy: The Unintended Consequences of Getting Tough on Illegal Immigration, *The L.A. Weekly*, December 5–11, 2003.

14. Peter Laufer, *Wetback Nation: The Case for Opening the Mexican-American Border* (USA: Ivan R. Dee Publisher, 2004).

15. Department of State, *U.S.-National Security Strategy: Prevent Our Enemies from Threatening Us, Our Allies, and Our Friends with Weapons of Mass Destruction*. Document found at the Department of State's Web page, http://www.state.gov/r/pa/ei/wh/15425.htm (Accessed on December 1, 2005).

16. *The New York Times*, February 11, 2005.

17. John Bailey and Jorge Chabat, *Transnational Crime and Public Security: Challenges to Mexico and the United States* (La Jolla, CA: University of California, 2002) 1.

18. "On Security," in Ronnie D. Lipschutz, ed., *On Security* (New York: Columbia University Press, 1995) 9.

19. Allan Bersin, "Statement before the U.S. House Committee on the Judiciary, Subcommittee on Immigration and Claims Hearing on *Border Security and Deterring Illegal Entry into the United States*," 105th Congress, First Session, 1997, House Report 105–32, 16.

20. An example of this kind of literature is Jon E. Dogherty's *Illegals: The Imminent Threat Posed by Our Unsecured U.S.-Mexican Border* (Nashville, TN: WND Books, 2004). Another example is Frosty Wooldrige's *Immigration's Unarmed Invasion: Deadly Consequences* (USA: Authorhouse, 2004). There are many other books sounding the same kind of alarm about the border.

21. John Kerry, *The New War: The Web of Crime that Threatens America's Security* (New York: Simon & Schuster, 1997) 149.

22. Katherine McIntire Peters, "Up against the Wall," October 1, 1996, in GovExec.com. Article found at http://www.govexec.com/archdoc/1096/1096s1.htm (Accessed on November 1, 2005).

23. See Mr. Bill O'Reilly's November 9, 2005, interview with Congressman Duncan Hunter at http://www.foxnews.com/story/0,2933,175030,00.html (Accessed on November 20, 2005).

24. See Congressman Tom Tancredo's Web page at the House of Representatives. Press release link at http://tancredo.house.gov/press/pressers/1212Tancredo51TerroristSuspectsCrossedBorderIllegally.htm (Accessed on December 13, 2005).

25. Pew Hispanic Center, *Latino Choices in News Media are Shaping Their Views of Their Communities, the Nation and the World*. Press release found at the Pew Hispanic Center Web page at http://pewhispanic.org/newsroom/releases/release.php?ReleaseID=10 (Accessed on December 2, 2005).

26. "Democracy's Ten Year Rut," *The Economist*, October 27, 2005.

27. The numbers are estimates from the Census Bureau. See them at the Census Bureau Web page http://www.census.gov/popest/estimates.php (Accessed on November 13, 2005).

28. The source of this and other numbers regarding Texas can be found in the Texas Comptroller of Public Accounts Web page at http://www.window.state.tx.us.specialrept/specialrept/snapshot (Accessed on November 29, 2005).

BIBLIOGRAPHY

ARTICLES

Bachelet, Pablo. "Tucson a Hub for Mexicans' Drug Trade." *Arizona Daily Star*, August 1, 2005.

Burnett, John. "Corruption at the Gates: Series Explores Lure of Money, Prestige among U.S. Border Agents." *National Public Radio*, September 12, 2002. http://www.npr.org/programs/atc/features/2002/sept/border_corruption (October 2, 2005).

Clark, Rebecca L. and Scott A. Anderson. "Illegal Aliens in Federal, State, and Local Criminal Justice Systems." *The Urban Institute*, June 30, 2000. http://www.urban.org/url.cfm?ID=410366 (October 15, 2005).

Cooper, Marc. "On the Border of Hypocrisy: The Unintended Consequences of Getting Tough on Illegal Immigration." *The L.A. Weekly*, December 5–11, 2003.

Dougherty, Jon E. "Lawmaker: Concern Rising Following Arrest of al-Qaeda Suspect in Mexico." *WorldNet Daily*, November 25, 2005. http://www.wnd.com/news/article.asp?ARTICLE_ID=47401 (November 7, 2005).

Flynn, Stephen. "The Neglected Home Front." *Foreign Affairs*, September/October 2004, 83(5): 20–33.

Gilot, Louie. "Researcher Says Math Can Protect Border." *El Paso Times*, December 12, 2005.

Green, Cynthia. "Federal Grand Jury Investigating Wal-Mart's Use of Undocumented Migrants." *The Labor Research Association*, September 18, 2005. http://www.laborresearch.org/story.php?id=332 (December 13, 2005).

Harman, Danna. "Mexican Drug Cartels: Wars Move Closer to the U.S. Border." *USA Today*, August 17, 2005. http://www.usatoday.com/news/world/2005-08-17-mexican-cartels_x.htm (October 30, 2005).

Hedges, Michael. "Bush Budget Scraps 9,790 Border Patrol Agents: President Uses Law's Escape Clause to Drop Funding for New Homeland Security." *The San Francisco Chronicle*, February 9, 2005.

Ibarra, Ignacio. "Border Group Claims WMD Test." *Arizona Daily Star*, July 22, 2004.

Jeffrey, Terence. "A Case of Selective Enforcement." *Town Hall*, November 4, 2005. http://www.townhall.com/opinion/columns/terencejeffrey/2003/07/02/170036.html (November 16, 2005).

McAuley, John. "Immigrants Keep U.S. Economy Supple." *Minnesota Star Tribune*, September 4, 2002.

Meissner, Doris. "Two Jobs for One INS." *The Washington Post*, April 9, 2002.

Milbank, Dana. "Bush Poised to Back New Border Agency." *The Washington Post*, March 19, 2002.

Milbank, Dana and Cheryl Thompson. "Panel Agrees on Plan to Split INS." *The Washington Post*, March 22, 2002.

O'Reilly, Bill. "Interview with Congressman Duncan Hunter." *The O'Reilly Factor*, November 9, 2005. http://www.foxnews.com/story/0,2933,175030,00.html (November 20, 2005).

Robbins, Ted. "Illegal Immigrant Deaths Burden Border Towns." *Nation*, October 6, 2005. http://www.npr.org/templates/story/story.php?storyId=4948382 (November 19, 2005).

Ruiz, Rubén. "Ejecutan a Tres Ex Policías." *El Imparcial*, June 7, 2005.

Singel, Ryan. "Passport Chip Criticism Grows." *Wired News*, March 31, 2005. http://www.wired.com/news/privacy/0,1848,67066,00.html?tw=wn_story_related (November 1, 2005).

Stock, Margaret D. and Benjamin Johnson. "The Lessons of 9/11: A Failure of Intelligence, Not Immigration Law." *Immigration Policy Focus*, December 2003, 2(3).

Strand, Paul. "Border Invasion: Stemming the Illegal Flood." *CBN News*, April 14, 2005. http://www.cbn.com/cbnnews/news/050414a.asp (November 23, 2005).

Thompson, Cheryl. "INS Role for the Police Considered." *The Washington Post*, April 4, 2002.

"AIC/Zogby Mexican Opinion Poll: Report." *Americans for Immigration Control, Inc.*, June 11, 2002. http://www.immigrationcontrol.com/AIC_Zogby_Mexican_Poll.htm (September 10, 2005).

"American Immigration: An Overview." *U.S. English, Inc.*, November 20, 2005. http://www.us-english.org/foundation/research/amimmigr/Chapter3.PDF (December 7, 2005).

"Attorney General Wants More Border Patrol Helicopters." *Aviation Today*, January 1, 2002. http://www.aviationtoday.com/cgi/rw/show_mag.cgi?pub=rw&mon=0102&file=0102civup.htm (December 9, 2005).

"Construcción de una Comunidad de América del Norte." *The Council on Foreign Relations*, November 25, 2005. http://www.cfr.org/content/publications/attachments/NorthAmerica_TF_final_esp.pdf (December 1, 2005).

"Democracy's Ten Year Rut." *The Economist*, October 27, 2005.

"Former EP Border Agent Sentenced for Letting Drug Couriers Pass." *El Paso Times*, November 23, 2005.

"Illegal Immigrants Are Bolstering Social Security with Billions." *The New York Times*, April 5, 2005.

"Illegal Immigration." *Migration News*, November 24, 2005. http://migration. ucdavis.edu/mn (December 1, 2005).

"Portrait of a Mexican Drug Lord." *CBS News*, December 24, 2003. http://www. cbsnews.com/stories/2003/10/24/world/main579960.shtml (October 10, 2005).

"Pot-Laden Truck Creates Armed Standoff." *El Paso Times*, November 19, 2005.

"Smugglers Getting Sneakier." *Arizona Daily Star*, December 26, 2004.

"Stryker Training." *The Monitor*, March 2005.

"Survey: Illegal Drugs: Stumbling in the Dark." *The Economist*, July 28, 2001.

"US Border a 'Safety Valve' for Latin Poor." *Providence Journal*, May 11, 2005. http://www.commondreams.org/views05/0511-26.htm (November 27, 2005).

BOOKS

Andreas, Peter. *Border Games: Policing the U.S.-Mexico Divide*. Ithaca, NY: Cornell University Press, 2001.

Bagley, Bruce M. and William O. Walker III. *Drug Trafficking in the Americas*. Boulder, CO: Lynne Rienner, 1994.

Bailey, John and Jorge Chabat. *Transnational Crime and Public Security: Challenges to Mexico and the United States*. San Diego: Center for U.S.-Mexican Studies, 2004.

Bentham, Jeremy and Miran Bozovic, Eds. *The Panopticon Writings*. London: Verso, 1995.

Blancornelas, Jesús. *El Cártel: Los Arellano Félix: La mafia más poderosa en la historia de América Latina*. Mexico, DF: Plaza y Janés, 2002.

Bossard, André. *Transnational Crime and Criminal Law*. Chicago: Office of International Criminal Justice, 1990.

Braunstein, Peter and Michael William Doyle. *Nation: The American Counterculture of the 1960s and '70s*. New York: Routledge, 2003.

Dougherty, Jon E. *Illegals: The Imminent Threat Posed by Our Unsecured U.S.-Mexican Border*. Nashville, TN: WND Books, 2004.

Dunn, Timothy J. *The Militarization of the U.S.-Mexico Border 1978–1992: Low-Intensity Conflict Comes Home*. Austin: University of Texas at Austin Press, 1996.

Foucault, Michel. *Discipline and Punish: The Birth of the Prison*. New York: Vintage Books, 1977.

Fuss, Charles M. *Sea of Grass: The Maritime Drug War, 1970–1990*. Annapolis, MD: Naval Institute Press, 1996.

Graebner Anderson, Annelise. *The Business of Organized Crime: A Cosa Nostra Family*. Stanford: Hoover Institution Press, 1980.

Kaplan, Lawrence J. and Dennis Kessler. *An Economic Analysis of Crime*. Springfield, IL: Thomas, 1976.

Kerry, John. *The New War: The Web of Crime that Threatens America's Security*. New York: Simon & Schuster, 1997.

Kurian, George T. *A Historical Guide to the U.S. Government.* New York: Oxford University Press, 1998.

Laufer, Peter. *Back Nation: The Case for Opening the Mexican-American Border.* Chicago, IL: Ivan R. Dee Publisher, 2004.

Lipschutz, Ronnie D., Ed. *On Security.* New York: Columbia University Press, 1995.

Marill, Robert Lee. *Patrolling Chaos: The U.S. Border Patrol in Deep South Texas.* Lubbock: Texas Tech University Press, 2004.

Mason Hart, Jason, Ed. *Border Crossings: Mexican and Mexican American Workers.* Wilmington, DE: SR Books, 1998.

Naylor, R. T. *Wages of Crime: Black Markets, Illegal Finance, and the Underworld Economy.* Ithaca, NY: Cornell University, 2002.

Orwell, George. *Nineteen Eighty-Four.* New York: Penguin Group, 2005. Entire text of the book can be found at: http://orwell.ru/library/novels/1984/english/en_p_1 (December 5, 2005).

Paredes, Américo. *A Texas-Mexican Cancionero: Folksongs of the Lower Border.* Austin: University of Texas Press, 1995.

Pozo, Susan. *Exploring the Underground Economy.* Kalamazoo: W. E. Upjohn Institute, 1996.

Pyle, David J. *The Economics of Crime and Law Enforcement.* New York: St. Martin's Press, 1983.

Ruso, Roberto. *Attitudes toward Immigrants and Immigration Policy: Surveys among Latinos in the U.S. and Mexico,* 2005. Text found at http://pewhispanic.org/files/reports/52.pdf (November 15, 2005).

Shannon, Elaine. *Desperados: Latin Drug Lords, U.S.A. Lawmen and the War America Can't Win.* New York: Penguin, 1989.

Stoddard, Ellwyn R. *U.S.-Mexico Borderlands Issues: The Binational Boundary, Immigration and Economic Policies: Borderlands Trilogy,* Vol. I. El Paso, TX: The Promontory, 2001.

Strange, Susan and Claire Sterling. *Crime without Frontiers.* New York: McGraw-Hill, 1995.

Torres, Juan Mora. *The Making of the Mexican Border.* Austin: University of Texas Press, 2001.

Wooldridge, Frosty. *Immigration's Unarmed Invasion: Deadly Consequences.* United States: Author House, 2004.

INTERNET

"Border line data." http://us-mex.irc-online.org/borderlines/PDFs/bl79.pdf (November 26, 2005).

"Population Statistics." http://www.scerp.org/population.htm (January 27, 2005).

"The 1853 Gadsden Purchase Treaty." http://www.yale.edu/lawweb/avalon/diplomacy/mexico/mx1853.htm (December 10, 2005).

"Immigrant Statistics." http://www.archives.gov/research_room/genealogy/immigrant_arrivals/mexican_border_crossings.html#special (February 1, 2005).

"Immigration Statistics." http://uscis.gov/graphics/shared/aboutus/statistics/legishist/456.htm (January 27, 2005).

"President Discusses Border Security and Immigration Reform in Arizona." *Speech.* http://www.whitehouse.gov/news/releases/2005/11/20051128-7.html (November 29, 2005).

"Bush Vows to Harden Border Policy." *Speech.* http://www.chron.com/disp/story.mpl/metropolitan/3489624.html (November 28, 2005).

"Governor Schwarzenegger Delivers a Speech on Closing Borders." *Speech.* http://www.foxnews.com/story/0,2933,153988,00.html (November 28, 2005).

"President Discusses War on Terror at National Endowment for Democracy." http://www.whitehouse.gov/news/releases/2005/10/20051006-3.html (November 29, 2005).

"Rethinking the Role of the U.S. Mexican Border in the Post-9/11 World." http://www.cfr.org/publication/6906/rethinking_the_role_of_the_us_mexican_border_in_the_post911_world.html (December 3, 2005).

"A Secure Europe in a Better World." http://ue.eu.int/uedocs/cmsUpload/78367.pdf (December 5, 2005).

"Militarizing the Border." http://mediafilter.org/CAQ/CAQ56border.html (December 10, 2005).

"The War on Drugs." http://www.pbs.org/wgbh/pages/frontline/shows/drugs/cron/ (December 9, 2005).

"Illegal Immigration and Enforcement along the U.S.-Mexico Border: An Overview." http://www.dallasfed.org/research/efr/2001/efr0101a.pdf (December 9, 2005).

Hear the story of drug smuggling through the Tohona O'odham Reservation on National Public Radio. http://www.npr.org/templates/story/story.php?storyId=1125387 (November 20, 2005).

"American Immigration: An Overview." *U.S. English Foundation.* http://www.us-english.org/foundation/research/amimmigr/Chapter3.PDF (November 20, 2005).

"Federal Grand Jury Investigating Wal-Mart's Use of Undocumented Migrants." http://www.laborresearch.org/story.php?id=332 (September 18, 2005).

Birda, Trollinger, Martinez, Eddings and Jewell v. Tyson Foods, Inc. http://www.vdare.com/misc/tyson_complaint.htm (September 18, 2005).

"Department of Justice Announces INS Restructuring Plan Splitting Service and Enforcement Functions." http://www.usdoj.gov (November 14, 2004).

"A Case of Selective Enforcement." http://www.townhall.com/opinion/columns/terencejeffrey/2003/07/02/170036.html (November 4, 2005).

"Sixty Percent Favor Barrier on Mexican Bodrer." http://www.rasmussenreports.com/2005/Immigration%20November%207.htm (November 15, 2005).

"H.R. 3162 RDS, 107th Congress, 1st Session. H.R. 3162 in the Senate of the United States." Patriot Act. http://www.epic.org/privacy/terrorism/hr3162.html (December 10, 2005).

"New Requirements for Travelers between the United States and the Western Hemisphere." http://travel.state.gov/travel/cbpmc/cbpmc_2223.html (December 5, 2005).

"Tightened Border in San Diego Shifts Strain to Areas East." http://www.signonsandiego.com/news/reports/gatekeeper/20040801-9999-1n1econ.html (November 29, 2005).

Katherine McIntire Peters. "Up against the Wall." http://www.govexec.com/archdoc/1096/1096s1.htm (November 1, 2005).

"Interview with Congressman Duncan Hunter." http://www.foxnews.com/story/0,2933,175030,00.html (November 20, 2005).

Pew Hispanic Center. "*Latino Choices in News Media are Shaping Their Views of Their Communities, the Nation and the World.*" http://pewhispanic.org/ newsroom/releases/release.php?ReleaseID=10 (December 2, 2005).

GOVERNMENT REPORTS

Bureau of Justice Statistics. *National Transportation Statistics 2005.* http://www.bts. gov/publications/national_transportation_statistics/2005 (October 5, 2005).

Bureau of Transportation Statistics. http://www.bts.gov/programs/international/ border_crossing_entry_data/us_mexico/pdf/entire.pdf (June 21, 2005).

Bureau of Transportation Statistics. *Major NAFTA Border Crossings: 1996–2000.* http://www.bts.gov/publications/transportation_statistics_annual_report/ 2001/html/chapter_07_table_01_219.html (November 5, 2005).

Congressional Research Service. *Border Security: Inspections, Practices, Policies, Issues,* May 26, 2004.

Congressional Research Service. *Border Security: The Role of the U.S. Border Patrol.* http://www.fas.org/sgp/crs/homesec/RL32562.pdf (September 7, 2005).

Congressional Research Service. *Homeland Security: Unmanned Aerial Vehicles and Border Surveillance,* February 7, 2005.

Drug Enforcement Administration. *Illegal Drug Price and Purity Report,* April 2003. http://www.usdoj.gov/dea/pubs/intel/02058/02058.html#2 (September 28, 2005).

Government Accountability Office. *Border Patrol Hiring: Despite Recent Initiatives, Fiscal Year 1999 Hiring Goal Was Not Met,* December 1999.

Government Accountability Office. *Tax Administration: IRS Needs to Consider Options for Revising Regulations to Increase the Accuracy of Social Security Numbers on Wage Statements,* (August 2004).

Government Accountability Office. *Social Security: Better Coordination among Federal Agencies Could Reduce Unidentified Earnings Reports,* (February 2005).

Government Accountability Office. *Immigration Enforcement: DHS Has Incorporated Immigration Enforcement Objectives and Is Addressing Future Planning Requirements,* October 2004.

Government Accountability Office. *Homeland Security: Overview of Homeland Security Management Challenges,* April 20, 2005.

Government Printing Office. *Remarks from former Customs and Border Protection Commissioner Robert Bonner.* http://permanent.access.gpo.gov/websites/ www.cbp.gov/xp/cgov/newsroom/commissioner/speeches_statements/ archives/2003/sept092003_2.xml.htm (November 30, 2005).

Homeland Security Department. *Testimony by Secretary Michael Chertoff before the House Homeland Security Committee,* April 13, 2005. http://www. dhs.gov/dhspublic/display?theme=45&content=4460> (December 1, 2005).

Homeland Security Department. *Testimony by Deputy Secretary of Homeland Security Admiral James Loy Before the Senate Select Committee on Intelligence.* http://www.iwar.org.uk/homesec/resources/natsec2005/loy.htm (November 5, 2005).

Homeland Security Department. http://www.dhs.gov/dhspublic/interapp/press_ release/press_release_0541.xml (October 19, 2005).

Office of Management and Budget. http://www.whitehouse.gov/omb/budget/fy2006/ dhs.html (December 8, 2005).

United States Congress. *Homeland Security Act Title IV.* http://www.dhs.gov/dhspublic/interweb/assetlibrary/hr_5005_enr.pdf (October 20, 2005).
United States Customs and Border Protection. *National Border Patrol Strategy.* http://www.customs.gov/linkhandler/cgov/border_security/border_patrol/national_bp_strategy.ctt/national_bp_strategy.pdf (September 7, 2005).
United States Department of State. http://usinfo.state.gov/eap/east_asia_pacific/chinese_human_smuggling/smuggling_in_the_press/crime.htm (November 4, 2005).
United States Department of State. U.S. Embassy in Mexico City. http://mexico.usembassy.gov/mexico/ep050610violence.html (October 30, 2005).
United States Department of State. *U.S.-National Security Strategy: Prevent Our Enemies from Threatening Us, Our Allies, and Our Friends with Weapons of Mass Destruction.* Document found at the Department of State's Web page, http://www.state.gov/r/pa/ei/wh/15425.htm (December 1, 2005).
United States House of Representatives. *"Testimony of Peter Gadiel before the Committee on the Judiciary."* http://judiciary.house.gov/OversightTestimony.aspx?ID=289 (November 5, 2005).
United States House of Representatives. "Statement before the U.S. House Committee on the Judiciary, Subcommittee on Immigration and Claims Hearing on *Border Security and Deterring Illegal Entry into the United States,*" 105th Congress, First Session, 1997, House Report 105-32, 16.
Congressman Tom Tancredo's Web page at the House of Representatives. http://tancredo.house.gov/press/pressers/1212Tancredo51TerroristSuspects-CrossedBorderIllegally.htm (December 13, 2005).

DATA

"Border-Wide Population Projections." http://www.scerp.org/population.htm (September 7, 2005).
"United States Census: Population Estimates." http://www.census.gov/popest/estimates.php (November 26, 2005).
"Americans for Immigration Control and Zogby Poll." http://www.immigrationcontrol.com/AIC_Zogby_Mexican_Poll.htm (September 10, 2005).
Thomas, Brenda and Tony Payan. "Survey of Recent Immigrants at the U.S. Consulate in Ciudad Juárez," 2003–2004.
"United States Census Bureau, Foreign Trade Division, Data Dissemination Branch." http://www.census.gov/foreign-trade/balance/c2010.html#2001 (November 5, 2005).
"Trade in Goods (Exports, Imports and Trade Balance) with Mexico." http://www.census.gov/foreign-trade/balance/c2010.html#199 (November 5, 2005).
The source of this and other numbers regarding Texas can be found in the Texas Comptroller of Public Accounts Web page at http://www.window.state.tx.us (November 29, 2005).

INTERVIEWS

Interview with a former member of the Juárez Cartel, who wished to remain anonymous. Interview conducted in Ciudad Juárez, Chihuahua, on August 3, 2005.

Interview with a federal court employee in El Paso, TX, who wished to remain anonymous. Interview conducted on August 18, 2005.

First Interview with "James," a trucking company operator who asked to remain anonymous, in San Antonio, TX. Interview conducted on August 5, 2005.

Second Interview with "James," a trucking company operator who asked to remain anonymous, in San Antonio, TX. Interview conducted on October 5, 2005.

Interview with a member of a drug cartel in Ciudad Juárez, Chihuahua. Interview conducted on August 4, 2005.

Interview with a federal court employee in El Paso, TX, who wished to remain anonymous. Interview conducted on August 18, 2005.

INDEX

About the Author

TONY PAYAN is Assistant Professor of International Relations and Foreign Policy at the University of Texas at El Paso. He is the author of *Cops, Soldiers, and Diplomats: Explaining Agency Behavior in the Drug War* (2006).